COLORADO
TRAVEL ✦ SMART

Poppy and Flatirons, Boulder

COLORADO

TRAVEL ✦ SMART®

Second Edition

Dianna Litvak

John Muir Publications
Santa Fe, New Mexico

For Brian, my endless source of love, support, and encouragement

John Muir Publications, P.O. Box 613, Santa Fe, New Mexico 87504

Printed in the United States of America
Second edition. First printing February 1999.

ISSN: 1099-646-X
ISBN: 1-56261-451-7

Editors: Peg Goldstein, Heidi Utz
Graphics Editor: Tom Gaukel
Production: Marie J.T. Vigil
Design: Janine Lehmann and Linda Braun
Cover Design: Janine Lehmann
Typesetting: Kathleen Sparkes
Map Illustration: American Custom Maps—Jemez Springs, NM USA
Map Style Development: American Custom Maps—Jemez Springs, NM USA
Printer: Publishers Press
Front cover photos: © Jack Olson
Back cover photo: © Curtis Martin

Distributed to the book trade by
Publishers Group West
Berkeley, California

HOW TO USE THIS BOOK

This *Colorado Travel•Smart* guidebook is organized in 14 destination chapters, each covering the best sights and activities, restaurants, and lodging available in that specific destination. Thanks to thorough research and experience, the author is able to bring you only the best options, saving you time and money in your travels. The chapters are presented in geographic sequence so you can follow an easy route from one to the next. If you were to visit each destination in chapter order, you'd enjoy a complete tour of the best of Colorado.

Each chapter contains:
- User-friendly maps of the area, showing all recommended sights, restaurants, and accommodations.
- "A Perfect Day" description—how the author would spend her time if she had just one day in that destination.
- Sightseeing highlights, each rated by degree of importance: ★★★—Don't miss; ★★—Try hard to see; ★—See if you have time; and No stars—Worth knowing about. (If the author considers a sight a waste of time, it isn't in this guide.)
- Selected restaurant, lodging, and camping recommendations to suit a variety of budgets.
- Helpful hints, fitness and recreation ideas, insights, and random tidbits of information to enhance your trip.

The Importance of Planning. Developing an itinerary is the best way to get the most satisfaction from your travels, and this guidebook makes it easy. First, read through the book and choose the places you'd most like to visit. Then study the color map on the inside cover flap and the mileage chart (page 12) to determine which spots you can realistically see in the time you have available and at the travel pace you prefer. Using the Planning Map (pages 10–11), map out your route. Finally, use the lodging recommendations to determine your accommodations.

Some Suggested Itineraries. To get you started, here are six itineraries of varying lengths, based on specific interests. Mix and match according to your interests and time constraints, or follow a given itinerary from start to finish. The possibilities are endless. *Happy travels!*

SUGGESTED ITINERARIES

With *Colorado Travel•Smart*, you can plan a trip of any length—a one-day excursion, a getaway weekend, or a three-week vacation—around any special interest. To get you started, the following pages contain six suggested itineraries geared toward a variety of interests. For more information, refer to the chapters listed—chapter names are bolded and chapter numbers appear inside black bullets. You can follow a suggested itinerary in its entirety, or shorten, lengthen, or combine parts of each, depending on your starting and ending points.

Discuss alternative routes and schedules with your travel companions—it's a great way to have fun, even before you leave home. And remember: don't hesitate to change your itinerary once you're on the road. Careful study and planning ahead of time will help you make informed decisions as you go, but spontaneity is the extra ingredient that will make your trip memorable.

© Unicorn/Dick Young

Lake San Cristobal near Lake City

Best of Colorado Tour

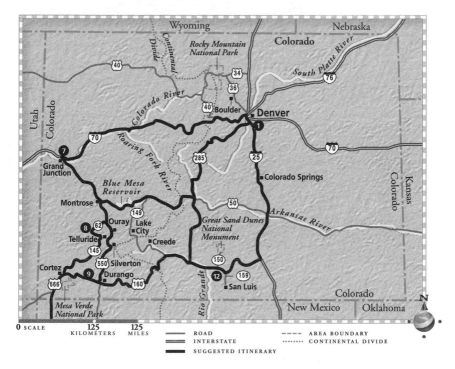

For those discerning travelers who want only the "crème de la crème" for their Colorado vacation, these are the places I recommend. You should know, however, that all of the destinations included in this book are "the best." Most everything about Colorado is superlative!

- **❶ Denver** (Denver Art Museum, Denver Public Library, Colorado History Museum, downtown, Cherry Creek)
- **❼ Grand Junction and the Grand Valley** (Colorado National Monument, Grand Mesa, Palisade wineries)
- **❽ Northern San Juan Mountains** (exploring Victorian mountain towns, hiking, mountain bike rides, and scenic driving)
- **❾ Durango and Cortez** (Ancestral Pueblo sites, Durango-Silverton Narrow Gauge Railroad)
- **⓬ San Luis Valley** (San Luis, Fort Garland Museum, Great Sand Dunes National Monument)

Time needed: 2 weeks

Nature Lovers' Tour

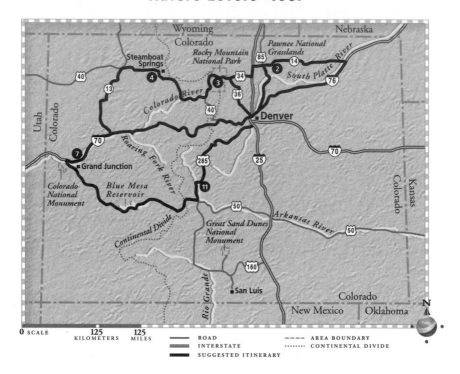

The variety of natural places found in Colorado is tremendous. This itinerary recommends a sampling of different regions, from prairie grasslands
to desert canyonlands to 14,000-foot peaks, all bursting with a diversity of
plant and animal life.

- ❷ **Pawnee Grasslands** (Pawnee Buttes)
- ❸ **Rocky Mountain National Park** (Trail Ridge Road, wildlife viewing, hiking)
- ❹ **Steamboat Springs** (Flat Tops Wilderness Area, Mt. Zirkel Wilderness Area)
- ❼ **Grand Junction and the Grand Valley** (Colorado National Monument)
- ⓫ **Upper Arkansas River Valley** (Fourteeners, hiking, mountain biking, river rafting)

Time needed: 1 to 2 weeks

Family Fun Tour

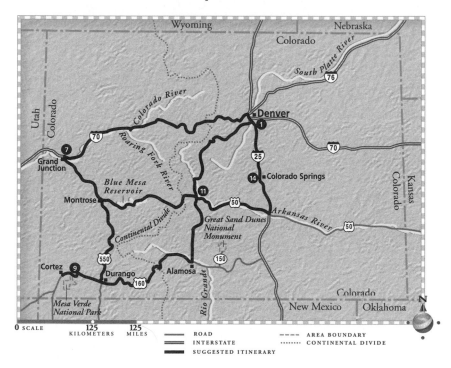

One thing everybody knows about kids is that they love dinosaurs. Families can visit the state's most famous paleontological specimens, embark on an exciting river-raft trip, wander through ancient dwellings, and stand on top of one of America's most famous mountains.

- ❶ **Denver** (Denver Museum of Natural History, Denver Zoo, Elitch Gardens Amusement Park, United States Mint)
- ❼ **Grand Junction and the Grand Valley** (Dinosaur Discovery Museum, Dinosaur Valley, dinosaur quarries)
- ❾ **Durango and Cortez** (Mesa Verde National Park, Durango-Silverton Narrow Gauge Railroad)
- ⓫ **Upper Arkansas River Valley** (river rafting)
- ⓮ **Colorado Springs** (Pikes Peak, United States Air Force Academy, Cheyenne Mountain Zoo, Cripple Creek)

Time needed: 10 days to 2 weeks

Arts and Culture Tour

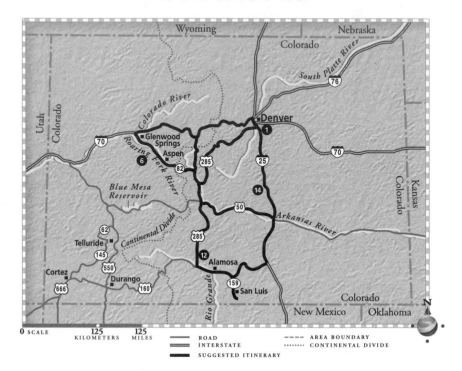

This itinerary gives you ideas for exploring the arts and cultures of Colorado—both past and present. The rich artistic traditions of several ethnic groups are especially highlighted.

- ❶ **Denver** (Colorado History Museum, Museo de las Americas, Black American West Heritage Museum, Denver Center for Performing Arts, galleries, cultural festivals)
- ❻ **Roaring Fork Valley** (Aspen, Glenwood Springs, galleries, festivals)
- ⓬ **San Luis Valley** (galleries and museums in La Garita, San Luis, Alamosa; Stations of the Cross, Our Lady of Guadalupe Church)
- ⓮ **Colorado Springs** (museums, Colorado Fine Arts Center, Manitou Springs, Van Briggle Pottery)

Time needed: 1 week to 10 days

Outdoor Recreation Tour

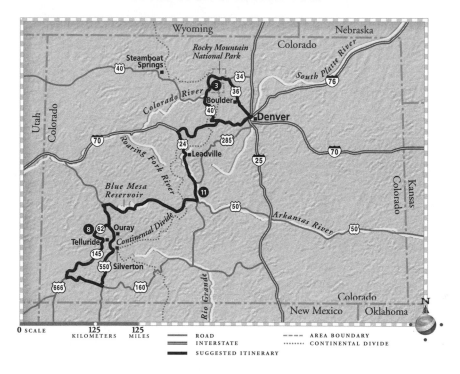

Colorado is famous for a staggering array of outdoor adventures. Wintertime is a skier's paradise; summer rewards outdoor enthusiasts with hikes up soaring peaks, white-water raft trips, and backpacking in the beautiful Colorado wilderness.

- ❸ **Rocky Mountain National Park** (hiking, backpacking, fishing, wildlife viewing, cross-country skiing, snowshoeing)
- ⓫ **Upper Arkansas River Valley** (Fourteeners, water sports, hiking, backpacking, fishing)
- ❽ **Northern San Juan Mountains** (Fourteeners, Telluride Ski Area, wilderness areas, hiking, mountain biking on four-wheel-drive roads and trails)

Time needed: 1 to 2 weeks

History Buffs' Tour

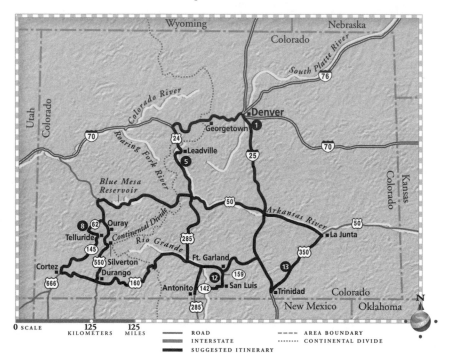

This itinerary guides you to significant historical sites in Colorado, steeped in the pasts of Native Americans, fur trade forts, early Hispanic settlements, ghost towns, and mountain towns that survived the bust years after the mineral rush.

- **❶ Denver** (Georgetown, Colorado History Museum)
- **❺ Leadville** (National Mining Museum, Tabor Opera House, Matchless Mine, Route of the Silver Kings)
- **❽ Northern San Juan Mountains** (ghost towns and mining districts)
- **⓬ San Luis Valley** (San Luis, Fort Garland Museum, Pikes Stockade, Cumbres & Toltec Scenic Railroad)
- **⓭ Santa Fe Trail** (Bent's Old Fort, Corazon de Trinidad National Historic District, Boggsville, Ludlow, Highway of Legends)

Time needed: 2 weeks

USING THE PLANNING MAP

A major aspect of itinerary planning is determining your mode of transportation and the route you will follow as you travel from destination to destination. The Planning Map on the following pages will allow you to do just that.

First, read through the destination chapters carefully and note the sights that intrigue you. Then, photocopy the Planning Map so you can try out several different routes that will take you to these destinations. (The mileage chart that follows will allow you to calculate your travel distances.) Decide where you will be starting your tour of Colorado. Will you fly into Denver, Colorado Springs, or Grand Junction, or start from somewhere in between? Will you be driving from place to place or flying into major transportation hubs and renting a car for day trips? The answers to these questions will form the basis for your planning.

Once you have a firm idea of where your travels will take you, copy your route onto the additional Planning Map in the Appendix. You won't have to worry about where your map is, and the information you need on each destination will always be close at hand.

© Unicorn/Robert Hitchman

Wildflowers in Yankee Bay Basin near Ouray

Planning Map: Colorado

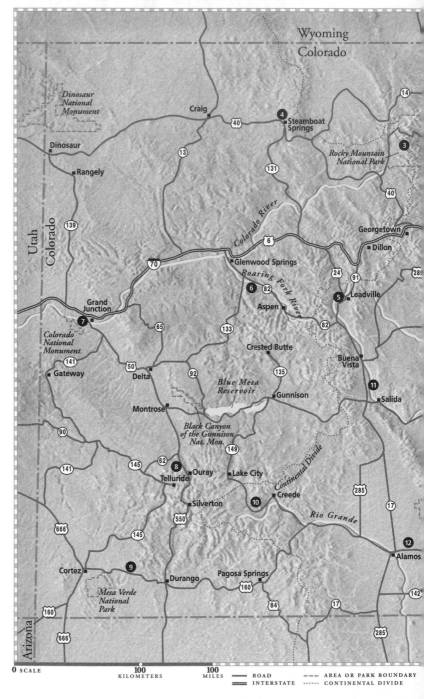

Wyoming
Colorado

Utah
Colorado
Arizona

Dinosaur National Monument
Craig
Steamboat Springs
Dinosaur
Rangely
Rocky Mountain National Park
Georgetown
Dillon
Glenwood Springs
Roaring Fork River
Aspen
Leadville
Grand Junction
Colorado National Monument
Crested Butte
Buena Vista
Gateway
Delta
Blue Mesa Reservoir
Gunnison
Salida
Montrose
Black Canyon of the Gunnison Nat. Mon.
Continental Divide
Ouray
Telluride
Lake City
Silverton
Creede
Rio Grande
Cortez
Durango
Pagosa Springs
Mesa Verde National Park
Alamos
Colorado River

0 SCALE **100** KILOMETERS **100** MILES

— ROAD   --- AREA OR PARK BOUNDARY
≡ INTERSTATE   ···· CONTINENTAL DIVIDE

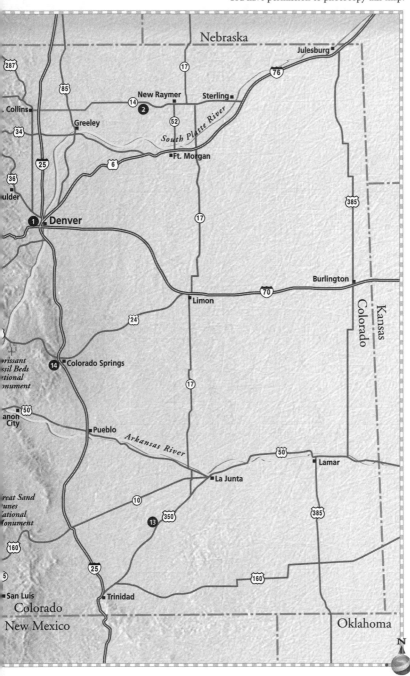

COLORADO MILEAGE CHART

	Grand Junction	Telluride	Durango	Leadville	Aspen	Salida	Alamosa	Creede	Trinidad	Colorado Spgs.	Denver	Estes Park	Greeley
Telluride	134												
Durango	168	124											
Leadville	179	245	264										
Aspen	134	281	321	60									
Salida	197	186	205	59	87								
Alamosa	268	268	150	141	169	68							
Creede	219	221	131	172	200	113	68						
Trinidad	380	367	261	252	268	181	111	179					
Colorado Spgs.	302	291	310	129	157	105	164	223	127				
Denver	258	340	359	113	173	154	213	262	195	68			
Estes Park	319	416	435	171	231	219	278	327	260	133	65		
Greeley	312	394	413	167	227	208	267	316	249	122	54	51	
Steamboat Spgs.	197	331	365	120	180	179	256	292	371	244	176	142	193

WHY VISIT COLORADO?

Pikes Peak, an imposing sentinel rising above Colorado's eastern plains, has intrigued people for generations. Its namesake, Zebulon Pike, regarded it as unclimbable and believed it must reach at least 20,000 feet above the valley floor. In fact, at 14,110 feet, it isn't even Colorado's highest mountain, ranking only 31st among 54 "Fourteeners" (peaks above 14,000 feet). But its sheer magnificence inspired famous words that are part of the American soul: "O beautiful, for spacious skies, for amber waves of grain, for purple mountain majesties above the fruited plain." Although poet Katherine Lee Bates wrote "America the Beautiful" many decades ago, Pikes Peak continues to inspire those seeing it for the first or the fiftieth time. This great mountain is a stalwart symbol for all that is magnificent, unique, and inspirational about Colorado.

As a Colorado native, I am privileged to introduce you to my state—all of it—from the eastern plains country to the high mountain valleys and the plateau lands of the western slope. This guide will acquaint you with Colorado's wilderness, its past, and its everyday wonders. My suggestions, which are based on my own experiences, will help you plan your journey, show you many rare and unusual places, and allow you to discover all that Colorado has to offer. My best advice would be to take your time and really get to know a place before rushing off to the next—it will all be waiting for you the next time you come.

HISTORY AND CULTURES

You will discover our diverse cultures, both past and present, in many places throughout Colorado. In fact, the landscape itself holds many clues—for those patient enough to find them—revealing mysterious stories about early human habitation. Although evidence is hard to find, we do know that people roamed this land at least 12,000 years ago, hunting huge animals such as woolly mammoth and bison. Other small family groups thrived here at least 9,000 years ago by hunting game and gathering roots and berries. They also made pottery and used bows and arrows introduced by other nomadic bands to the east.

More tantalizing clues begin to appear with the Fremont peoples, who lived in the red sandstone canyons of the Colorado Plateau near present-day Grand Junction from A.D. 500 to 1450. On the canyon walls they inscribed detailed scenes and figures, such as the mythical humpbacked flute player, Kokopelli, and drilled complex hole patterns on the mesa tops, revealing their sophisticated knowledge of the solar system. Their rock art, and that of many other native tribes, graces many isolated spots in western Colorado. Stumbling upon it provides a rare chance to ponder the message behind these stylized human and animal images.

The remains of the Ancestral Pueblo peoples in the Four Corners region (where the corners of Colorado, Utah, Arizona, and New Mexico meet) provide clues to the most enigmatic era in Colorado's prehistory. These ancestors of the modern Pueblo and Hopi tribes in Arizona and New Mexico lived for many years in southwestern Colorado, where mountain streams and fertile soil supported large villages. But then the ancient Pueblos simply vanished from their homes in Colorado. Several plausible explanations have sparked lively debates over their mysterious disappearance.

For thousands of years, the Utes claimed Colorado's extensive mountain ranges as their homeland, typically traveling short distances between the high and low country as the seasons changed. By 1600, the tribe acquired horses brought to the New World by Spanish explorers and adapted them to their daily needs. Horses caused dramatic changes in the Utes' mobility, as tribal members began to venture farther onto the foothills and plains, fighting with Plains Indians tribes over choice hunting grounds and buffalo herds. These Plains tribes, including the Comanche, Kiowa, Cheyenne, Arapaho, Plains Apache, Pawnee, and Shoshone, also competed against one another for control of the Great Plains region of Colorado, Kansas, and Nebraska. They followed the seasonal migrations of gigantic herds of American buffalo, relying on the animals for their clothing, shelter, and sustenance.

Hispanos from northern New Mexico first moved into southern Colorado 450 years ago—more than three centuries before white settlers claimed the land for homesteads and cattle ranches. Extended families began filtering into southern Colorado to tend sheep and farm, establishing *plazas* and *placitas* along fertile river valleys such as *El Huerfano* (the Orphan) and *El Rio de las Animas Perdidas en Purgatorio* (the River of Souls Lost in Purgatory). The rich legacy of these pioneering families lives on today in the San Luis Valley.

In 1821 Mexico wrested its independence from Spain and established an important trading relationship with the United States, a practice illegal under Spanish rule. The international boundary between the neighboring countries was the Arkansas River, which, from its headwaters in the central Rockies near Leadville, courses through what is now southeastern Colorado. Traders from both countries ventured between Missouri and Santa Fe on the Santa Fe Trail, sometimes using the mountain branch of the trail that followed the Arkansas River.

The most important stopping point on the Arkansas River in United States territory was Bent's Old Fort (near present-day La Junta), established in 1834, where Plains Indian tribes agreed to trade buffalo robes, furs, and horses with enterprising merchants and traders. The fort brought together three distinct cultural groups, all of whom played major roles in Colorado's rich and storied history: Plains Indians, Mexicans, and Euro-Americans. For this reason it is perhaps the most important reconstructed historical site in Colorado.

Zebulon Pike, an American explorer, entered Colorado in 1806, followed by Stephen Long in 1820, to document the inhabitants and resources of the vast new territory that had been added to the United States with the Louisiana Purchase. Both explorers believed present-day Nebraska, Kansas, and eastern Colorado were an arid wasteland, best left to the "wild" peoples and animals that inhabited it. The formidable Rocky Mountains to the west were seen as a great wilderness in which only seasoned mountain men and Indians could survive. But everything changed in 1858, when prospectors announced to an eager nation the discovery of "color" at the confluence of Cherry Creek and the South Platte River, today the very heart of Denver. As reports of "gold!" filtered back to the states, hundreds of thousands of people willing to risk everything for a chance to get rich quick flooded Pikes Peak country.

With increased settlement, the United States government grew more interested in the immense agricultural and mineral wealth of Colorado Territory. As a result, the native tribes were forced to relinquish their cherished ancestral lands. A sad footnote of this painful time in Colorado history remains: Of the many tribes that once claimed parts of Colorado, only the Ute Mountain Ute and Southern Ute tribes retain a minuscule portion of their original lands in the extreme southwestern corner of the state.

Settlement, mining, and industry, the visible products of a tamed frontier, rapidly transformed Colorado's landscape. Bonanza towns such as Aspen, Georgetown, and Leadville left significant marks on history. From their births as infant mining camps they matured into adolescent towns. But once the minerals played out, these settlements became washed-up relics of a bygone era. Several former boom towns languished until the joys of mountain living and tourism hastened in a new boom era.

In the late 20th century, Colorado wrestles with its ever-expanding popularity. During the last decade alone, its cities and towns have grown by leaps and bounds—and growth continues with no end in sight. More and more people, grown weary of the hustle and bustle of their own cities, have turned to Colorado as a place to escape, hoping life here will be simple, relaxed, and healthy. Many Coloradans now find themselves scrambling to preserve the past, their cherished way of life, and the remaining wilderness and open spaces from the damaging effects of rapid growth.

THE ARTS

You'll find a refreshing variety of arts and culture in Colorado, from the time-honored and traditional to the cutting-edge and unconventional. Denver hosts a multitude of events, including concerts, symphonies, gallery openings, museum exhibitions, theater, and dance performances.

Denver's friendly neighborhood gatherings take the form of festivals, such as the Chile Festival, Black Arts Festival, and Cherry Blossom Festival. The Cherry Creek Arts Festival, held each Fourth of July, features the best regional art.

But Denver doesn't hold a monopoly on Colorado arts—many communities have long-standing artistic traditions and diverse selections of events, museums, and galleries. Aspen is an international mecca for musicians, artists, scientists, and others, proudly offering a wide variety of arts for such a small community. For more than 100 years, Colorado Springs and neighboring Manitou Springs have attracted artists, many of whom came to cure their tuberculosis but ended up staying a lifetime. This has resulted in an eclectic collection of museums, architecture, and galleries. The San Luis Valley is a haven for artists who continue to practice centuries-old arts passed down to them by their Hispanic ancestors. Their tinwork, religious objects, weavings, sculpture, and jewelry are widely available in many towns in the valley. And in the Four Corners region, the Ute Mountain Ute and Southern Ute tribes display locally produced works including silver jewelry, unique pottery, and visual arts.

Artists' collectives in places like Boulder, Salida, Alamosa, and Durango have increased statewide appreciation of the arts. Special art exhibits, workshops, classes, poetry readings, theater, and dance performances now occur daily throughout Colorado.

CUISINE

During your Colorado visit, be prepared to sample many different foods, from Western-style barbecue to tequila-braised calamari. Traditional Colorado foods feature a variety of wild game—venison, buffalo, elk, rabbit, pheasant, quail, duck, goose, and even wild turkey. The Rocky Mountain trout is always a sumptuous dinner entrée, often baked or sautèed in creamy butter. And with hundreds of cattle ranches throughout the state, you can expect only the best cuts of aged beef.

During late summer and fall, farmers sell their fresh hand-picked vegetables and fruits at homemade stands lining the highways. Legendary Rocky Ford cantaloupes, grown in a small agricultural community in the Arkansas River Valley, are noted for their sweet aroma and taste. The fertile Grand River Valley is prime orchard country, where peaches, plums, and apricots bask in the gentle "peach wind" that wafts through the valley, as do numerous vineyards. Near the Grand Mesa, in Cedaredge, are seemingly endless rows of apple trees, sources of the most crisp and flavorful apples in the state.

Professional Colorado chefs use only the freshest ingredients in their creations, varying their menus according to the seasonal availability of locally grown produce. Many restaurants employ an innovative cooking style, matching old favorites with new ingredients, such as grilled salmon rubbed with chipotle and red chile, pasta dishes enhanced by complex Asian flavors, or thick T-bone steaks topped with a dollop of fresh salsa.

While authentic Mexican and Tex-Mex (Mexican with a Texas twist) have been established favorites in Colorado for decades, new Southwestern cuisine is a more recent arrival. Southwestern cooking features traditional pueblo foods from New Mexico (black beans, corn, and green chile) paired with unusual ingredients, such as duck, lamb, or goat cheese. In addition, a plethora of ethnic restaurants offers the best in international cooking.

Resort towns such as Aspen, Telluride, and Steamboat Springs are known for their cafés and bistros, many started by European ski enthusiasts. Like most Colorado cities, these towns also have numerous health-food stores and restaurants specializing in distinctive vegetarian cuisine. In rural areas the food remains traditionally Western—just like the good ol' days—with the finest steaks and wild game accompanied by fresh vegetables and homemade potato dishes.

Although beer might not qualify as "cuisine," microbreweries proliferate in the state, with 60 or so establishments causing a sensation in beer drinking. Microbreweries feature a range of beers to please any taste, from light ales to heavy porters, and often vary them according to season. The hearty fare served at many pubs is in a class by itself, with tempting appetizers, pastas, soups, and main-course selections featuring beer as a central ingredient.

FLORA AND FAUNA

The High Plains that blanket eastern Colorado are generally too dry for trees, except along streams or rivers. Swaying grasses and prickly cacti cover the prairie, which erupts with an assortment of wildflowers each spring. Grassland birds have adapted to the scarcity of trees by nesting and rearing their young on the ground. You will see Colorado's state bird, the lark bunting, as well as hawks and eagles, which feast on rattlesnakes and small rodents scampering through the brush. Rabbits, coyotes, foxes, pronghorn antelope, prairie dogs, gophers, and owls are other significant prairie species.

Much of Colorado is a semiarid desert, reaching elevations between 5,000 and 10,000 feet. The San Luis Valley, the Yampa River Valley near Steamboat Springs, and the Dolores River Canyon west of Grand Junction are all examples of Colorado's high deserts. Desert shrubs such as rabbit brush, sagebrush, and greasewood have uniquely adapted to the region by using their long roots to capture moisture deep under the ground.

Piñon-juniper woodlands, such as those found at Mesa Verde, are often referred to as "pygmy forests" because their trees are stunted and gnarled, soaking up only 10 to 20 inches of moisture each year. Juniper berries and piñon nuts provide nourishment for several species, such as elk, mule deer, bighorn sheep, quail, chipmunks, and squirrels.

Ponds, lakes, marshes, creeks, and rivers cover only 3 percent of the state but support 90 percent of its wildlife. Lush vegetation marks water location in this arid land, with tangles of cattails, bulrushes, willows, and cottonwoods lining the waterways. Migrating birds rest near water during the spring and fall, when sightings of great blue herons, waterfowl, and sandhill cranes delight wildlife viewers. Beavers invent dams on the streams, while fish—both native and introduced species—thrive in Colorado's waters.

Denver and Colorado Springs are situated on the eastern fringe of foothills, where thickets of scrub oak and mountain mahogany present beautiful fall colors. Beyond the foothills, ponderosa pines (with a bark that smells like vanilla), Douglas firs, and lodgepole pines begin to make their first appearance. Mice, chipmunks, foxes, black bears, scrub jays, and warblers harvest abundant seeds, fruits, and nuts from the vegetation during the fall, while mountain lions, bobcats, owls, and mule deer scavenge year-round.

At altitudes of approximately 10,000 feet, in places like the northern San Juan Mountains and the Creede and Lake City regions, are Colorado's subalpine forests. The temperature here is much cooler, and abundant snowfall makes this ecosystem moist. Hardy trees of the subalpine forest include the Engelmann spruce, subalpine fir, and aspen, with its distinctive white bark and quaking leaves. Bristlecone pines, the oldest trees in Colorado (some are 2,000 years old), also live here. Visitors to the subalpine in the spring and summer are delighted by its symphony of wildflowers, including avalanche lilies, Indian paintbrush, golden banner, and columbines (the Colorado state flower). Elk graze here in the summer but move to lower elevations in winter. Year-round residents include snowshoe hares and weasels that change their summer and winter colors to match the surrounding environment, and black bears that hibernate throughout the long winter months.

Colorado's alpine tundra begins at treeline, between 11,500 and 12,000 feet, where talus-covered mountains are barefaced. Alpine tundra regions include the highest parts of Rocky Mountain National Park and the Sawatch Range near Leadville and Salida. Trees living directly at treeline are warped by harsh winds and subzero temperatures. Ground-covering tundra plants can withstand the arctic cold above treeline but are extremely fragile and immediately destroyed upon human contact. The wildflowers at these elevations sport brilliant colors that actually convert light into heat and help them survive. The few animals that inhabit the tundra include marmots, playful pikas, ptarmigans, and sparrows.

LAY OF THE LAND

Colorado's lowest point is 3,387 feet above sea level, where the Arkansas River crosses into Kansas. Its highest point is the second highest mountain in the contiguous 48 states, Mt. Elbert, at 14,433 feet—which means that elevation can vary more than 11,000 feet. In between are gently rolling plains, soaring peaks, deep canyons, flat-topped mesas, and rushing rivers.

With more than 50 Fourteeners, this state is truly a mountaineer's paradise. Most ranges run primarily from north to south, such as the Front Range, which is easily accessible from Colorado Springs and Denver, and the Sangre de Cristo and Sawatch Ranges, framing the western and eastern boundaries of the San Luis Valley. Other ranges are angled differently, from east to west or at a 45-degree angle, such as the San Juan Mountains in southwestern Colorado and the Book Cliffs near Grand Junction.

Winding its way through the high peaks of Colorado is the Continental Divide, a crest of mountains and passes from which the continent's streams drain either to the Atlantic or Pacific Ocean. Coloradans refer to residents living west of the divide as "west slopers," while those to the east are "front rangers." A sometimes serious rivalry exists between these two groups, especially when it comes to the availability of water resources.

Several major rivers headwater at the crest of the Divide. The Colorado River begins as a playful mountain creek high above Grand Lake in Rocky Mountain National Park and courses through Colorado's western slope into Utah. It gathers strength with several western tributaries before entering the Grand Canyon in Arizona. Further west, it is captured behind Hoover Dam near Las Vegas and finally ends its journey at the Gulf of California. Because it supports agriculture and water consumption throughout the West, by the time it reaches the Gulf, its resources are entirely depleted.

The fabled Rio Grande begins on the eastern slope of the San Juan Mountains, flowing through southern Colorado and New Mexico until it forms the border between Texas and Mexico. The Arkansas River is born in the Sawatch Range amongst Colorado's highest peaks. It flows through the river canyons near Salida that are wildly popular with river rafters, before continuing its long continental journey to the Mississippi River. On the eastern side of the Mosquito Range, the Platte River originates as a rushing mountain river that flows northward through Denver, where it begins to flatten (similar to a plate, for which it is named), then continues its course through the northeastern plains of Colorado and Nebraska as the South and North Platte Rivers.

OUTDOOR ACTIVITIES

The best way to experience Colorado is to take part in any number of outdoor activities. Recreation here holds something for people of all ages and abilities. More than 23.9 million acres of public land provide plenty of room to "get lost" in the great outdoors. Before embarking into Colorado's wilderness, purchase a wilderness license ($1) from a local outfitter or sports store. The fees fund search-and-rescue operations in the state, including yours if you need it.

Colorado's mountains support more than 20 downhill ski resorts in addition to scores of cross-country centers and miles of back country trails. If you've been scared off by the notoriously exorbitant cost of a ski vacation, rest easy. While it's true that some ski areas are extremely pricey, others cater to budget and beginner skiers, something particularly pleasing for families. Besides, there are plenty of other things to do in Colorado during the winter—snowshoeing, cross-country skiing, ice skating, dipping in hot springs—that don't require a costly lift ticket.

River rafting on high mountain streams is Colorado's second most popular activity, behind skiing. Any type of river trip is possible, from calm and relaxed floats to white-knuckle adrenaline rushes. The river rafting season usually begins in May, when the mountain snowmelt turns calm rivers into raging torrents, and peaks in June and July. River outfitters rent equipment, lead float trips, and impart important lessons and instructions to help you enjoy your trip.

Fishing is a favorite pastime in Colorado. Opportunities range from fly-fishing in cold streams and rivers to dropping a line from a boat, canoe, or shore. The regulations in each part of the state vary greatly; contact the Division of Wildlife (see "Resources" at the end of this chapter) for up-to-date information. Before heading out to enjoy your day, pick up a fishing license, required for those over age 15.

Non-motorized recreational options abound. You can take short walks along bike paths or nature trails in urban areas, seek out longer day hikes in one of several national forests or parks, or plan an overnight or multiday excursion through untouched wilderness. Bicycling, on both dirt trails and roadways, is also extremely popular. Bike trails lace the entire state—in urban areas, in rural towns, and through a network of mountain trails fanning out into the back country.

Understandably, one of Colorado's most popular outdoor activities is scenic driving, simply taking your time to travel through the state and making several stops along the way. Interstate travelers miss out on much of Colorado's scenery, history, and wildlife. In 1991 Governor Roy Romer instituted a Scenic Historic Byways program, which now recognizes 22 scenic routes throughout the state. These noninterstate routes appear on the state map. The Colorado Historical Society's interpretive signs, found at major rest areas and scenic overlooks, offer information about the state's cultural and natural history. Whatever outdoor activity you choose in Colorado, enjoy!

PLANNING YOUR TRIP

HOW MUCH WILL IT COST?

Your trip to Colorado can be as expensive or as inexpensive as you want—it really depends on the condition of your pocketbook. I tend to be a budget traveler, so I have passed on several money-saving recommendations in the food and lodging sections of each chapter. But if I have come across a place where spending a little extra money is definitely worth it, I let you know. Be sure to ask about AAA or any other discounts that may apply. Ask if your travel agent is a member of a consortium, which provides better lodging rates.

Parts of Colorado are less expensive than others. Take, for example, Fort Morgan, Alamosa, or La Junta, where prices are generally a quarter of what they would be in Denver, Durango, or Telluride. These out-of-the-way destinations offer completely different visitor experiences than their well-known counterparts, and I strongly urge you to take advantage of them. You won't soon forget a journey out to the Pawnee Grasslands, the San Luis Valley, or the Santa Fe Trail region.

You will also see a huge difference in lodging rates according to the high tourist season in each destination. Ski resorts such as Aspen, Steamboat Springs, and Telluride are expensive during the winter, especially late December to late March. But during spring and fall their prices drop 10 to 20 percent, if not more, a bonus for travelers who like to visit a place when it is less crowded. Their summer rates are also lower than you might expect. Other destinations, such as the San Luis Valley, Upper Rio Grande Valley, and Rocky Mountain National Park, are nearly deserted during the winter, and prices are lowered at these times to attract visitors.

Let's say you've purchased your airline ticket, rented a car, and are ready to hit the road. If you like to camp and buy your food at a local market instead of eating every meal out, you should budget $15 to $20 per person, per day. If you don't like to camp, expect to spend an average of $60 to $75 per person, per day (prices based on double occupancy at budget accommodations and two to three moderately priced meals). The amount of money you spend on gas depends on your vehicle; airfare and rental fees are also variable. Add another $10 per day to visit museums, parks, and attractions, then budget how much you can spend on souvenirs or presents.

WHEN TO GO

Colorado is a wonderful place to visit at any time of year, but you should schedule your trip according to your interests. If you like to downhill ski, you'll want to come sometime between Thanksgiving weekend and the end of April, although the ski season has been known to last until the Fourth of July at higher elevations. Keep in mind that winter is also the most treacherous time to drive in Colorado, as winter storms can close passes and highways. Even in early and late summer, rain and snowstorms at higher elevations can make driving extremely dangerous. Many campgrounds and RV parks also close during the winter.

When the snow begins to melt in the high country (usually by mid-May), mountain dirt roads and trails become one messy pile of mud. The high country is often inaccessible for driving, hiking, or mountain biking until things dry out, usually by mid-June. Spring is a great time to visit western and eastern Colorado, before the summer heat begins. Summer and autumn are ideal for hiking and backpacking in the higher mountain elevations.

Throughout Colorado, outdoor festivals take place every weekend during the summer. I have given you approximate dates for some of the larger events, so you can plan accordingly. During the more popular festivals, it can be tough (and sometimes downright impossible) to book a room in a place overrun with festival goers.

If you are a warm-weather traveler and like to beat the crowds, consider planning your trip before Memorial Day or after Labor Day. During these months, the weather is still pleasant for sightseeing, and many families can't travel because the kids are in school. You may have your chosen destination all to yourself.

CLIMATE

The most prominent feature of Colorado's weather is that it is exceptionally fickle. The state's extreme differences in elevation mean that weather patterns vary considerably from one place to the next. For example, eastern Colorado can be locked in a torrential downpour while western Colorado remains dry as a bone. This wide range of climatic variation can occur even in a space of less than 30 miles. To make things even more exciting, on any given day a region might see a variance of 50-plus degrees in a 12-hour period, with sub-zero temperatures in the morning soaring to 50 degrees by 2 p.m.

The climate is greatly affected by the position of mountain ranges in the central and western parts of the state, where mountains can either shield or trap a valley in harsh weather. Mountain valleys can be much colder than the mountains themselves in the winter months, because cold air from higher elevations sinks to the valley floor.

Although Colorado's weather does vary, you can always depend on the fact that bad weather never sticks around for long. A bitter winter snowstorm will almost always be followed by a sunny day that quickly melts the snow at lower elevations. This pattern can make winter in Colorado downright enjoyable. During the spring and fall, the state is usually blessed with long periods of dry, pleasant weather often punctuated by sudden rain or snowstorms. The summer months are hot in the lower elevations (temperatures average around 80 degrees but have been known to climb into the 100s for days at a time), but thunderstorms regularly cool things off in the late afternoon.

Always be prepared for changes in weather conditions and expect precipitation at any time, even on clear and sunny days. When exploring the high country, be sure to summit above timberline before noon, and hightail it back down to the trees as soon as possible. The last place you want to be during an afternoon lightning storm is at the top of a

COLORADO'S CLIMATE

Average daily high and low temperatures in degrees Fahrenheit, plus monthly precipitation in inches:

	Colorado Springs	Denver	Grand Junction	Telluride
Jan.	41/16	43/17	36/15	37/6
	.30	.47	.59	1.4
March	49/24	51/26	54/31	42/13
	.88	1.1	.82	1.6
May	69/42	69/44	75/48	62/30
	2.3	2.4	.76	1.7
July	85/57	87/59	92/64	77/41
	2.9	1.7	.62	2.5
Sept.	75/61	77/48	81/53	69/34
	1.3	1.1	.89	2.1
Nov.	50/25	52/26	51/28	46/15
	.47	.69	.63	1.5

mountain. Always bring rough-weather gear, such as a raincoat, heavy pants, a hat, and gloves, when exploring the high country, to protect yourself from hypothermia during a sudden storm. And because the sun shines brightly in Colorado all year round, always wear sunscreen and a hat, especially at higher elevations.

TRANSPORTATION

Those flying into Colorado can choose from several airports, depending on where your vacation begins. Denver International Airport (DIA) is the sixth largest airport in the country. Situated a half-hour east of metropolitan Denver, the new airport cost $5 billion to build. It features a unique peaked roof that resembles a series of white tents, and inside, local and national artists have created a multitude of murals, paintings, sculpture, and mosaics (the bill for the art alone was $7.5 million). The concourses are filled with retail shops and restaurants rivaling those found in any American mall.

DIA is the first stop for most major flights into Colorado, which gives you some flexibility in planning your trip. You can fly directly into Denver, rent a car, and begin your trip there, or take a connecting flight to another Colorado airport. These include the Colorado Springs airport (just an hour south of Denver along the Front Range), or the major Western Slope airports of Grand Junction, Eagle, Montrose, or Durango (especially helpful if you want to spend most of your time in the western part of the state).

Many rental car companies are located at DIA. Be sure to compare prices of national companies with those of locally owned companies for the best deal. Each rental agency has fleets of minivans and four-wheel-drive vehicles, the most popular rentals in the state. Many travelers, especially Europeans, like to rent recreational vehicles to undertake their road trip in comfort.

Once you're on the road in the vehicle of your choice, you will find driving around Colorado an extremely pleasurable experience. Driving to and from these destinations can be easily accomplished by any type of vehicle. However, several scenic drives follow some pretty rough roads, unsuitable for two-wheel-drive vehicles and RVs. You can rent a four-wheel drive at the outset (a smart idea if you plan to be driving during the winter months) or when you reach a certain destination, as many towns have companies that rent vehicles for just that purpose.

When driving through Colorado, you should always check road

conditions by calling the Colorado Department of Transportation
Road Conditions Hotline, 303/639-1111 or 639-1234. Or call the local
sheriff's department or state patrol office for an up-to-date report.

While train travel is not the most convenient method of getting
around Colorado, several train excursions do exist. Enjoy a gorgeous
trip through the Rocky Mountains and the incomparable Glenwood
Canyon by taking an Amtrak train from Denver's Union Station to the
resort town of Glenwood Springs (see the Roaring Fork Valley chapter). This is a great way to see the scenery without having to drive. For
more information, call Amtrak at 303/534-2812 or 800/872-7245.
There are also two excellent historical narrow-gauge railroads: the
Durango & Silverton and the Cumbres & Toltec, which offer a great
chance to see the beauty of the mountains by rail.

CAMPING, LODGING, AND DINING

Should you choose to camp during your stay in Colorado, thousands
of opportunities await you. You won't spend more than $10 per
night to camp at a public site, or more than $20 per night at a private
site. Some campsites are accessible from the highway, others are tucked
along a remote county or forest road, and still others can be reached
only by foot. Most private campgrounds cater to RVs, providing long
pull-through sites, electricity, and water. Some even have swimming
pools, hot tubs, horseback rides, and fishing access right from your
campsite. Call ahead to make reservations at a private RV park, especially during the summer months. Many private campgrounds are
closed during the late fall, winter, and early spring.

Public sites usually don't offer the same services as private campgrounds, but most do have water and restroom facilities. The more
popular national parks have several large campgrounds with hundreds
of sites open year-round. The options within national forests tend to
be fairly rustic and accommodate fewer people. If you are traveling
through Bureau of Land Management land, you can usually just pull
off the road and pick your site—it's all public land and all available
for camping.

Even if you plan on camping most of the time during your trip to
Colorado, some nights you may just need a bed. You don't necessarily
have to pay an arm and a leg to find a decent place. I have not recommended any chain hotels or motels because they are usually all the
same and many more personable exist.

If you are traveling on a limited budget, you may want to take advantage of cozy bed-and-breakfasts that offer lower rates if you have to walk down the hall to use the bathroom (remember, the rate also includes breakfast). Motor motels and rustic cabins, also very affordable, usually have small kitchenettes. Historic hotels, inns, and rustic lodges tend to be slightly more expensive, but their rates vary according to season. Often these accommodations include a full breakfast, with some providing other meals as well. The only catch about staying in such places is that they often have strict reservation policies, requiring at least 30 days' cancellation notice. The rooms are usually nonsmoking, and children and pets are not always welcome. The amenities at such accommodations are truly special because the innkeepers will often provide fresh flowers, robes, reading material, and other personal touches usually unheard of in the hotel/motel industry.

On the upper end of the lodging scale are those legendary places you should know about just in case you receive a windfall and want to spend it all in one night. These accommodations range from a resplendent historic hotel to a special suite in a bed-and-breakfast, where the hosts do their best to treat you like a king or queen.

The dining recommendations in this book vary widely and should satisfy your requirements for any type of meal. Because you will spend your vacation doing a variety of things, you will want to have a variety of meals, with different prices, tastes, and ambience. You might want to grab a bagel before hiking or search out the best diner in town for a steaming platter of eggs, hash browns, and toast for under $3. Lunch might find you eating a burger or diving into a substantial salad while sitting on a sunny patio people-watching, while dinner can range from a hearty ethnic meal to a feast of prime rib with a bottle of wine. The dining possibilities in each destination are usually diverse enough to allow you to choose from the frugal to the extravagant.

RECOMMENDED READING

A wealth of knowledge exists in the numerous books written on many different Colorado subjects. I have recommended a few— actually only a fraction of my favorites—to enhance your trip. Most of these books are still in print and can be found at major bookstores. If you have trouble locating one, contact the bookstore at the Colorado Historical Society, 303/866-3682, or the Tattered Cover Bookstore, 303/322-7727 or 800/833-9327.

For the best book on the prehistory and history of Colorado's Native Americans, turn to *People of the Red Earth*, by Sally Crum. In addition to nicely presenting the information for laypeople, she provides lists of important archaeological sites that you may also wish to visit. In *Bent Fort*, David Lavender captures the essence of the cultural and economic interactions of fur traders, merchants from Missouri, Plains Indians, and Mexicans who met at the isolated Arkansas River fort beginning in 1834.

The Colorado Book, edited by Eleanor Gehres et al., is a compendium of fiction, nonfiction, history, art, poetry, and music, all about Colorado. This indispensable volume does a nice job of assembling the best of the best in Colorado writings. To step into the shoes of an earlier Colorado traveler, find a copy of Isabella Bird's *A Lady's Life in the Rocky Mountains*. This intrepid Englishwoman thrived on adventure travel and made several trips abroad—by herself—during her exciting life. She trekked through Colorado during the late 1870s, when she stayed, among other places, in Estes Park and climbed Longs Peak in a pair of borrowed boots many sizes too large. Bird's insights into Colorado during this period are priceless.

The *Colorado Wildlife Viewing Guide*, by Mary Taylor Gray, is a well organized and carefully researched guide with suggestions on what types of wildlife to look for in national parks, wildlife refuges, national forests, and state wildlife areas, as well as in lesser-known county and municipal parks. Gray's maps and place descriptions are excellent. Wildflower enthusiasts will want to use the two volumes of *Colorado Wildflowers*, by G. K. Guennel, as their bible; the books include full-page glossy photos of wonderfully diverse specimens.

For a general synopsis of Colorado history, I recommend *A Colorado History*, by Carl Ubbelholde, Maxine Benson, and Duane Smith, as the most comprehensive and informative. While not a full-fledged historical book, *Across Colorado: Recipes and Recollections*, Thomas J. Noel and the Volunteers of the Colorado Historical Society, is a wonderful collection of recipes, legends, photographs, and other interesting historical facts about the state. Likewise, Thomas J. Noel's *Buildings of Colorado* is a great volume for anyone interested in visiting venerable old structures while on vacation.

Volumes have been written about Colorado's mining camps, but several books approach the subject in a more entertaining and casual manner. *Images of the San Juans*, by P. David Smith, is a photographic history of the San Juans filled with fascinating images of their early settlement and mining industry. *The Life of an Ordinary Woman*, by Anne Ellis, is a touching diary written by a woman who lived in several Colorado mining camps. Ellis compellingly describes, with stark realism, the everyday issues faced by women in these harsh places and tells with humor and insight how they coped. For an informative guide with directions to many of Colorado's most famous ghost towns, pick up a book by Muriel Sibell Wolle, *Stampede to Timberline: The Ghost Towns and Mining Camps of Colorado* or *Timberline Tailings: Tales of Colorado's Ghost Towns and Mining Camps*.

For information on hikes within the state, one of the best guides available is *100 Hikes in Colorado*, by Scott S. Warren. Should you be traveling with children, I highly recommend a book written by two intrepid moms, Marty Meitus and Patty Thorn, called *Places to Go with Children in Colorado*. The authors impart several fresh ideas that make traveling fun for children and recommend many "child-friendly" places throughout the state.

For more suggestions on camping and other rustic accommodations, turn to *Colorado RV Parks* and *Colorado Cabins, Cottages, and Lodges*, both written by Hilton and Jenny Fitt-Peaster, who know the cabins and RV parks like their own backyard. And *Absolutely Every Bed and Breakfast in Colorado (Almost)*, edited by Alan Stark et. al., offers helpful summaries of hundreds of bed-and-breakfasts within the state.

RESOURCES

Bed & Breakfast Innkeepers of Colorado: P.O. Box 38416, Colorado Springs, CO 80937-8416; 800/83-BOOKS.

Bureau of Land Management: 2850 Youngfield, Lakewood, CO 80215; 303/239-3600.

Colorado Association of Campgrounds, Cabins, and Lodges: 5101 Pennsylvania Avenue, Boulder, CO 80303; 303/499-9343.

Colorado Bicycle Program: 4201 East Arkansas Avenue, Room 225, Denver, CO 80222; 303/757-9982.

Colorado Cross Country Ski Association: Box 1292, Kremmling, CO 80459; 800/869-4560.

Colorado Department of Transportation: Road Conditions, 4201 East Arkansas, Denver, CO 80222; 303/639-1111 or 303/639-1234.

Colorado Division of Parks and Outdoor Recreation: 1313 Sherman Street, Suite 618, Denver, CO 80203; 303/866-3437.

Colorado Division of Wildlife: 6060 Broadway, Denver, CO 80216.

General information, 303/297-1192; fishing information, 303/291-7533; up-to-date fishing reports, 303/291-7534; camping information, 303/291-7532.

Colorado Dude & Guest Ranch Association: P.O. Box 300, Tabernash, CO 80478; 970/887-3128.

Colorado Mountain Club: 710 10th Street, Golden, CO 80401; 303/279-3080.

Colorado Ski Country USA: 1560 Broadway, Denver, CO 80203; 303/837-0793.

Colorado State Patrol: 700 Kipling, Denver, CO 80215; 303/239-4500.

Colorado Travel and Tourism Authority: 707 17th Street, Denver, CO 80202; 800/265-6723.

Denver Metro Convention and Visitors Bureau: 280 14th Street, Denver, CO 80202; 303/892-1505.

National Park Service: 12795 West Alameda Parkway, Lakewood, CO 80225; 303/969-2000.

United States Forest Service: P.O. Box 25127, Lakewood, CO 80225; 740 Simms, Lakewood, CO 80225; 303/275-5350.

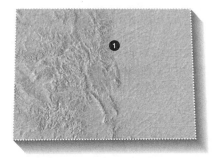

1
DENVER

In November 1858, the confluence of Cherry Creek and the South Platte River, formerly an Indian camping ground, erupted into a brawling boom town swarming with enthusiastic gold seekers, schemers, and promoters. The banks of the waterways would forever be changed by the discovery of precious metals in the mountains to the west. Early Denver pioneers maneuvered to make the settlement bigger and better than its counterparts on the eastern fringe of the Rocky Mountains. Their efforts paid off, as Denver is the largest center for commerce, industry, and trade in the Rocky Mountain West.

Although dubbed the "Queen City of the Plains," Denver's connection to the mountains stretching across its western horizon cannot be overstated. These peaks are a haven and escape for Denverites, and their proximity to the sprawling metropolis makes this city one of the best places to live in the country. The 1990s have heralded phenomenal growth for Denver and its expansive suburbs, with more than 2 million people now living in the metropolitan area. Denver boasts a state-of-the-art airport, an innovative municipal library, world-class museums, four professional sports teams, and an eclectic entertainment scene. The city is a major visitor destination in itself, and many people spend a few days exploring it before heading into other parts of Colorado. ◼

DENVER

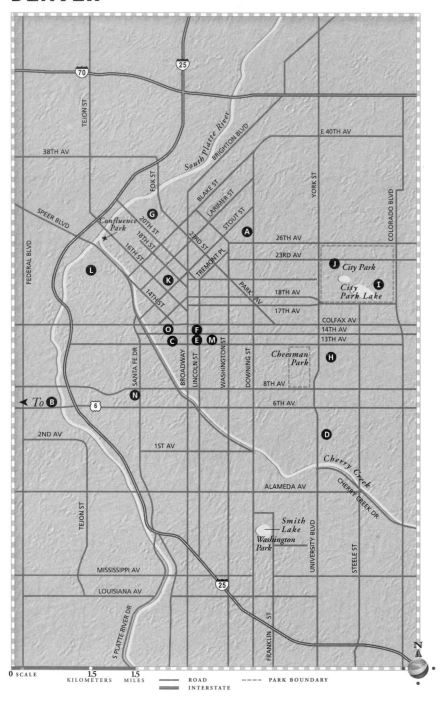

Sights

Ⓐ Black American West Museum

Ⓑ Buffalo Bill Memorial Museum and Grave

Ⓒ Byers-Evans House and Denver History Museum

Ⓓ Cherry Creek

Ⓔ Colorado History Museum

Ⓕ Colorado State Capitol

Ⓖ Coors Field

Ⓒ Denver Art Museum

Ⓗ Denver Botanic Gardens

Ⓘ Denver Museum of Natural History/Planetarium/IMAX Theater

Ⓒ Denver Public Library

Ⓙ Denver Zoo

Ⓚ Downtown

Ⓛ Elitch Gardens Amusement Park

Ⓜ Molly Brown House

Ⓝ Museo de las Americas

Ⓞ United States Mint

Note: Items with the same letter are located in the same area.

A PERFECT DAY IN DENVER

Spend the day exploring Denver's downtown. Museum buffs can visit two excellent regional venues: the Denver Art Museum and the Colorado Historical Society in the Civic Center Cultural Complex. Nearby are the pedestrian Sixteenth Street Mall, Larimer Square, and Lower Downtown, with shops, coffeehouses, bars, and restaurants. In the evening treat yourself to one of the city's excellent restaurants, then check out local listings for concerts, plays, movies, or special events in the metro area.

SIGHTSEEING HIGHLIGHTS

★★★ **Colorado History Museum**—The museum highlights Colorado's multifarious history through permanent and changing exhibits. It tells the stories of explorers, mountain men, Native Americans, pioneers, and diverse ethnic groups in Colorado. Of note are permanent exhibits on the Cheyenne Dog Soldiers, a prominent band of the Cheyenne Indian tribe, and the role of Hispanos in Colorado's history.

Details: *1300 Broadway; 303/866-3682. Mon–Sat 10–4:30, Sun noon–4:30. $3 adults, $2.50 seniors and students, $1.50 ages 6–16.*

Combination ticket for the Byers Evans House and Denver History Museum: $5 adults, $4 seniors and students, $2 children. (2 hours)

★★★ **Denver Museum of Natural History**—In addition to many unique exhibits, dioramas, and interactive programs, this museum has a fascinating permanent dinosaur exhibit called *Prehistoric Journey*. Visitors are transported to the age of the dinosaurs through a state-of-the-art eco-environment simulating that of the dinosaurs billions of years ago. Several dinosaur skeletons in the museum's voluminous collection have been painstakingly reassembled, and the informative exhibit provides all the relevant details.

The **Planetarium** and **IMAX theater** are also part of the Denver Museum of Natural History complex. The Planetarium presents laser shows and multimedia attractions, while the IMAX theater projects films on a screen four and a half stories high and five stories wide, immersing the audience in stunning cinematography. Shows run every hour, starting at 11 a.m. Daytime planetarium shows are included in the price of museum admission. IMAX admission: $5 adults, $4 children and seniors. Museum and IMAX combination ticket: $9 adults, $6 children and seniors.

Details: 2001 Colorado Blvd. on the east end of City Park; 303/322-7009. IMAX information: 303/370-6300. Daily 9–5 $6 adults, $4 seniors and ages 3–12. (half day)

★★★ **Denver Public Library**—Directly west of the Colorado History Museum is the Denver Public Library, designed by world-renowned architect Michael Graves. This addition to the historic Central Library resembles a medieval city, with its contrasting shapes, heights, and colors. The $75 million expansion made this public library the largest between Chicago and Los Angeles.

It's worth a trip inside to view the library's architectural details. Wood-paneled walls, intriguing murals in the spacious atrium, and a limestone floor with actual fossils adorn this stunning piece of architecture. On the fifth floor are the Western history and genealogy collections, including the Gates Western History Reading Room. At the center of the room is a dramatic wooden derrick, harkening back to Colorado's mining and oil-drilling days. Western art graces the walls, including the dramatic landscape painting *Estes Park*, by Albert Bierstadt.

Details: 10 W. 14th Ave., 303/640-6200. Mon–Wed 10–9, Thu–Sat 10–5:30, Sun 1–5 p.m. (30 minutes)

★★★ **Denver Zoo**—More than 3,500 animals live in Denver's city zoo, located next to the Denver Museum of Natural History. The zoo constantly strives to update its exhibits, and new animals arrive periodically. One highlight is Tropical Discovery, a simulated rainforest habitat that includes vibrant, colorful fish aquariums and a collection of exotic snakes living in temple wall ruins. In the Northern Shores exhibit, polar bears swim underwater, and sea lions and seals playfully course through outdoor pools.

Details: E. 23rd St. and Steele, between York St. and Colorado Blvd. in City Park; 303/331-4110. Daily 10–5. $6 adults, $3 seniors and ages 4–12. (2–3 hours)

★★ **Colorado State Capitol**—To the east of the Civic Center Park is the classical Colorado State Capitol, embellished with dramatic entryway murals, gilded stairways, and an eye-catching gold dome. Enjoy a stunning 360-degree view of the mountains, plains, and city from the upper rotunda.

Details: Between Sherman and Lincoln Sts. on Colfax (15th Ave.); 303/866-2604. Free tours weekdays 9–3. (30 minutes)

★★ **Denver Art Museum**—Connected by a small walking plaza to the west of the Denver Public Library is the Denver Art Museum. This municipal museum boasts strong early British, American Indian, Pre-Columbian, Spanish Colonial, and Western American collections. It presents several changing exhibits annually. You'll find an excellent restaurant on the lower level, open during museum hours.

Details: 100 W. 14th Ave. (14th and Bannock); 303/640-2793. Tue–Sat 10–5, Wed 10–9, Sun noon–5. $4.50 adults, $3.50 seniors and students, under five free. Free to all on Saturday. (2 hours)

★★ **Denver Botanic Gardens**—In the midst of a bustling city, the Denver Botanic Gardens provide a quiet oasis of trees, plants, flowers, and birds. The alpine garden has a wide assemblage of mountain flora from around the world. Nearby, the Japanese garden has a serene goldfish pond and small tea house imported from Japan. Several unique festivals and special events occur here during the warmer months.

Details: 1005 York St. (eastern end of Cheesman Park); 303/331-4010. Daily 9–5. $3 adults, $1.50 seniors and students, $1 ages 6–15. (1½ hours)

✩✩ **Downtown Denver**—The historic heart of Denver has been the focus of an exciting rejuvenation in recent years. Many renovated warehouses and office buildings in Lower Downtown (dubbed LoDo) now accommodate restaurants, bars, galleries, lofts, and specialty stores. The urban improvements were spurred by the opening of **Coors Field** at 20th and Blake, the home of the Colorado Rockies, Denver's major league baseball team. Designed as a tribute to old-time downtown baseball parks, Coors Field has natural grass and 48,000 seats arranged so that fans sit close to the action. Tickets are often available for many of the games; call the Colorado Rockies at 800/388-7625. **Elitch Gardens Amusement Park** (I-25 and Speer; 303/595-4386) features many rides, including the Twister, a wooden roller coaster, and the Colorado River water ride. The park is prominently located in the Platte River Valley, a downtown urban area, and is open daily in summer. Admission is $24 for those over 48 inches tall, $14 for those under 48 inches. Discounts for seniors.

Details: Denver Metro Convention and Visitors Bureau, 280 14th St., 303/892-1505. (half–full day)

✩ **Black American West Museum**—Situated in the historic Five Points neighborhood, this heritage center chronicles the lives of African American cowboys, soldiers, and pioneers who came to the West and Colorado after the Civil War. Many people consider this museum the best source of information about African Americans in the West.

Details: 3091 California St. (at the northeast end of the light-rail system); 303/292-2566. Wed–Fri 10–2, Sat and Sun noon–5. $3 adults, $2 seniors, $1 ages 13–17; 50¢ ages 4–12. (1 hour)

✩ **Buffalo Bill Memorial Museum and Grave**—Buffalo Bill (William F. Cody), arguably the most famous man of his time, died at his sister's home in Denver in 1915. Thousands of people filed past his body on display in the state capitol. Even though Buffalo Bill wished to be buried in the town of Cody, Wyoming, his wife instructed Denver officials to bury him here, on top of Lookout Mountain just west of town. The Buffalo Bill Memorial Museum displays rare memorabilia from this showman, army scout, and frontier legend.

Details: 987½ Lookout Mountain Road (take I-70 west to exit 256); 303/526-0747. May–Oct daily 9–5. Winter Tue–Sun 9–4. $3 adults, $2 seniors, $1 ages 6–15. (1 hour)

✭ **Byers-Evans House and Denver History Museum**—Housed in the former home of two prominent Denver families and filled with Victorian furnishings, this facility also includes an innovative interactive computer program providing interesting facts about Denver's history.
Details: 1310 Bannock St.; 303/620-4933. Tue–Sat 10–4, Sun 1–4. $3 adults, $2.50 seniors and students, $1.50 ages 6–16. (1 hour)

✭ **Cherry Creek**—For a fun afternoon of window shopping or spending money with wild abandon, head to Cherry Creek, southeast of downtown at First Avenue and Steel Street. The shopping mall features well-known retailers such as Neiman Marcus, Saks Fifth Avenue, and Williams and Sonoma, in addition to hundreds of specialty stores.

Just north of the mall is **Cherry Creek North**, a delightful area with restaurants, boutiques, and great coffee shops. The multi-storied **Tattered Cover Bookstore**, on the corner of Steele and First Avenue, 303/322-7727, is one of Denver's most treasured institutions. Its wooden shelves are stocked with every conceivable type of printed material. Scattered throughout the maze of bookshelves are plush loveseats and overstuffed chairs, perfect for spending a quiet afternoon browsing through books, magazines, and newspapers. The coffee shop on the first floor will tempt you with delectable pastries and desserts; check out the Fourth Story Restaurant for more serious lunch and dinner options. Lower Downtown also hosts a Tattered Cover bookstore, on the corner of 16th and Wynkoop, 303/436-1070.
Details: 3000 E. First Ave., 303/355-4223. (2 hours)

✭ **Molly Brown House**—The fabulously wealthy Molly Brown never cared that Denver's high society found her gauche and uncultured. After she survived the disastrous *Titanic* shipwreck, she became known as "Unsinkable Molly Brown" and was the subject of a Broadway play of the same name. The movie *Titanic* again made Molly the talk of the town. Historic Denver, a preservation agency, has restored her luxurious mansion into a Victorian museum, with guided tours and afternoon teas.
Details: 1340 Pennsylvania; 303/832-4092. Tue–Sat 10–4, Sun noon–4, open Mon in summer. $5 adults, $3.50 seniors, $1.50 ages 6–12. (1 hour)

✭ **Museo de las Americas**—Seated at the nucleus of Denver's Hispanic community, this museum exhibits Hispanic art, culture, and history. Changing displays focus on Latin America and the American Southwest.
Details: 861 Santa Fe Dr.; 303/571-4401. Tue–Sat 10–5. $3 adults, $2 seniors, $1 students. (1 hour)

✸ **United States Mint**—The basement of this formidable building houses the second largest storehouse of gold in the country; only Fort Knox's is bigger. In addition to free weekday tours of the coin-minting process, you can also view several excellent displays on the history of the U.S. Mint and Treasury.

Details: 320 W. Colfax Ave. at Cherokee St.; 303/405-4761. Mon–Fri 8–2:45, tours leave every 30 minutes. Admission is free. (1 hour)

FITNESS AND RECREATION

More than 130 miles of bike paths lace the metro area, connecting Denver to its outlying suburbs. One of the more popular paths, the **Cherry Creek Trail**, can be accessed behind the Cherry Creek Shopping Center. If taken north five miles, the trail ends up in **Confluence Park**, where gold was discovered in 1858 at the confluence of the South Platte River and Cherry Creek. Eight miles south is **Cherry Creek Reservoir**, a popular recreation spot for volleyball, windsurfing, waterskiing, and Jet Skiing.

Denverites love their many well-kept neighborhood parks, such as **Washington Park** in south Denver, and **Cheesman Park**, in the Capitol Hill neighborhood west of the Botanic Gardens. Both have loops for jogging, walking, Rollerblading, and biking, and acres of fields for playing soccer, volleyball, or ultimate Frisbee. Enjoy beautiful scenery, a picnic, or a short hike at such nearby state parks as **Castlewood Canyon** and **Roxborough**, both south of Denver.

FOOD

The cuisine of Denver is superb—from Colorado specialties to a variety of ethnic offerings. However, with more than 2,000 restaurants in the metro area, recommending only a few is difficult! My recommendations are places I like to go for special occasions, with dinner entrees usually within the $11 to $22 range, or restaurants at which you can expect quality food for reasonable prices.

Restaurants have proliferated downtown during the past few years, with several steakhouses, breweries, and sports bars dominating the scene. But a number of restaurants have also withstood the test of time, such as **Mori Japanese Restaurant**, 2019 Market, 303/298-1864, in the backyard of Coors Field. Its extensive menu features only the freshest sushi and sashimi, as well as mouth-watering seafood soups, teriyaki, and tempura. The **Wazee Supper Club**, 1600 15th St., 303/623-9518, has retained its funky neighborhood atmosphere in the midst of a changing downtown. Pizzas are first-rate, with heaping amounts of toppings and a fresh, flaky crust. Serving food until 1 a.m., the restaurant is frequented by many regulars who can't stay away from the pizza.

South of downtown, at East Eighth Ave. and Lincoln Street, is **Le Central**, 303/863-8094, billed as the "affordable French restaurant." Serving Denverites for years, this popular place is perfect for a romantic evening or a relaxing brunch. Its ample portions and interesting menu feature seasonal ingredients and wild game. Reservations recommended.

Near the University of Denver campus, at the intersection of Evans Street and University Boulevard, is **Coos Bay Bistro**, 2076 S. University Boulevard, 303/744-3591. The bistro calls its cuisine "Californian–northwest Italian," but this label doesn't begin to describe their wonderful creations, featuring fresh salads, pizzas, tapas, pastas, and seafood. For authentic Mexican food, head to **El Noa Noa**, 722 Santa Fe Drive (near the Museo de las Americas), 303/623-9968. Serving breakfast, lunch, and dinner every day but Sunday, the restaurant boasts a beautiful outdoor patio. Here you'll find such traditional combinations as smothered enchiladas, wonderful chiles rellenos, and huevos rancheros.

In Cherry Creek North is **Mel's Bar & Grill**, 235 Fillmore Street, 303/333-3979, operated by two longtime Denver restaurant owners whose experience shows in the atmosphere and menu, featuring contemporary American foods with Mediterranean influence. **Zaidy's Deli of Cherry Creek**, 121 Adams, 303/333-5336, serves traditional deli fare, with thick sandwiches, breakfasts, and traditional Jewish cooking such as lox, bagels, chopped liver, and chicken noodle soup. The enormous potato latke–lox combo is incredible.

Looking for a quick and healthy meal or a well-stocked salad bar? Try **Alfalfa's Market**, 900 East 11th Avenue, 303/ 832-7701; or 201 University Boulevard, 303/320-0700. Alfalfa's is a natural and gourmet foods grocery store, deli, and bakery that prepares healthy and satisfying hot meals (eggplant lasagna, pasta, roasted chicken) for relatively inexpensive prices. For a great deal in fast, healthy, and inexpensive food, try the fat burritos at **Chipotle's**, 745 Colorado Boulevard, 303/333-2121; or downtown at 1600 California or 1620 Market. Ask for a chicken fajita burrito—a blend of rice, beans, seasoned chicken, and your choice of salsa, $4.95.

DENVER

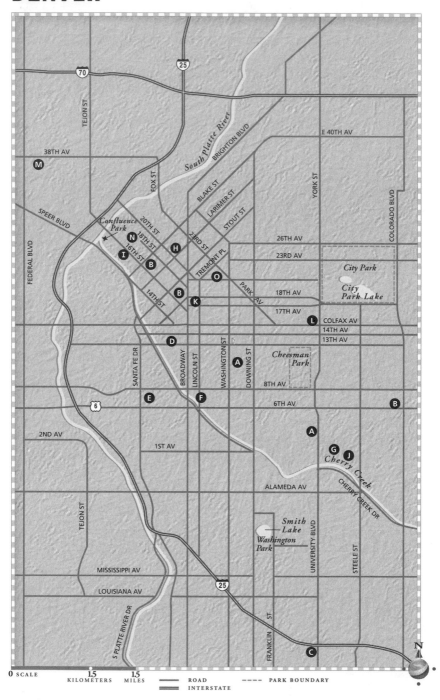

Food

- **Ⓐ** Alfalfa's Market
- **Ⓑ** Chipotle's
- **Ⓒ** Coos Bay Bistro
- **Ⓓ** Dozen's
- **Ⓔ** El Noa Noa
- **Ⓕ** Le Central
- **Ⓖ** Mel's Bar & Grill
- **Ⓗ** Mori Japanese Restaurant
- **Ⓘ** Wazee Supper Club
- **Ⓙ** Zaidy's Deli

Lodging

- **Ⓚ** Brown Palace Hotel
- **Ⓛ** Castle Marne
- **Ⓜ** Lumber Baron Inn
- **Ⓝ** Oxford Hotel
- **Ⓞ** Queen Anne Inn

Dozen's, 236 West 13th Avenue, is a great place for breakfast, brunch, or lunch. It's conveniently located near the attractions of the Civic Center Cultural Complex. The menu includes fluffy omelets, egg and vegetable skillets, and a range of healthy sandwiches under $7.

LODGING

The elegant **Brown Palace Hotel**, 321 17th Street, at Tremont Place, 800/321-2599 or 303/297-3111, is the grande dame of all Denver hotels, built in 1893 to attract a first-class clientele. Its distinctive triangular Renaissance structure sits prominently among Denver's skyscrapers. The hotel's galleried atrium lobby is adorned with tapestries, a terrazzo floor, and onyx arches. The rooms feature either Victorian or art deco furnishings. Rates depend on availability and the season but generally range between $180 and $250 a night. The Brown offers a special deal if you call within 30 days of the time you wish to stay. If a room is available, they will offer it at reduced rates.

The **Oxford Hotel**, 1600 17th Street, 800/228-5838 or 303/628-5400, is another of Denver's elegant historic hotels. It's within a stone's throw of both Coors Field and Lower Downtown's booming restaurant, bar, and gallery scene. Rates range between $139 and $299, depending on the season and availability. The hotel restaurant and pub, McCormick's, specializes in seafood, and its quirky art deco martini bar, the Cruise Room, is one of Denver's most popular night spots.

Bed-and-breakfasts are often more economical and comfortable options; you'll find several near downtown cultural attractions and restaurants. The **Queen Anne Inn**, 2147 Tremont Place, 303/296-6666, is a well-known inn housed in two shingled Victorian structures. Some rooms feature jet tubs or spas, and amenities include hot/cold apple cider, a hot breakfast each morning, and the opportunity to taste a different Colorado wine each evening. Double rooms range from $75 to $145. Another well-appointed bed-and-breakfast near downtown is the **Castle Marne**, 1572 Race Street, 303/331-0621 or 800/926-2763. With amenities such as robes, Jacuzzis, and fresh flowers, this is a great place to be pampered. Rates, including a full breakfast with homemade breads and muffins, range from $85 to $220. The owner will also serve a six-course candlelight dinner for $120.

The **Lumber Baron Inn**, 2555 West 37th Avenue, 303/477-8205, is an 1890 Queen Anne mansion in the north Denver Highlands neighborhood. The owners restored the inn and its original furnishings, creating a lovely bed-and-breakfast. Five suites, ranging from $125 to $195 a night, feature private whirlpool tubs. The inn offers several special packages, such as a murder mystery night, offering a unique variation from the normal bed-and-breakfast routine.

NIGHTLIFE

Denver offers the kind of big-city nightlife that will satisfy just about any taste. When you get to town, pick up a copy of the independent weekly newspaper *Westword* or the Friday entertainment section of either the *Denver Post* or *Rocky Mountain News* for a listing of weekly plays, concerts, lectures, dance performances, films, and gallery offerings.

Several art deco movie theaters have been converted into concert venues offering a great variety of live music, from salsa, country, big band, and alternative to plain old rock 'n' roll. The **Bluebird Theater**, 3317 East Colfax Avenue, 303/ 322-2308; the **Ogden Theatre**, 935 East Colfax Avenue, 303/831-9448; and the **Paramount Theatre**, 1631 Glenarm Place, 303/534-8336, always have something interesting going on, such as comedy acts, cult movies, or concerts.

About a dozen microbreweries cluster in downtown Denver. While each brews distinctive beers, the **Wynkoop Brewing Company**, 1634 18th Street (18th and Wynkoop), 303/297-2700, is a head above the crowd. The brewpub is across from Union Station, in an 1880s warehouse on an historic commercial street. The establishment has grown to three levels, with comedy or jazz in the basement, a restaurant and bar on the first level, and a sea of pool tables upstairs. Another popular brewpub is the **Broadway Pub**, 2441 Broadway, 303/292-2555, a relaxed place for a beer and pizza frequented by those who shy away from the big-screen TVs and commotion of downtown's sports bars.

The **Denver Center for the Performing Arts**, 13th and Curtis, is the city's first-class entertainment complex, encompassing nine separate venues. The circular Boettcher Concert Hall hosts the Colorado Symphony Orchestra, and the Temple Hoyne Buell Theatre holds traveling shows and nationally acclaimed performances. The complex's other, smaller theaters feature everything from dramatic stage plays to musicals. Current attractions: 303/893-3272. Box office: 303/893-4100.

In addition to the big-name acts, Denver's independent theaters present everything from avant-garde productions to traditional comedies and dramas. **Jack's Theater**, 1553 Platte, 303/433-8082, and the **Avenue Theater**, 2119 East 17th Avenue, 303/321-5925, are just two of the many playhouses in the metro area.

Last, but certainly not least, Denver is the proud home of four professional sports teams. During your stay, you can catch a variety of games, including basketball (the Nuggets), baseball (the Rockies), football (the Broncos), and hockey (the Avalanche). For ticket information, contact the **Ticket Connection**, 303/758-1999, or look in the "Easy Reference Guide" in any Denver phone book.

SIDE TRIP: BOULDER

Located about 45 miles northwest of Denver on U.S. Highway 36, Boulder is one of Colorado's most handsome towns. The **University of Colorado** campus sprawls just south of downtown Boulder, along Broadway, with ivy-covered red sandstone buildings. After exploring campus and "the Hill" just across the street, wander a few more blocks down North Broadway to the **Pearl Street Mall and Historic District**. The interesting boutiques, galleries, street performers, and excellent restaurants lining this walking mall are popular with CU students, Boulder residents, and visitors.

Boulderites are diehard sports enthusiasts, and everywhere you look, people are out walking, jogging, in-line skating, and biking. The many open-space parks surrounding the town lend themselves to wonderful hikes. One of the more popular is the Mesa Trail,

BOULDER

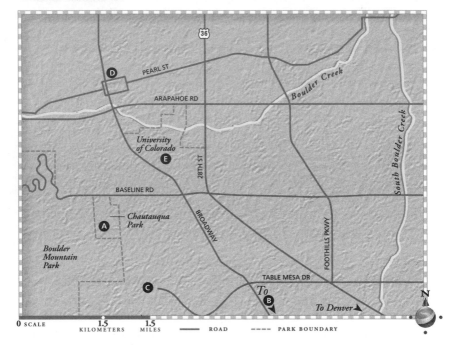

Sights

Ⓐ Chautauqua Park and Auditorium

Ⓑ Eldorado Canyon

Ⓒ National Center for Atmospheric Research

Ⓓ Pearl Street and Historic District

Ⓔ University of Colorado

which links several parks along the Flatirons, a series of uplifted sandstone slabs and prominent Boulder landmarks. You can hike portions of the trail from **Eldorado Canyon**, the **National Center for Atmospheric Research** (see below), and **Chautauqua Park and Auditorium**.

Situated below the Flatirons is the National Center for Atmospheric Research (NCAR), 1850 Table Mesa Drive (west end),

303/497-1174, a center for weather and climate research. Acclaimed architect I. M. Pei designed this distinctive structure, inspired by Anasazi cliff dwellings at Mesa Verde. Inside, you can wander through several interesting scientific weather displays and observe the super computers in the lower level of the building. The open space area behind NCAR, a great place for a picnic, has several connecting hiking trails. Free admission; guided tours available.

SIDE TRIP: GEORGETOWN AND SILVER PLUME

For an entertaining day trip from Denver, head to these historic Victorian towns 45 miles west of Denver on I-70. Rich gold deposits lured many eager prospectors to this valley, but the silver mines of Georgetown and Silver Plume turned out to be the choice prize of this region. Both towns peaked in the 1870s, when their forward-thinking citizens built churches, hotels, homes, a city park, flagstone sidewalks, and a large school building to demonstrate the permanence of their settlements. Much of the early architecture of these towns has been lovingly preserved, and today Georgetown and Silver Plume comprise a National Register Historic District.

When the Colorado & Southern Railroad steamed through the valley in 1885, these isolated towns finally linked to the burgeoning settlement of Denver and beyond. But the Colorado & Southern had to struggle mightily to build their rails the short distance between Georgetown and Silver Plume. In just two miles, the train scaled an elevation of 600 feet, causing it to twist and turn over trestles, loops, and curves totaling over four miles of track.

In 1939, after declining mining activity and the effects of the Depression, the Colorado & Southern Railroad rails were sold for scrap. The Colorado Historical Society purchased the property in the 1950s, finally restoring the route to its former glory in 1975. Renamed the **Georgetown Loop**, the narrow-gauge train ride now includes a visit to the historic **Lebanon Silver Mine**, an authentic silver mine reachable only by rail. Walking shoes and a jacket make the tour more comfortable. The regular round-trip train ride takes an hour and 10 minutes, the silver mine tour adds an extra hour and 20 minutes. Tickets for the round-trip tour, which can start from either Georgetown or Silver Plume, are $11.95 adults, $7.50 children 3–15. The Lebanon Silver Mine tour costs $4 adults, $2 children. Old Georgetown Station, 11th and Rose Streets; 970/569-2403. Denver line: 303/670-1686 or

GEORGETOWN AND SILVERPLUME

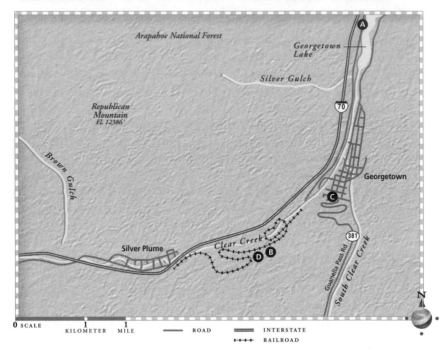

Sights

Ⓐ Georgetown Bighorn Sheep Viewing Site

Ⓑ Georgetown Loop

Ⓒ Hamill House

Ⓓ Lebanon Silver Mine

800/691-4FUN. Memorial Day through October 1, trains depart approximately every hour and 20 minutes every day.

A herd of 150 to 200 bighorn sheep can often be seen grazing on ridges high above Georgetown. The Colorado Division of Wildlife constructed the **Georgetown Bighorn Sheep Viewing Site** east of town, with viewing scopes and interpretive signs about the herd. Volunteers staff the viewing station at certain times to answer questions.

The streets of Georgetown and Silver Plume can accurately be described as whimsical and otherworldly. Spend some time wandering, poking into galleries, specialty shops, and bookstores. The **Hamill House** (Third and Argentine Streets; 303/569-2840), a restored structure dating to 1867, has an interesting past as the former home of one of the richest men in Clear Creek County, William Arthur Hamill. Operated today by the Georgetown Society, an agency dedicated to preserving many of the town's historic structures, the home is filled with 1880s furnishings and artifacts.

HELPFUL HINT

When visiting the Civic Center, park your car for the day in the lots at 13th Avenue and Broadway, since most downtown attractions are within walking distance. The nearby 16th Street Mall Shuttle offers a free quick ride to Larimer Square, Lower Downtown, and the Coors Field area.

2

PAWNEE GRASSLANDS

While Colorado's soaring mountains and ski resorts are well known to people across the globe, the high plains grasslands that blanket the eastern third of the state are often overlooked. This common oversight is unfortunate, as Colorado's plains boast ample sightseeing, unpretentious beauty, and comfortable hospitality. People who view the plains only as an unchanging, flat landscape are missing out on the diverse nature of this expansive region, with its rolling hills, canyons, and abundant wildlife.

The Pawnee Grasslands are an isolated patchwork of public and private lands in northeastern Colorado, accessible from Fort Collins to the west, Sterling to the east, and Fort Morgan to the south. Gravel county roads form a grid across the landscape, and most are navigable by any type of vehicle. When the roads get wet or muddy, however, they are usually impassable. Before visiting the area, inquire about road conditions at the Pawnee National Grasslands headquarters in Greeley, 666 O Street, 970/353-5004. Start with a full tank of gas and plenty of water and food, especially if you plan to stay overnight, because this is remote country. And stay only on designated roads in the grasslands; never trespass on private land. ◣

PAWNEE GRASSLANDS

Sights

Ⓐ Crow Valley Recreation Area

Ⓑ Fort Morgan Museum

Ⓑ Rainbow Bridge

Ⓑ Riverside Park

Ⓒ Pawnee Buttes

Ⓓ Overland Museum

Note: Items with the same letter are located in the same town or area.

A PERFECT DAY IN THE PAWNEE GRASSLANDS

Journey across Colorado's northeastern plains to visit Pawnee Buttes, two striking bluffs rising from this vast landscape. Take advantage of the hikes, mountain bike rides, or scenic drives possible in the Pawnee National Grasslands. Along the way, stop to stretch your legs in shady places like Grover or the Crow Valley Recreation Area.

GRASSLANDS WEATHER, ECOLOGY, AND HISTORY

Plains weather is always unpredictable. A sweltering, sunny summer day can suddenly turn stormy and cool with a spectacular show of thunder and lightning. Temperatures from September to early November are usually pleasant, and heavy rainfall from April to June helps carpet the prairie with wildflowers. The grasslands can even be delightful on a mild winter day.

Dominated by short grasses such as buffalo and blue grama, the grasslands are punctuated by stands of giant cottonwood trees growing along creeks and streams. Birds of prey soar overhead in the wide sky, swift foxes dart through the shrubs, and prairie dogs poke their heads out of their burrows. Owls, ferrets, badgers, gophers, and rattlesnakes also live in underground caves and passages, allowing them to escape from summer's unrelenting heat.

The nutritional grasses of these vast high plains once supported millions of bison. Plains Indians laying claim to these premier hunting grounds include the Comanche, Lakota, Cheyenne, and Arapaho tribes. It is puzzling that these grasslands are named for the Pawnee Indians, as this area was not part of their traditional homeland. The Pawnee lived near the Loop River in present-day Nebraska, and if these longstanding enemies of the Lakota, Cheyenne, and Arapaho ventured onto these plains to hunt bison, they did so at great peril. Many battles occurred here because of Pawnee encroachments.

The grasslands receive only about 14 inches of precipitation annually, most of it falling during the spring months. Drought-resistant vegetation and animals flourish, practicing unique adaptations that capture every last drop of moisture. If you visit the grasslands during a wet year, you might be fooled into thinking that this is fertile agricultural land. That's what happened when thousands of optimistic homesteaders moved here during a rash of wet years in the 1880s. The country hummed with several farming settlements, all visited by the railroad.

The craze back then was something called "dry farming," a practice that didn't require extensive irrigation ditches to support wheat, hay, or alfalfa crops. Farmers dug deep furrows in their fields and rested them every other year to attract whatever moisture was lingering in the air. However, they disturbed the ground surface so much that all the topsoil blew away in the Dust Bowl of the 1930s. During these years, this land was devastated by drought, strong winds, and hard winters, forcing most luckless and bankrupt farmers off their lands.

Only a few families managed to eke out a living in the years following the Depression. Shortly thereafter, the Soil Conservation Service purchased large parcels of the prairie and began to teach farming and irrigating practices better suited to the high plains environment. Today a handful of cattle ranchers lease grazing land from the United States Department of Agriculture through the Pawnee National Grasslands. Skeletons of homes, barns, and cemeteries dot the landscape, reminders of the earlier agricultural boom times. Although much of the natural environment has been disturbed by plowing and overgrazing, a few sections remain unspoiled, such as near the Pawnee Buttes, where native grasses and plants can still be seen.

SIGHTSEEING HIGHLIGHTS

★★★ **Pawnee Buttes**—These two sedimentary buttes have resisted the erosional forces of wind and water for millions of years and are well-known sentinels of the northeastern plains. Plains Indian tribes often gathered at the buttes in the midst of their vast bison hunting grounds. The plains rise gently at this spot, revealing an expansive view of the prairie and the Rocky Mountains to the west. Far off in the distance, you can see Longs Peak, a landmark visible throughout the northeastern plains. *Centennial*, James Michener's epic book about Colorado, focuses on this part of the state. He named the buttes Rattlesnake Buttes for good reason—keep an eye out for these creatures sunning on the rocks.

Thirty million years ago this area supported large populations of ancestral mammals. Paleontologists began excavating fossilized bones here in the 1870s, discovering many skeletons resembling modern-day rhinoceroses, horses, camels, and turtles. Several mammal skeletons excavated from the buttes can be seen at the Denver Museum of Natural History. Discoveries of ancestral horse skeletons from this location contributed significantly to understanding how the horse evolved into its modern form.

The three-mile round-trip hiking trail to the buttes wends through swaying grasses, yucca plants, and prickly pear cacti, ending at the base of the west butte. Eagles, hawks, and falcons nest at the small ridge near the buttes. Cliff access is closed during springtime to protect the young broods.

Details: *Northeast of Briggsdale. (2½ hours)*

★★ **Crow Valley Recreation Area**—This quiet and shady area has a developed campground, picnic area, and baseball diamond. Also on the grounds is the **Steward J. Adams Educational Site**, a center for studying grasslands ecology.

During your visit look for a host of birds, such as golden eagles, ferruginous hawks, prairie falcons, and burrowing owls. The mountain plover is the unofficial grasslands mascot, recently added to the state's endangered species list. These birds lay their eggs in the grass. Listen for the singing of the western meadow lark and the lark bunting, Colorado's state bird.

The Audubon Society often takes bird-watching groups to the grasslands and has prepared a 36-mile self-guided tour. The tour begins at the recreation area and proceeds through the western grasslands. There is also a 12-mile mountain bike loop.

Details: *Quarter-mile north of Briggsdale on Hwy. 14. For a map and information, contact the Pawnee National Grasslands, 666 O Street, Greeley, 970/353-5004. (half day)*

✴ **Fort Morgan**—Established in 1864, Fort Morgan protected travelers from Indian attacks on the South Platte River Trail into Denver. In later years the settlement evolved into a thriving agricultural center. Just after the turn of the century, the Great Western Sugar Company built a sugar beet processing factory in town that supported hundreds of local farmers. Sugar beet farming attracted diverse ethnic groups, such as Volga Germans (German-speaking people from the Volga River Valley in Russia) and Japanese, who started out working as field laborers and later bought their own farms. Many descendants of these ethnic groups still remain in the area. Hispanics also came from southern Colorado and northern New Mexico to work the fields, although fewer of them stayed as permanent residents. Located across from Riverside Park on Highway 52, Fort Morgan's historic sugar beet processing factory continues to convert northeastern Colorado's sugar beet harvest into refined white sugar.

The free **Fort Morgan Museum** (414 Main St.,970/867-6331) features an extensive Native American artifact collection exclusively from northeastern Colorado, encompassing over 13,000 years. The museum also proudly displays the belongings of its famous resident, Glenn Miller, in addition to first-rate exhibits on regional history. Inquire here about a walking tour of historic Fort Morgan and its National Register properties, and driving tours to nearby wildlife areas.

Riverside Park, a 240-acre wildlife preserve that protects the riparian ecosystem of the South Platte River, is located on Highway 52, the southern portal of the Pawnee Pioneer Trail Byway. One of the park's main features is **Rainbow Bridge**, a National Historic Civil Engineering Landmark, with a unique patented rainbow arch design. When built in 1922, the bridge formed the longest rainbow arch in the world.

Details: Fort Morgan Chamber of Commerce, 300 Main St., 970/867-6702 or 800/354-8660. (half day)

✴ **Sterling**—After the discovery of gold in the mountains west of Denver in 1859, legions of opportunists packed up and rushed to present-day Colorado in hopes of striking it rich by mining, farming, or raising cattle to feed the new residents. Many travelers started their journey on the great Oregon Trail, which began in Independence, Missouri, and followed the Platte River through Nebraska. Those destined for the new Colorado settlements headed toward the confluence of the South Platte and Platte Rivers, today just east of the Colorado/Nebraska border near the town of Julesburg, then followed the South Platte all the way into Denver. This cutoff, which became known as the **South Platte Trail**, brought thousands of settlers into fledgling Colorado Territory, established in 1861.

Sterling's history is filled with rich tales of the trail and hardships encountered by those who undertook the long journey. The free **Overland Museum** (Centennial Square on Highway 6 off I-76; 970/522-3895) displays early trail artifacts and items from the first settlers of this area. The museum also has excellent replicas of animal fossils similar to those found near the Pawnee Buttes. Pioneer farm machinery, a Concord stage, native grasses, and wildflowers grace the exterior of the building.

Details: Sterling Chamber of Commerce, 109 N. Front St., 970/522-5070. (2 hours)

FITNESS AND RECREATION

Jackson Lake State Park, northwest of Fort Morgan on State Highway 144, offers boating, camping, fishing, and wildlife viewing. Species seen here include doves, pheasants, pelicans, beavers, badgers, and waterfowl. **Riverside Park**, north of the intersection of Highways 52 and 6 in Fort Morgan, is a great place to jog, walk, enjoy a picnic, or swim in the public pool. The park also has fishing ponds and extensive nature paths.

FOOD

While in Grover, you just might crave an authentic milkshake. Lucky for you, the **Grover Market Basket**, 970/895-2215, on the corner of Custer and Chatoga Avenues, serves the thickest one in town. In addition to jumbo burgers and Philly steak sandwiches, you'll also find such Saturday night specials as top sirloin, shrimp, or T-bone steak, chicken-fried steak, or a burrito plate, all including dessert. A small market here sells groceries and supplies.

Pawnee Station, on Highway 14 in New Raymer, 970/437-5726, is another grasslands restaurant. It has full breakfasts, hamburgers, steaks, and daily specials for under $5.

In Sterling, the smoke-free **T. J. Bummer's**, 203 Broadway, 970/522-8397, serves hearty burgers, steaks, and chicken dishes ranging from $3 to $12. Locals recommend **Delgado's**, 116 Beach, 970/522-0175, featuring a range of Mexican specialties and combination platters.

PAWNEE GRASSLANDS

ROAD
INTERSTATE

SCALE

0   20
KILOMETERS

0   20
MILES

Food

- Bisetti's
- CooperSmith's
- Country Steak-Out
- Delgado's
- Grover Market Basket
- Memories Restaurant
- Pawnee Station
- T. J. Bummer's

Lodging

- Central Motel
- Elk Echo Ranch
- Fountain Lodge
- Mulberry Inn

Lodging *(continued)*

- Oakwood Inn
- West Mulberry Street Bed and Breakfast Inn
- West Pawnee Ranch

Camping

- Steward J. Adams Campground
- Buffalo Hills Camper Park
- Jackson Lake State Park
- Pioneer Mobile Home Park
- Riverside Park
- Wayward Wind Campground

Note: Items with the same letter are located in the same town or area.

In Fort Morgan, the **Country Steak-Out**, 19592 East Eighth Avenue, 970/867-7887, serves a mean chicken-fried steak, with dinners starting at $6 and going up to $20 for prime rib or lobster. **Memories Restaurant**, in the Park Terrace Inn, 725 Main, 970/867-8205, offers Italian and Mexican entrees as well as superb steaks. Lunch and dinner range from $5 to $10.25.

Many further restaurant options exist in nearby Fort Collins. For fine Italian cuisine, **Bisetti's**, 120 South College Avenue, 970/493-0086, specializes in homemade pasta and seafood dishes, ranging from $8.95 to $15.95. **CooperSmith's**, 5 Old Town Square, 970/498-0483, is a traditional English-style pub and restaurant. Its in-house brewery features a wide variety of well-crafted selections, and its cooks prepare several dishes ($5–$13) from beer recipes. Next door is CooperSmith's Billiards, with professional billiard tables, serving pizzas from a wood-burning oven. The billiards room is open daily until 1:30 a.m.

LODGING

Lodging within the remote grasslands country is hard to come by, but several bed-and-breakfasts have recently opened, offering a unique opportunity to experience the peacefulness of the grasslands. The **Elk Echo Ranch**, 47490 Weld County Road 155, 970/735-2426, is located five miles north of the intersection of County Road 155 and Highway 14, four miles east of Stoneham. It sits on a majestic 1,000 acres that include elk and buffalo herds. The owners take guests to visit the elk, providing a rare chance to see these beautiful animals up close. Rates are $99 per couple.

The **West Pawnee Ranch**, located northwest of Grover, 970/895-2482, is open year-round. The three guest rooms range from $50 to $90, with a full ranch breakfast including frittatas and sticky buns. The ranch also serves additional meals, which comes in handy since area restaurants close early. Guests can enjoy horseback rides on the ranch, providing a great opportunity to see birds and other wildlife on the plains.

In Sterling, the **Fountain Lodge**, 619 North Third, 970/522-1821, is an eccentric motor court, with lighted fountains shimmering in the courtyard. The modern **Oakwood Inn**, 810 Division Avenue, 970/522-1416, has rooms beginning at $29.95.

In Fort Morgan, the **Central Motel**, 201 West Platte Avenue, 970/867-2401, is clean and hospitable. Rates range from $36.95 to $46.95.

As the largest town near the Pawnee Grasslands, Fort Collins offers the most choices for lodging, ranging from standard motels to bed-and-breakfasts. The **Mulberry Inn**, located just off I-25 at exit 269A, 970/493-9000, has rooms from $55 to $100. Near the Colorado State University campus is the **West Mulberry Street Bed and Breakfast Inn**, 616 West Mulberry Street, 970/221-1917. This turn-of-the-century Four Square home is filled with period furnishings. Year-round rates range from $56 per single to $150 for a six-person suite. A full breakfast includes quiche, omelets, crepes, or homemade baked goods.

CAMPING

The only campground in the Pawnee Grasslands is the **Steward J. Adams Campground**, in the Crow Valley Recreation Area just north of Briggsdale. Managed by the Pawnee National Grasslands, it is shaded by numerous tall cottonwoods that line Crow Creek.

More than 200 camping spots for trailers, RVs, or tents can be found in **Jackson Lake State Park**. Facilities include running water, showers, and toilets. The park is northwest of Fort Morgan on Highway 144, near the town of Orchard. For more information, call 970/645-2551. Free camping is available at Fort Morgan's **Riverside Park**.

RV camping can be found at **Pioneer Mobile Home Park**, 300 East Harmony Road, I-25 exit 265; the park is four and a half miles west on Harmony Road, near downtown Fort Collins, 970/226-3325. In Sterling, the **Buffalo Hills Camper Park**, 22018 Highway 6 East, 970/522-2233 or 800/569-1824, is a full-service camping spot with hookups, picnic tables, and group camping. Fort Morgan also has its own camping park, the **Wayward Wind Campground**, near I-76 off exit 75A, 970/867-8948.

Scenic Route:
Pawnee Pioneer Trails Byway

The Pawnee Pioneer Trails Scenic and Historic Byway starts in the agricultural town of Ault on Highway 85, 14 miles east of Fort Collins. The route is marked by blue columbine signs and is part of the state's scenic byway program.

Drive east on Highway 14 through a long stretch of irrigated farmlands. Look for a change in the passing landscape along the way. Suddenly you leave the green fields behind and enter the golden grasses of the natural prairie at the border of **Pawnee National Grasslands**, about 13 miles east of Ault. Next you come upon the hamlet of **Briggsdale**, once a successful farming center but today merely a fraction of its former size. Many artifacts of a bygone era have been preserved in the **Briggsdale Museum**, in a former one-room schoolhouse, open only by appointment. If you'd like to see it, ask at the Briggsdale Market.

At Briggsdale, take County Road 77 north past the Crow Valley Recreation Area and continue north about 15 more miles until you reach County Road 120. Take this road east to the pleasant town of **Grover**. Grover sits in a naturally irrigated pocket on the grasslands,

PAWNEE PIONEER TRAILS BYWAY

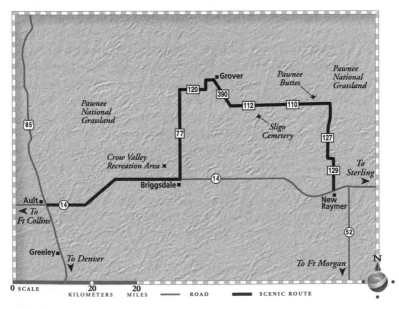

and its residents have enjoyed relative prosperity from ranching over the years. The **Grover History Museum** is in the former railroad depot. Across the way is a grain elevator on the National Register of Historic Places. You can just imagine railcars pulling in at the depot and men loading grain from the high elevator. The museum has many unique artifacts donated by the community, a display about the Pawnee Buttes, and an historic fire engine. It's usually open during the summer on Sunday from 1 to 4 p.m. The museum is free, but donations are appreciated.

From Grover, continue on County Road 120 until it dead-ends into County Road 390. This flat, wide road is the former route of the Chicago, Burlington, and Quincy Railroad, the lifeline of the prairie settlements. Continue on this stretch until you come to County Road 112, then turn east. Approximately two miles down the road, you will see a weathered wooden gate marking the lonely, windswept **Sligo Cemetery**. The struggles of homesteaders in Sligo, a community that once numbered 100 people, are poignantly remembered in this cemetery. Many young people who died from illnesses or injuries are buried here.

After visiting the cemetery (be sure to close the gate behind you), continue another five miles on County Road 112 until you intersect County Road 107, where you will head south and east to County Road 685, which takes you to the **Pawnee Buttes Trail Head**, on top of a broad ridge. Once you've hiked around the buttes, return to County Road 112 and head south and east, roughly following County Roads 110, 110.5, and 115. Ignore the changing road numbers—just continue to head east until you come to the intersection of County Road 127. Drive south, then transfer to County Road 129, which takes you into the tiny town of **New Raymer**, on State Highway 14. There's a gas station here in case you are running low. From New Raymer, it's 27 miles south to Fort Morgan, 25 miles east to Sterling, 50 miles west to Ault, and 65 miles west to Fort Collins. ◼

3

ROCKY MOUNTAIN NATIONAL PARK

Rocky Mountain National Park was dedicated on September 4, 1915, to preserve and protect the alpine ecology, wildlife, and vegetation of this spectacular portion of the central Rocky Mountains. The many individuals who had tirelessly lobbied for national park status savored their victory. At last, the glorious Rockies were protected from logging, grazing, and development.

In the mid-1970s, more than 90 percent of Rocky Mountain National Park was designated as wilderness area, ensuring that no roads, structures, or other human comforts would be constructed. At the same time, park administrators confronted the problem of overwhelming public interest in the park—it was being "loved to death." While the park remains popular with visitors, you can still beat the crowds and find many places in which to appreciate the vast beauty of these mountains in silence and solitude.

Access to Rocky Mountain National Park is through two gateway communities: Estes Park on the eastern side (65 miles from Denver on Highway 36), and Grand Lake on the western side (a little more than 100 miles from Denver on Highways 40 and 34). These communities are connected by Trail Ridge Road, Highway 34, which traverses the width of the park. The eastern side of the park receives twice as many visitors as the western because it is closer to several large communities along the Front Range, including Denver, Boulder, Fort Collins, and Loveland. While facilities within the park are limited, the towns of Grand Lake and Estes Park have all necessary services. ■

ROCKY MOUNTAIN NATIONAL PARK

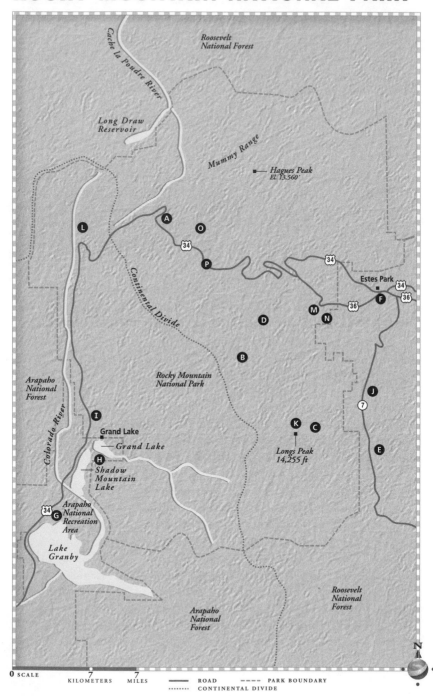

Sights

- Ⓐ Alpine Visitor Center
- Ⓑ Bear Lake Trailhead
- Ⓒ Chasm Lake
- Ⓓ Cub Lake
- Ⓔ Enos Mills Cabin
- Ⓕ Estes Park Area Historical Museum
- Ⓖ Farr (Granby) Pump Plant
- Ⓗ Grand Lake
- Ⓘ Kawuneeche Visitor Center
- Ⓙ Lily Lake Visitor Center
- Ⓚ Longs Peak
- Ⓛ Lulu City Trail
- Ⓜ Moraine Park Museum
- Ⓝ Park Headquarters
- Ⓕ Stanley Hotel
- Ⓞ Toll Memorial
- Ⓟ Trail Ridge Road

Note: Items with the same letter are located in the same area.

A PERFECT DAY IN ROCKY MOUNTAIN NATIONAL PARK

I like the western, or Grand Lake, side of the park because it's less crowded than Estes Park, which is more accessible to Front Range visitors. Get oriented at Kawuneeche Visitor Center, then take a two- to three-hour hike on the Lulu City Trail or any other trail that suits you. Afterward, drive over Trail Ridge Road to Estes Park, stopping at several places along the way to experience the alpine tundra environment.

NATURAL FEATURES OF ROCKY MOUNTAIN NATIONAL PARK

The Continental Divide, the "Backbone of the Nation," snakes through the western portion of Rocky Mountain National Park. From this spine, alpine streams flow either east toward the Atlantic Ocean or west toward the Pacific Ocean. Major rivers cascading to the east are the St. Vrain, Big Thompson, and Cache La Poudre, while to the west, the mighty Colorado River springs forth from an unassuming place north of Grand Lake.

Powerful mountain-building forces lifted ancient rocks to form these mountains approximately 70 million years ago. Arctic glaciers sculpted away the ancient bedrock, forming mountains, canyons, and U-shaped valleys. Several active glaciers remain on the north-facing slopes of some of the park's mountains.

Three different life zones are preserved here: the montane zone, with vegetation such as Ponderosa pine, Douglas fir, lodgepole pine, and quaking aspen; the subalpine zone, with Englemann spruce, alpine fir, and the gnarled limber pine; and the alpine zone, beginning at treeline (10,500 feet), with hardy ground-covering vegetation. An array of wildflowers flourish throughout the elevations, such as the Rocky Mountain iris, Indian paintbrush, alpine forget-me-not, sunflowers, blue columbine, and arctic gentian.

The autumn elk mating season at Rocky Mountain National Park is legendary. Each evening at dusk, the bulls vie for prominence by battling and bugling, a thrilling combination of loud whistles and grunts. A large herd resides in the higher reaches of the park during the summer but descends into the lower elevations in the fall. Mule deer can usually be seen browsing meadow grasses along park roads, but moose, coyote, and bear are harder to spot.

Native bighorn sheep herds were practically devastated in the central Rockies at the turn of the century because of disease. The herd has since grown back, thanks to several protectionist measures taken by the National Park Service and the U.S. Forest Service in adjoining Arapaho National Forest.

SIGHTSEEING HIGHLIGHTS

★★★ **Hiking**—Hiking trails in Rocky Mountain National Park vary widely in terrain and scenery. Some follow lazy meadow streams, others cross rushing waterfalls or form narrow footpaths along canyon walls, and still others take you to elevations so high you feel like you're on top of the world. With more than 355 miles of hiking trails, the park offers a wide range of options to suit any taste. Several trails are fully accessible to visitors with disabilities.

Trails beginning from the **Bear Lake Trailhead**, on the east side of the park, are by far the most popular. A shuttle bus will take you from the Glacier Basin parking area on Bear Lake Road to the trailhead. The trails here will be crowded during the summer, especially on weekends, while many others are virtually empty.

One of the finest hikes in the eastern park travels to **Chasm Lake**, roughly 11 miles round trip. Its trailhead is at the Longs Peak Ranger

Station, nine miles south of Estes Park on Highway 7. This trail can be snow-covered until late June, and patches of snow remain here all summer. There are no really steep sections, but the hike does climb from 9,400 feet to 11,850 feet. A shorter and more moderate hike to **Cub Lake** begins near Moraine Park campground. The lake is usually layered with a delicate pattern of green water lilies, and beaver ponds cluster along the way. The hike is four and a half miles round trip and gains about 750 feet in elevation.

On the west side, the **Lulu City Trail** is a moderately strenuous path that follows the Colorado River to the former mining settlement of Lulu City, a booming gold rush town in 1880. Miners never found a large cache of minerals here, so the town eventually died. The six-mile round-trip hike is fairly level; it begins at the Colorado River Trailhead.

Details: Park Headquarters, 970/586-1206. Summer 8–9, winter 8–5.

✩✩✩ **Trail Ridge Road**—Trail Ridge Road is the highest continuously paved road in the United States, with a total length of 48 miles between the eastern and western portals of Rocky Mountain National Park. Even though it climbs to 12,183 feet in elevation, the road never exceeds a 7-percent grade. Construction crews began developing the road in 1931, continued through the harsh winter of 1932, and finally opened it in 1933. The road became an instant success, coinciding with the American craze for auto touring. Thousands of visitors swarmed to "the playground of the Rockies" to experience elevations of 12,000 feet from the comfort of their own cars.

The road stays open from Memorial Day until the first heavy snowfall, usually mid-September or October. However, inclement weather during the middle of the summer can make driving conditions treacherous in a matter of minutes and force the road to close. Avoid driving if there is any risk, as several fatalities have occurred. Be sure to get out of the car at the numerous scenic overlooks and trails along the roadway. Bighorn sheep and elk herds can often be spotted grazing on the exposed hillsides. Dramatic views seen from this staggering elevation include deep canyons, pristine snowfields, and the towering cliffs of the Continental Divide. A one-mile round-trip hike to the **Toll Memorial**, a monument to an early superintendent of Rocky, departs from the Rock Cut Trailhead about six miles east of the Alpine Visitor Center. Several interpretive signs along the trail explain features in the landscape. When hiking, stay only on established trails to avoid damaging fragile tundra vegetation.

Details: *U.S. Highway 34 between Estes Park and Grand Lake. Road open Memorial Day–mid-Sept or mid-Oct. (2 1/2-hour drive one way)*

✰✰ **Enos Mills Cabin**—Enos Mills first visited this region during the summer of 1884, at the age of 14. He fell in love with the Central Rockies at first sight and returned every summer thereafter to work as a hiking guide up Longs Peak. Later in life, he purchased the Longs Peak Inn, where he catered to visitors for many years. Mills became a devoted disciple of naturalists such as John Muir, Ralph Waldo Emerson, and Henry David Thoreau. He also authored his own books describing the glorious wilderness of the Rockies, their flora and fauna, and his many exciting adventures exploring the region. His efforts in lobbying for National Park designation earned him the nickname "Father of Rocky Mountain National Park." The one-room log cabin where Mills lived for many summers is now a museum.
   Details: *Eight miles south of Estes Park on Hwy. 7; 970/586-4706. Memorial Day–Labor Day daily 10–5, in winter by special appointment. Donations are requested. (1 hour)*

✰✰ **Rocky Mountain National Park Activities and Visitor Centers**— When you enter the park, stop at one of the visitor centers to learn about the many programs, such as short, ranger-led nature walks, campfire programs, and longer hikes to more isolated destinations. Several activities are designed just for kids. Rangers at **Park Headquarters**, on the eastern side of the park, 970/586-1206, issue backcountry permits and suggest activities suited to your tastes and length of visit. Summer hours are 8 to 9. The **Kawuneeche Visitor Center**, on the western side of the park, 970/627-3471, has several excellent exhibits on wildlife, vegetation, and park history. Especially helpful are the displays recommending activities according to your length of stay. Rangers here also issue backcountry permits. Summer hours are 7 to 7. During winter, Kawuneeche and Park Headquarters both stay open daily 8 to 5. Park Headquarters also hosts a Saturday evening program in its auditorium throughout the winter. Other programs resume in late June.
   Several of the park's seasonal visitor centers are open from 9 to 5 during summer. The **Moraine Park Museum** is located two and a half miles southwest of Park Headquarters on the east side. The Denver Museum of Natural History has designed several interactive exhibits here about the geology and natural history of the park. The **Alpine Visitor Center** sits atop Fall River Pass on Trail Ridge Road. Its

exhibits focus on the ecosystem of arctic tundra. South of Estes Park on Highway 7 is the **Lily Lake Visitor Center**, providing nature walks, ranger-led activities, and information on area resources.

✪ **Estes Park**—In 1860 Joel Estes first gazed upon the high mountain valley known today as Estes Park, completely awestruck by its beauty. Seeking a ranch with prime grazing lands, the Estes family was one of the first to settle this pristine land. The family struggled in their lonely paradise, subsisting mainly on wild game and selling surplus meat in Denver. The long, isolating winters taxed their stamina and patience, but they remained in Estes Park for many years.

Shortly thereafter, Estes Park and Longs Peak came to be highly regarded by pleasure travelers for mountain sightseeing, hunting, and fishing. Several individuals with an eye for promotion shaped the region into a first-rate visitor destination. The inventor of the Stanley Steamer automobile, F. O. Stanley, came to Estes Park because of illness, but found his health improved in the pure mountain air. He opened the acclaimed Stanley Hotel in June 1909, which remains an imposing Estes Park landmark today. Do you remember the creepy Stephen King novel *The Shining*? King spent several nights at the Stanley writing his thriller, and the hotel's exterior was featured in the

© Jack Olson

Rocky Mountain National Park

movie starring Jack Nicholson. Popular for lodging and receptions, the refurbished **Stanley Hotel** offers year-round entertainment and dining. Call 970/586-3371 or 800/976-1377 for more information.

Summer brings a host of festivals to Estes Park, with special **Sunday Concerts** sponsored by the Stanley Hotel, the **Scandinavian Mid-Summer Festival**, and the **Estes Park Music Festival** on Monday evenings in midsummer. Elkhorn Avenue is bursting with art galleries and specialty shops. For more information on concerts and galleries, contact the Estes Park Visitor Center, 800/443-7837 or 970/586-4431.

For a taste of history, visit the **Estes Park Area Historical Museum** (200 Fourth Street, Estes Park; 970/586-6256). Exhibits portray the history of the resort, with displays geared toward children. The museum is open daily in summer; limited hours rest of the year.

Details: Estes Park Chamber of Commerce, 500 Big Thompson Ave., 800/44-ESTES or 970/586-4431. (full day)

✯ **Farr (Granby) Pump Plant**—The Colorado–Big Thompson Water Diversion Project is a massive irrigation system that diverts water from the Colorado River through an underground tunnel beneath the Continental Divide. The water is then pumped to farms, ranches, and municipalities in northern Colorado. When engineers promoted the idea of a tunnel in the 1930s, environmentalists heatedly argued against it, claiming that water diversion was contrary to the conservation and preservation ideals of national parks. But agricultural interests reigned, and the government decided to siphon waters meant for the Continental Divide's western slope to the eastern side instead.

The system can deliver up to 310,000 acre feet of water annually to municipal, industrial, and agricultural users on the eastern slope. Water is stored in Lake Granby, then funneled through the Alva Adams Tunnel beneath the Continental Divide at Longs Peak. Engineers tried especially hard to hide the results of construction. The project involves five reservoirs, two pump plants, and endless miles of canals and pipelines. Tours include a half-hour movie about the construction of the Colorado–Big Thompson project and its association with water diversion along the Front Range. Visitors may also view the pumping equipment at the plant.

Details: County Rd. 64 (10 miles north of Granby on Hwy. 34); 970/627-3406. Free public tours Memorial Day–Labor Day 8–4 hourly except at noon. (1 hour)

✵ **Grand Lake**—Established in the 1870s, Grand Lake provided supplies to fledgling silver camps in the central Rocky Mountains. After the mining fizzled, Grand Lake, like Estes Park, became a resort. Located on Colorado's largest natural lake, this small village still attracts many visitors, who enjoy motor-boating, sailing, fishing, and windsurfing on Grand Lake and Lake Granby. Every Fourth of July, the town sponsors a spectacular fireworks display over Grand Lake.
Details: Grand Lake Chamber of Commerce, Hwy. 34 and W. Portal Rd., 800/531-1019 or 970/627-3402. (full day)

✵ **Longs Peak**—Named for Stephen H. Long, the military explorer who first recorded seeing this imposing mountain near present-day Fort Morgan in 1820, Longs Peak is the highest mountain, at 14,255 feet, within the boundaries of Rocky Mountain National Park. This enormous landform can be seen from many high points on the northern plains.

The trail to the flat-topped summit of Longs Peak is no ordinary walk in the woods. It is perhaps one of the hardest of Colorado's Fourteeners to climb. Yet many people attempt to scale the peak without adequate preparation. The 16-mile round-trip hike starts at the Longs Peak Ranger Station south of Estes Park, beginning at 9,300 feet and climbing 4,855 feet to the summit. Hikers fit for a strenuous journey and accustomed to the altitude will certainly revel in this challenge, but others might wish to enjoy the beauty of Rocky Mountain National Park on a more moderate trail (see "Hiking" and "Fitness and Recreation"). If you do attempt the climb, be sure to start at dawn, reach the summit, then make it below treeline by noon to avoid any afternoon storms on top of the peak.
Details: Hike begins at Longs Peak Ranger Station south of Estes Park. (2 days)

FITNESS AND RECREATION

Rocky Mountain National Park offers a host of outdoor activities. Hiking is by far the preferred recreational pursuit here in the summertime, in addition to horseback or bike rides on **Bear Lake Road, Trail Ridge Road**, or the **Horseshoe Park/Estes Park Loop**. Bicyclists pay a $3 park-entry fee, good for seven days. Backpackers relish the park's remote backcountry, which hold numerous opportunities to "get lost" for a time. Fly-fishing on the **Big Thompson River** is also widely enjoyed. For information on good fishing spots, guided fishing trips, or

ROCKY MOUNTAIN NATIONAL PARK

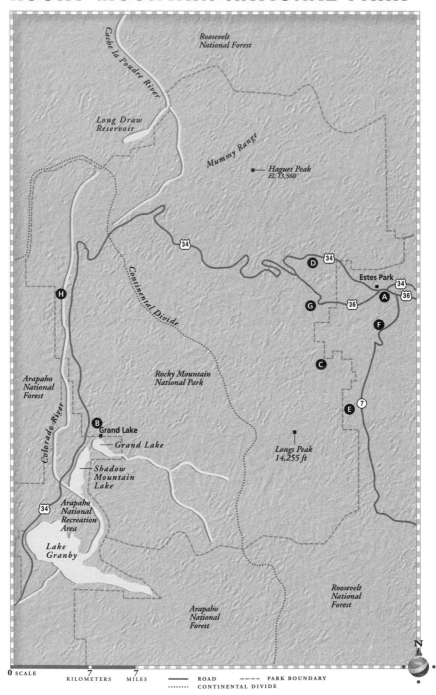

Cache la Poudre River

Roosevelt
National Forest

Long Draw
Reservoir

Mummy Range

■ Hagues Peak
EL 13,560'

34

D

34

Estes Park

34

Continental Divide

H

G

36

A

36

F

Arapaho
National
Forest

Rocky Mountain
National Park

C

E

7

B
Grand Lake

Colorado River

— Grand Lake

— Shadow
Mountain
Lake

Longs Peak
14,255 ft

34

Arapaho
National
Recreation
Area

Lake
Granby

Roosevelt
National
Forest

Arapaho
National
Forest

N

0 SCALE
7   7
KILOMETERS   MILES

ROAD

PARK BOUNDARY

CONTINENTAL DIVIDE

Food

Ⓐ Black Canyon Inn

Ⓑ Caroline's Cuisine

Ⓑ Chuck Hole

Ⓐ Dunraven Inn

Ⓑ E. G.'s

Ⓐ Estes Park Brewery

Ⓐ Pippi's Place

Ⓑ Rapids Restaurant

Lodging

Ⓐ Baldpate Inn

Ⓑ Daven Haven Lodge

Lodging (continued)

Ⓑ Soda Springs Ranch

Ⓐ Trapper's Motor Inn

Ⓒ Spirit Mountain Ranch

Camping

Ⓓ Aspenglen Campground

Ⓑ Elk Creek Campground

Ⓒ Glacier Basin Campground

Ⓔ Longs Peak Campground

Ⓕ Mary's Lake Campground

Ⓖ Moraine Park Campground

Ⓗ Timber Creek Campground

Note: Items with the same letter are located in the same area.

fly-fishing lessons, visit **Colorado Wilderness Sports**, 358 East Elkhorn Avenue, Estes Park, 970/586-6548.

Technical rock climbing is a popular sport here, but only experienced mountaineers should attempt it. Several climbing schools in the area offer instruction. For more information contact the **Colorado Mountain School**, Estes Park, 970/586-5758.

Winter in the park is a treat because you see more wildlife than people. Rangers in Rocky Mountain National Park often lead special cross-country skiing tours on the weekends. Near the park entrance is the **Grand Lake Touring Center**, 970/627-8008, featuring more than 17 miles of groomed trails, half- or full-day rentals, and lessons on request.

FOOD

Pippi's Place, a bakery and coffeehouse in Estes Park, 361 South St. Vrain Avenue, 970/586-9299, is the perfect place to go for a hearty breakfast before hitting the trail. It serves breakfast and lunch daily. The menu includes waffles, croissants, sandwiches, and soups for $5 to $7.

A lively place to quaff some homemade beers and enjoy a burger or pizza for under $10 is the **Estes Park Brewery**, 470 Prospect Village Drive, 970/586-5421. The **Dunraven Inn**, 2470 Highway 66, 970/586-6409, serves Italian entrees such as manicotti, lasagna, ravioli, shrimp scampi, lobster, or steak, ranging from $10 to $20. For an elegant meal, try the **Black Canyon Inn**, 800 MacGregor Avenue (Devil's Gulch Road), 970/586-9344. House specialties are freshly and creatively prepared, with seafood, wild game, poultry, veal, and pasta ($15–$20). Open for lunch Wednesday through Sunday 11:30 to 2 and for dinner 5 to 9.

In Grand Lake, the **Chuck Hole**, 1119 Grand Avenue, 970/627-3509, is the place to go for breakfast or lunch, with breakfast platters of eggs, hash browns, or pancakes, and sandwiches and burgers for lunch. Also on Grand Avenue is **E. G.'s**, 970/627-8404, a restaurant and lounge offering interesting twists on Colorado cuisine, such as fried calamari, Baja fish tacos, French onion soup, shrimp enchiladas, baby back ribs, or stuffed chicken breast with sun dried tomato pesto. The **Rapids Restaurant**, 209 Rapids Lane, 970/627-3707, in a rustic log cabin, is a nice place to go for a romantic dinner, with entrées such as prime rib, pasta, and poultry ranging from $11 to $20. Open summer nights 5 to 9:30, until 10 on Friday and Saturday. The restaurant is closed in November, and on Monday and Tuesday evenings from October through the last weekend in May.

South of town, at the Soda Springs Ranch, is **Caroline's Cuisine**, 970/627-9404. Specialties include beef, seafood, poultry, and pasta entrées, plus wonderful salads, fresh bread, and homemade soups.

LODGING

Families often prefer to take in the Western-style activities at one of the many dude ranches surrounding Rocky Mountain National Park. Contact the Colorado Dude & Guest Ranch Association, P.O. Box 300X, Tabernash, CO 80478, 970/724-3653, ext. 40, for a list of area ranches.

Both Estes Park and Grand Lake have varied lodging options, with numerous motor courts, bed-and-breakfasts, and historic cabins. Most accommodations stay open year round, but some close November through April.

For a full list of lodging in Estes Park in a wide price range, contact the Estes Park Accommodations Association, 800/44-ESTES. Two of my favorites: The **Baldpate Inn**, 4900 South Highway 7, 970/586-6151, is a rustic and comfortable lodge, cleverly named after the key collection featured in *Seven Keys to Baldpate*, written by Earl D. Biggers in 1917. The plot of this mystery involves seven people who each believe they hold the only key to an isolated mountain hotel. The inn is open from Memorial Day to October 1, with rates ranging from $80 to $140. The Baldpate also maintains a wonderful restaurant. Budget-minded travelers should check out the **Trapper's Motor Inn**, 553 West Elkhorn Avenue, 970/586-2833. It's the best bet for clean, well-kept rooms, starting at $32 in the winter and $52 in the summer.

On the Grand Lake side of the park, **Spirit Mountain Ranch**, 970/887-3551 or 800/887-3551, sits on 72 acres of secluded property surrounded by public lands. The ranch is a great place for hiking, skiing, and bird-watching, with more than 50 species of birds seen in the area. Rates, including a full breakfast, range from $100 to $125.

The **Daven Haven Lodge**, 604 Marina Avenue, 970/627-8144, stays open year round. The cabins here cater to families, sleeping up to nine, and range from $68 to $125. The **Soda Springs Ranch**, 9921 Highway 34, 970/627-8125, has condominiums ranging from $85 to $180. Open year round, the ranch is four miles south of Grand Lake.

CAMPING

Campsites within the park fill quickly from mid-June to mid-August. On the Estes Park side, the **Moraine Park Campground** and the **Glacier Basin Campground** can accommodate RVs or tents. To make advance reservations for either campground, call 800/365-CAMP. Other park campgrounds do not require reservations but fill up quickly on a first-come, first-served basis. **Longs Peak** and **Aspenglen**, on the east side, are for tents only. And on the west side, the **Timber Creek Campground** accommodates either RVs or tents.

Backcountry camping is allowed within the park, and permits are issued from May to mid-August for $10. Contact the Backcountry Office, 970/586-1242, for more information. The office issues permits for a maximum of seven nights, and you must give them an idea of where you'll be camping. Fires are allowed only at sites with fire rings.

Those seeking private RV campgrounds can try the **Elk Creek Campground**, 143 County Road 48, north of Grand Lake on Highway 34, at the west entrance to Rocky Mountain National Park, 970/627-8502 or 800/ELK-CREEK. In Estes Park, **Mary's Lake Campground**, 2120 Mary's Lake Road, 970/586-4411 or 800/445-MARY, has a playground on the shores of Mary's Lake, campfire pits, and picnic tables.

4

STEAMBOAT SPRINGS

A hardy Western lifestyle prevails in northwestern Colorado, where cattle and sheep ranching began in the late 1870s and still thrives today. Some of the world's largest underground coal mines west of Steamboat Springs generate more than one-third of Colorado's power and provide coal to a multitude of national and international industries. Thrown into this ranching and mining mix is the Steamboat Springs Ski Area, a world-renowned ski resort nicknamed Ski Town USA. Long before the ski area became an international sensation, Steamboat Springs residents exploited the natural ski paradise to their best advantage, sending dozens of hometown athletes to compete in the winter Olympics.

The Continental Divide skirts Steamboat Springs to the east and north, with Muddy Pass and Rabbit Ears Pass providing access through the formidable mountain barrier. Up north is the Mount Zirkel Wilderness Area, a wild and untouched region buttressed by the Park Range. To the southwest are the high tablelands of the Flat Tops Wilderness Area. The Yampa River, which originates in the Flat Tops, flows through the heart of northwestern Colorado and provides a rich habitat for a variety of plants and animals. Beavers, Canadian geese, bald eagles, great blue herons, and the greater sandhill crane all live along the river. Gigantic herds of deer, elk, and antelope roam the high mountain valley, as do bighorn sheep, moose, and a fairly large herd of wild mustangs in Sandwash Creek Basin near Craig. With all of this natural beauty, Steamboat Springs visitors have many opportunities to experience Colorado's mountains firsthand. ◨

STEAMBOAT SPRINGS AREA

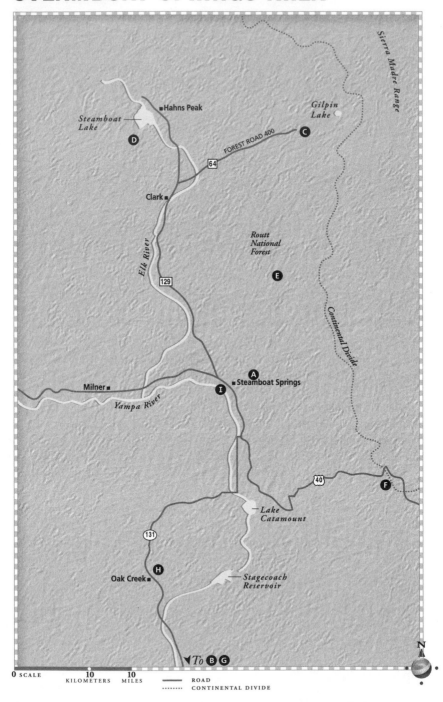

Sights

Ⓐ Fish Creek Falls

Ⓑ Flat Tops Wilderness Area

Ⓒ Gilpin Lake Trail

Ⓒ Gold Creek Lake Trail

Ⓓ Hahn's Peak/Steamboat Lake State Park

Ⓔ Mt. Zirkel Wilderness

Ⓕ Rabbit Ears Pass

Ⓒ Three Island Lake Trail

Ⓖ Trappers Lake

Food

Ⓗ Chelsea's

Camping

Ⓑ Flat Tops Wilderness Area

Ⓘ Ski Town KOA Campground

Ⓓ Steamboat Lake and Pearl Lake State Park

Note: Items with the same letter are located in the same town or area.

A PERFECT DAY IN STEAMBOAT SPRINGS

Start the morning off early and drive to either the Mount Zirkel or Flat Tops wilderness areas, where you can enjoy the beautiful surroundings with a scenic drive and hike. Bring a picnic lunch. Later, return to Steamboat Springs and get ready for a bubbling mineral bath at the hot springs pool in Steamboat Springs or in the nearby Strawberry Hot Springs. For a truly romantic evening, visit Strawberry Hot Springs at night, to soak under a twinkling blanket of stars. Explore town after enjoying dinner at one of the many restaurants.

SIGHTSEEING HIGHLIGHTS

★★★ **Flat Tops Wilderness Area**—South of Steamboat Springs is an exceptionally wild and scenic area known as the Flat Tops. The **Flat Tops Trail Scenic and Historic Byway** starts in Yampa, travels through two national forests (Routt and White River), and ends in the town of Meeker. It takes approximately two and a half hours to drive the byway, not including stops along the way. Although half of this 82-mile drive is unpaved, it is still adequate for two-wheel-drive vehicles, except when wet. The road is closed to cars in winter, when it becomes a favored spot for cross-country skiers.

The Ute Indians used a series of ancient trails across the Flat Tops when traveling between their winter grounds in the White River Valley and summer grounds in the Yampa River Valley. Beginning in the 1820s, fur trappers were lured here by the Yampa's huge beaver populations. Each summer, the Utes and mountain men journeyed to a predetermined place for a rendezvous, where agents from the fur companies swapped traps, gunpowder, bullets, utensils, and other supplies for large quantities of beaver pelts.

On the west end of the Flat Tops are lands formerly within the White River Indian Agency, set aside for the Utes after white settlers took their lands in the central mountains of Colorado. Nathan Meeker, an unyielding man appointed as Indian agent, attempted to convert the Utes to white ways by teaching them farming. He was murdered during an uprising at the agency in 1879. As a result, the Utes at White River Agency were removed from their Colorado homeland to the Uintah-Ouray Reservation in northeastern Utah.

United States Forest Service architect Arthur Carhart visited the Flat Tops Timber Reserve, the predecessor to the national forest, in the early 1900s to make recommendations for development around the serene **Trappers Lake**. But after viewing the splendid natural environment, he realized that constructing roads and homes would destroy the very wilderness that made the area so special. His defiant stand against development helped pave the way for further legislation, finally resulting in the 1964 Wilderness Act, which protected unspoiled sections of nature. The Flat Tops became a wilderness area in 1975. From the eastern portal of the byway at Yampa, the access road (Forest Road 205) to Trappers Lake is approximately 40 miles. From there, the lake is another seven to eight miles.

Details*: For additional information, contact Routt National Forest in Yampa, 300 Roselawn, 970/638-4516. (full day)*

★★★ **Mount Zirkel Wilderness**—Straddling the Park Range of the Continental Divide northeast of Steamboat, the Mount Zirkel Wilderness embraces numerous alpine lakes, tundra, forests, and the Elk and Encampment Rivers. Several moderate hikes climb to several tranquil mountain lakes from branching forks at this trailhead. These include the **Gold Creek Lake Trail**, **Three Island Lake Trail**, and the **Gilpin Lake Trail**, which terminates at the Continental Divide. **Mount Zirkel**, elevation 12,180 feet, in the northern reaches of the wilderness boundary, can be reached via a long, exhilarating day hike for experienced hikers.

Details: From Steamboat Springs, drive two miles on Highway 40 to County Road 129. At County Road 64 (Forest Rd. 400), turn right. The road parallels the Elk River for approximately 30 to 45 minutes before you reach the parking area and trailhead at Slavonia. For more detailed information and a topographical map of the area, contact the Hahns Peak Ranger Office, 57 10th St., Steamboat Springs; 970/879-1870. (half–full day)

✪✪✪ **Steamboat Ski Area**—Steamboat residents are delighted to boast that approximately 40 hometown athletes have made it to the Winter Olympics, a number that beats any other ski town in the country. Winter sports are a passion here, beginning when early residents used skis for transportation during winter. And it isn't just downhill skiing that steals the spotlight, as snowboarding, ski jumping, freestyle, and cross-country skiing have all been mastered by local favorites.

Steamboat Ski Area is an exceptional mountain for intermediate skiers, but there's also plenty here for their beginning or advanced peers. The term "champagne powder" is often used to describe the light, fluffy snow that usually blankets these mountains by December or January. The area offers kids programs, lessons, and the Billy Kidd Center of Performance Skiing, which specializes in coaching intermediate and advanced skiers. You might want to take a snowboarding lesson, especially if you've never skied before, as some people say snowboarding is easier to learn than downhill skiing. In mid-January professional rodeo cowboys from the National Western Stock Show in Denver converge on the mountain to display their skiing finesse (or lack thereof).

Steamboat Ski Touring Center, 970/879-8180, has 20 miles of groomed cross-country trails that meander along Fish Creek near the alpine ski area. Admission is $10 for a full day, and $8 for a half-day, beginning after 1 p.m. Rental equipment and lessons are available.

Rabbit Ears Pass is a paradise for backcountry Nordic skiers. Its summit is actually a long meadow, interspersed with evergreens and gentle hills. Many consider this the best place to cross-country ski in Colorado, for its solitude, scenery, and voluminous snow. Several trails, for all abilities, begin near the high point of the pass, about 25 miles southeast of Steamboat Springs on Highway 40.

Carl Howelsen brought competitive and recreational ski jumping to Steamboat Springs and taught many local kids how to jump during the long winter months. The jumping hills at **Howelsen Park**, used by Olympic ski jumpers and national competitors, are the largest and most complete in the United States. The ski area has novice slopes open for nighttime skiing until 9 p.m., an outdoor ice-skating rink, and approximately seven miles of groomed cross-country trails. In summer the area offers horseback riding, mountain biking, skateboarding, roller skating, and in-line skating. To reach the park, take Highway 40 into Steamboat, turn left at Fifth Street, and drive two blocks across the bridge. Take a right in front of the rodeo stands. For general information, call 970/879-4300.

Details: *Steamboat Ski & Resort Company, 970/879-6111. Area generally open Thanksgiving–mid-April. (1–3 days)*

★★ **Fish Creek Falls**—East of Steamboat is Fish Creek Falls, a natural waterfall spilling into a steep canyon within Routt National Forest. At the turn of the century, local families made day trips to the falls, where they would picnic among the rocks and catch large volumes of fish for winter. In the 1930s the Civilian Conservation Corps improved the area, constructing a road, picnic facilities, and a trail to the falls.

While many people visit the 280-foot falls, located a short way up a wheelchair-accessible trail, fewer continue along the trail destined for Long Lake, seven miles up the steep Fish Creek Canyon. This can be an invigorating day hike or overnight trip.

Details: *From Steamboat Springs, take S. Lincoln Street (Hwy. 40) to Third Street and turn east. When you reach Oak Street (which turns into Fish Creek Falls Road), turn right and drive about three miles to the parking lot. For more information, contact the Hahn's Peak Ranger Office, 57 10th St., Steamboat Springs; 970/879-1870. (1 hour–full day)*

★★ **Hahn's Peak and Steamboat Lake State Park**—The Hahn's Peak Mining District first attracted gold prospectors in 1865. The low-grade ore here never kept things hopping, although a short revival did occur in 1872, when hydraulic mining operators used a staggering amount of water to recover a small amount of gold. The **Hahn's Peak Schoolhouse**, on the National Register of Historic Places, displays artifacts from the earliest settlement in northwest Colorado. The museum is open Memorial Day through Labor Day. To visit it, ask at the Things 'n' Stuff store in Hahn's Peak Village.

At the foot of Hahn's Peak, **Steamboat Lake State Park** is a peaceful reservoir developed in 1967 by the damming of Willow Creek. Although a reservoir, a natural ecosystem similar to those of other alpine lakes has developed here. The water is used as a backup supply for the Colorado Ute Power Plant near Craig, should the Yampa River run low. It has never been needed for that purpose, and many visitors come here to enjoy the scenery, camping, swimming, and fishing. Horseback rides are available, and boats can be rented at the marina. The park staff offers interpretive and kids' programs throughout the summer.

Details: Steamboat Lake State Park, County Rd. 129; 970/879-3922. Call the park for more information on Hahn's Peak. (2 hours)

✰✰ **Steamboat Springs Swimming Pool**—You will welcome a soak in these soothing hot springs after a hard day of outdoor activity, be it skiing, hiking, mountain biking, or even wildlife viewing. The Steamboat Sanitarium Association, incorporated near the turn of the century, officially inaugurated a longstanding local tradition of using the mineral springs gurgling in town. Heart Spring feeds these four outdoor mineral pools, each from 99 to 102 degrees Fahrenheit. You can also get a massage here, dry out in a sauna, swim in the lap pool, or play on the water slide.

Details: 136 Lincoln Ave., Steamboat Springs; 970/879 1828. Weekends 8–9:45, weekdays 7–9:45. $5 adults, $2 ages 3–12, $3.50 ages 13–17. Massages are $50 an hour, $30 per half-hour. 10 water slide rides $3.50, plus pool admission. (2 hours)

✰ **Strawberry Park Hot Springs**—One of the better-known hot springs in Colorado, Strawberry Park lies six miles north of Steamboat Springs. The springs are a popular destination for mountain bikers, cross-country skiers, snowshoers, and the less intrepid who drive up the gravel access road to Hot Springs Creek. Especially inviting during the chilly winter months, these 100-degree waters do the trick in warming up cold toes and fingers. Another great way to partake is by moonlight, to stargaze while you luxuriate.

Details: From Steamboat Springs take Seventh Street to Park Road and turn north to Hot Springs Creek; 970/879-0342. Daily 10 a.m.–midnight (no admission after 11 p.m.) $5 adults until 5, $7 Mon–Thu after 5, $10 Fri–Sun after 5. Minors are not allowed in the springs after dark. (2 hours)

✰ **Tread of the Pioneers Museum**—Established in an historic home built in 1900, the historical ski collection displayed here demonstrates the love of this sport in Steamboat Springs. Donated artifacts tell an engaging history of the town, established by a pioneer family in 1875.

Details: *Eighth and Oak Sts. Steamboat Springs; 970/879-2214. Ski season Mon–Sat 11–5, summer daily 11–5. $3 adults, $2 seniors. (30 minutes)*

✫ **Walking tour of the springs**—Numerous mineral springs rise to the surface in Steamboat Springs, which is named for a particularly noisy spring that reminded early residents of steamboats chugging up the Mississippi. The Chamber of Commerce has prepared a two-mile walking tour, with an accompanying brochure that includes interesting history and facts about the springs. Except for Heart Spring, which feeds the Steamboat Springs Pool, the springs are too cold for dipping—but the walk provides a nice diversion from shopping, skiing, or hiking.
Details: *Steamboat Springs Chamber of Commerce, 1255 S. Lincoln Ave., 970/879-0880. Mon–Sat 8–7, Sun 8–5. (1 hour)*

✫ **Routt County rodeos**—The residents of northwestern Colorado take their horse-riding and cattle-roping skills seriously. On summer weekends, rodeos bring out the best in local, and sometimes national, competition. County fairs take place during the late summer. If you're here at that time, be sure to go, as they feature a rodeo, live entertainment, kids' activities, and livestock judging.
Details: *Contact the Steamboat Chamber of Commerce, 970/879-0880, for more information on Routt County rodeos. (2 hours)*

FITNESS AND RECREATION

Winter sports are the premier recreational attraction here, but summer also brings a host of exciting outdoor activities. You can ride the wild **Yampa River** on the flotation device of your choice, or try the kayaking course set up on the river's path through town. Numerous hiking, backpacking, and camping options exist in the millions of acres of remote public lands surrounding Steamboat.

Mountain bikers of all abilities will delight in the rides possible on the slopes of **Steamboat Ski Area**, from easy jaunts on relatively flat terrain to goosepimple rides down precipitous mountain slopes. For an intermediate adventure, the **Spring Creek Trail** is perfect; advanced riders will be challenged by the dirt paths on the **Rabbit Ears Continental Divide Trail**. Stop in the **Ski Haus**, 1450 South Lincoln Avenue, 970/879-0385, to rent a bike or ask for trail information.

Families will find several other options besides skiing in winter and

hiking in summer. The **Yampa River Core Trail** is a four-mile path
linking downtown Steamboat with the ski area. The trail is paved and
has an adjoining gravel path to accommodate all types of activities,
from Rollerblading to stroller-walking. Kids also love the indoor
climbing gym called **Vertical Grip**. You can take a nature trail up
Mount Werner, the Steamboat ski area hill, where you will be
rewarded by majestic views of the **Yampa River Valley, Continental
Divide**, and **Flat Tops**. Or, ride the **Silver Bullet Gondola** to the top
of Mount Werner, from mid-June through late September.

Consider taking a hot-air balloon trip for the most panoramic view
of the stunning scenery of northwestern Colorado. You will rise 2,000
to 3,000 feet above the ground in a colorful balloon that holds four to
six people. Two companies offering balloon flights are **Balloons Over
Steamboat**, 970/879-3298, and **Pegasus Balloon Tours**, 970/879-
9191 or 800/748-2487. The trips cost $85 for a half-hour and $160 for
an hour, and children 5–12 fly for $55 for a half-hour and $100 for an
hour. Balloons fly year-round, starting at 7 a.m. in the summer, and at
9 a.m. during the winter, weather permitting. Both companies ask you
to make reservations at least one day in advance.

FOOD

Winona's Restaurant, 617 Lincoln Avenue, 970/879-2483, is especially known for its breakfasts, with omelets, waffles, and French toast.
Winona's also serves light lunch and dinner entrées such as sandwiches,
salads, and soups, all under $10. Open 7 to 9, except during the off-
season, when it closes at 3. For a substantial meal, head over to the
Old Town Pub, 600 Lincoln Avenue, 970/879-2101, where you can
feast on T-bone steak, prime rib, baby back ribs, seafood, pasta,
chicken sandwiches, or burgers, from $6.95 to $20.95.

If you'd like to share a pizza, **Cugino's Pizzeria**, 825 Oak Street,
across from the Tread of Pioneers Museum, 970/879-5805, is the place
to go. Large pizzas range from $8.50 to $19.75. Deliveries available
from 5 to 9:30 p.m.

To really treat yourself, visit **L'apogee**, 911 Lincoln Avenue,
970/879-1919, a classic French restaurant featuring specialties such as
Colorado lamb, filet mignon, duck, veal, and seafood ($20 to $36 for à
la carte entrees). L'apogee serves dinner nightly from 5:30 to 10. The
restaurant also contains **Harwig's**, a French bistro, serving Oriental-
and French-influenced dishes ($7 to $15) until 11 p.m. nightly.

STEAMBOAT SPRINGS

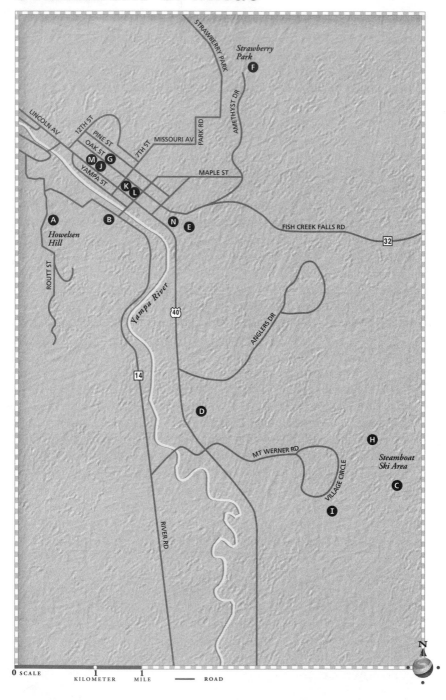

Sights

Ⓐ Howelsen Park

Ⓑ Routt County rodeos

Ⓒ Steamboat Ski Area

Ⓓ Steamboat Ski Touring Center

Ⓔ Steamboat Springs
   Swimming Pool

Ⓕ Strawberry Park Hot Springs

Ⓖ Tread of the Pioneers Museum

Food

Ⓖ Cugino's Pizzeria

Ⓗ Heavenly Daze

Food (continued)

Ⓘ La Montaña

Ⓙ L'apogee/Harwig's

Ⓚ Old Town Pub

Ⓛ Steamboat Brewery & Tavern

Ⓚ Winona's Restaurant

Lodging

Ⓜ Hotel Bristol

Ⓕ Perry-Mansfield School
   and Camp

Ⓝ Rabbit Ears Motel

Ⓕ Strawberry Park Hot Springs
   Cabins and Campground

Note: Items with the same letter are located in the same area.

Another favorite Steamboat restaurant is **La Montaña**, 2500 Village Drive, 970/879-5800, which has two different menus, featuring Tex-Mex (burritos, enchiladas, etc.) from $10 to $15 and Southwestern gourmet, with dinner entrées from $15 to $25.

The brewery near the ski area, **Heavenly Daze**, Ski Time Square, 970/879-8080, has made a name for itself with its raspberry wheat beer. It also serves pub food, with a large selection of burgers and sandwiches under $10 and a full range of dinner entrées from $10 to $18. The downstairs pool hall also has microbrews on tap. Another excellent microbrewery downtown is the **Steamboat Brewery & Tavern**, Fifth Street and Lincoln Avenue, 970/879-2233, where you can relax with a homemade beer and well-prepared meal, or munch on a great assortment of appetizers (under $10).

The town of Oak Creek, about 20 miles south of Steamboat on Highway 131, is a funky collection of buildings, shops, and restaurants. It's also home to one of the best restaurants in the region, **Chelsea's**, 970/736-8538, which specializes in Szechuan Chinese cuisine, as spicy as you can stand it. The chef prepares such succulent dishes as Peking duck ($23 for two people) or crispy chicken ($14.95 for two) if you call ahead two days in advance. Other features include wonderful shrimp dishes for around $10.50, chicken dishes starting at $7.75, as well as soup, egg rolls, and fried rice. Open for dinner Tuesday through Sunday.

LODGING

From mid-December to January 1, lodging prices in Steamboat are as steep as the surrounding mountains. Weeknights and off-peak week-ends bring more reasonable rates, and lodging deals abound during the summer. Accommodations are available in three general areas: down-town Steamboat Springs, close to the shops and restaurants; near the ski resort; or at a variety of ranches, cabins, and bed-and-breakfasts surrounding town. The largest variety of lodging options can be found near the ski resort, with numerous hotels, motels, condominiums, and homes. Call Steamboat Central Reservations, 800/922-2722, depart-ment 300, for information on ski resort lodgings. Be sure to ask for special rates on lift tickets or children's lessons.

My recommendations are based on some of the better lodging deals available in the area. For inexpensive and very rustic digs, head up to **Strawberry Park Hot Springs Cabins and Campground**, 44200 Routt County Road 36, 970/879-0342, where cabins rent for less than $35 on weeknights, $40 on weekends. Or pitch a tent for $25 on weeknights, $30 weekends. These prices also include hot springs admission. Strawberry Park also offers more deluxe accommodations in an 1890s railroad car, with a private bath, refrigerator, and futon for $75 a night. The **Perry-Mansfield Performing Arts School and Camp** north of Steamboat, 40755 Routt County Road 36, 800/538-7519, maintains six rustic cabins on a beautiful property. The camp offers a variety of options, from a one-bedroom lodge to a cabin that can sleep up to 10 people ($105 to $350). They are available year-round but on a more limited basis during summer camp season. Scheduled theater and dance performances take place during the sum-mer. To reach both the hot springs cabins and the camp, head north on Seventh Street until you reach Missouri Avenue, then turn right. When you come to Park Road (County Road 36), head north and fol-low the signs to either location.

One of the better lodging options downtown is the **Hotel Bristol**, 917 Lincoln Avenue, 970/879-3083. This recently upgraded inn has 22 rooms with either private or shared baths. Rates start at $44 in the summer, and average around $80 in the winter, except during the peak season, and include a full breakfast, hot tub, and ski lockers. Also downtown is the famous marquee of the **Rabbit Ears Motel**, 201 Lincoln Avenue, across from the Steamboat Hot Springs, 800/828-7701 or 970/879-1150. Doubles at this clean, well-kept hotel average $69 in summer, $89 in winter, including a continental breakfast. Some rooms have microwaves and refrigerators.

CAMPING

Most campgrounds in the **Flat Tops Wilderness** have fishing access, restrooms, and trash receptacles. Several are located on the base of Forest Road 205, at Trappers Lake. Look for **Bucks, Trapline, Cutthroat, and Shepherds Rim**.

You can also camp at **Steamboat Lake** and **Pearl Lake State Park**, north of town about 30 miles. Fees are $7 at Pearl Lake, and from $9 to $12 at Steamboat Lake. Steamboat Lake maintains showers and a small concession stand.

Open year-round, **Ski Town KOA Campground**, two miles west of Steamboat Springs on Highway 40, 970/879-0273, features a general store, Laundromat, and pool.

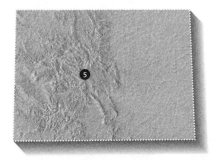

5
LEADVILLE

West of Leadville is the imperial Sawatch Range, birthplace of the Arkansas River and home to Colorado's highest mountains. To the east are the lower but no less magnificent peaks of the Mosquito Range. In some of the most violent upheavals on the continent, geologic forces lifted these mountains to heights of more than two miles above sea level, while pressures deep within the earth forced mineral-rich liquids into great fissures. These minerals precipitated a mining boom of epic proportions and created Leadville, Colorado's most memorable mining town. At 10,430 feet, Leadville is also the highest incorporated town in the United States.

After gold was discovered in the Rocky Mountains west of Denver in 1858, prospectors scoured every gully and hill in the surrounding region. In 1860 a group struck pay dirt southwest of present-day Leadville, in a place called California Gulch. This rush didn't last long since a perplexing black dirt clung to the gold, making separation of the ore almost impossible. A miner finally had the black dirt assayed and discovered it was a lead carbonate, chock-full of profitable silver. The second and more fevered rush to California Gulch began in 1877, attracting 20,000 people by 1880. Leadville became a maze of ramshackle tents, half-finished buildings, hotels, saloons, and bordellos.

For more than a century, the town has weathered the mining industry's booms and busts. Its most recent incarnation is as a tourist destination. Fascinating history and the beautiful Rockies are the primary attractions for visitors. ◼

LEADVILLE AREA

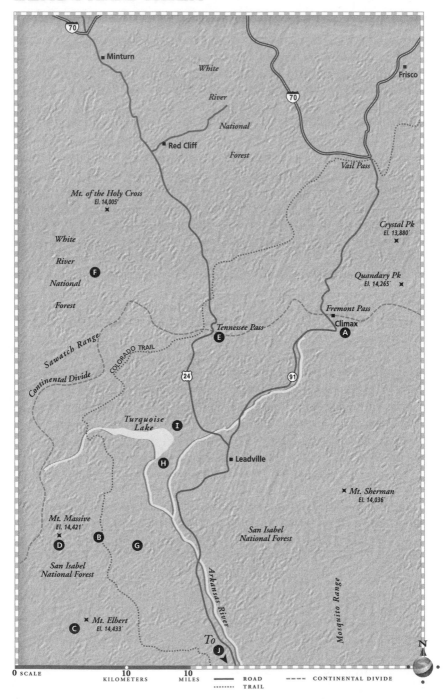

Sights

Ⓐ Climax Molybdenum Mine

Ⓑ Colorado Trail

Ⓒ Mt. Elbert

Ⓓ Mt. Massive

Ⓔ Ski Cooper/Camp Hale

Ⓕ Tenth Mountain Division Hut System

Camping

Ⓖ Elbert Creek Campground

Ⓖ Half Moon Campground

Ⓗ Sugar Loafin' Campground

Ⓘ Turquoise Reservoir

Ⓙ Twin Lakes

Note: Items with the same letter are located in the same area.

A PERFECT DAY IN LEADVILLE

Leadville's charm lies in its rich history. The town and nearby mining district comprise a National Historic Landmark District, where many structures, built with the most luxurious appointments at the height of mining activity, have been restored to their original splendor. Explore Leadville's historic attractions, such as the National Mining Hall of Fame & Museum, the Tabor Opera House, or the Healy House. Then take a scenic drive through the "Route of the Silver Kings" to see the remnants of the frenzied mining activity that took place in these hills.

SIGHTSEEING HIGHLIGHTS

★★★ **Hiking**—The possibilities for hiking in this region's crisp mountain air are endless. In the Sawatch Range, Colorado's two highest Fourteeners—**Mount Massive** (14 miles round trip, to an elevation of 14,421 feet) and **Mount Elbert** (nine miles round trip, to an elevation of 14,433 feet)—present formidable challenges. Both begin just above the Halfmoon Campground in the San Isabel National Forest. You can reach the trailhead by driving south on Highway 24 to Malta. Head west (right) on Highway 300 until you reach road 160, which takes you to road 110, along Halfmoon Creek and to the campground. While it is possible to hike either Elbert or Massive in one day, be prepared for a lengthy and strenuous journey that will last from dawn to dusk. Bring lots of food, water, and sufficient clothing to anticipate weather changes.

The **Colorado Trail** skirts Leadville to the west on its 500-mile journey between Denver and Durango. Access the trail at the summit of Tennessee Pass or in the San Isabel Forest near the town of Twin Lakes. For more information on these or any other hikes in the region, contact the San Isabel National Forest, 2015 North Poplar Street; 719/486-0749.

Additional stunning hikes with rustic lodges along the way can be found in the **Tenth Mountain Division Hut System**'s 350 miles of backcountry trails. The "huts" are actually large and comfortable solar-powered log cabins that sleep up to 16 people. Situated in the pristine wilderness, they include wood-burning stoves for cooking and heating. The huts stretch along trails between Vail, Leadville, and Aspen in White River National Forest. The difficulty of the terrain varies, and trips can be geared toward your ability level. In addition to hiking, activities on the trails include mountain biking, backcountry skiing, and snowshoeing. You must reserve huts in advance ($22–$36 per person, per night). For more information, contact the Tenth Mountain Division Hut Association, Aspen; 970/925-5775.

★★★ **National Mining Hall of Fame & Museum**—Leadville is the home of the nation's mining museum, authorized through an act of Congress and presidential approval in 1988. During a period of 130 years, mineral production in the region has grossed approximately $2 billion. It is fitting that this nonprofit museum, dedicated to the science, industry, and history of mining, is located in such a rich mineral-producing district.

Exhibits include many priceless minerals, some loaned by the Smithsonian and the Harvard Mineralogical Museum, in addition to educational exhibits on different types of mining. Two full-size replicas of underground mines—hard rock and coal—illustrate day-to-day experiences in the lives of miners.

Details: *120 W. Ninth St.; 719/486-1229. Oct–Apr Mon–Fri 10–2, May–Sept daily 9–5. $3.50 adults, $3 seniors, $2 ages 6–12. (2 hours)*

★★★ **Route of the Silver Kings**—Situated east of Leadville is the Leadville Mining District, a 20-square-mile pocket containing such minerals as gold, silver, lead, zinc, copper, and iron. The district is littered with abandoned and dilapidated structures from previous mining operations, all reminders of its potent effects on the landscape. Forgotten head frames, chutes, dumps, cables, and cars lie dormant throughout the area.

You may be tempted to explore these old structures and mineshafts—but don't. They are unstable and extremely dangerous. It's best to stay on the road and view them from a distance. Most of the mining roads, accessible from both Seventh and Fifth Streets, can be driven by any type of car. This is a great place for a mountain bike ride or leisurely walk. The Leadville Chamber of Commerce, on the corner of Ninth and Harrison, provides a brochure about the "Route of the Silver Kings," detailing its mines and the men who worked them— some made colossal fortunes, while others lost their last dollar.

Details: Leadville Chamber of Commerce, 809 Harrison Ave.; 719/486-3900. Daily 10–5. (2 hours)

★★★ **Tabor Opera House**—Horace A. Tabor, Leadville's first mayor and later a U.S. senator, built this distinguished and elegant opera house in 1879. The famous author Oscar Wilde visited Leadville on April 14, 1882, and delivered a lecture on the "ethics of art" to a full audience at the opera house. Many audience members admitted no understanding or interest in this subject but still had a hearty good time at the lecture. Afterward, they escorted Wilde to the Matchless Mine for a private tour, then served him a balanced three-course meal of whiskey, whiskey, and whiskey. When Wilde wrote about his Leadville visit in later years, he was most impressed with the sign above the piano in a local saloon that read: "Please do not shoot the pianist. He is doing his best."

Wilde was just one celebrity of many who visited Leadville to entertain, and be entertained in, its rowdy atmosphere. Presiding over the merriment, the Tabor Opera House brought culture and refinement to the young town and was a great asset to the mining camp.

Tabor lost the house in 1893 with the crash of the silver market. It changed hands several times, until it was saved in 1955 by a dedicated resident who restored the structure and much of its original furnishings and decor. Memorabilia from notable events is on display, and it continues as a venue for films, lectures, theater, and exhibits.

Details: 306–310 Harrison Ave.; 719/486-1147. June–Oct Sun–Fri 9–5:30, Nov–May by appointment. $4 adults, $2 ages 6–12. (1 hour)

★★ **Climax Molybdenum Mine**—A huge stock of molybdenum, a mineral used to harden steel, sits at the summit of Fremont Pass. The sprawling complex constructed by the Climax Mining Company became one of the world's largest underground mines. By the mid-1950s, molybdenum mining had taken over as the dominant industry in Lake County. Highly prized during both World Wars, the mineral was used in the construction of stainless steel, aircraft, automobiles, and in later years, spacecraft.

The company developed a town, also called Climax, at the 11,318-foot summit of Fremont Pass. Climax was the highest town in the United States until it closed in 1963. It housed miners and their families and included a school, hospital, and even its own ski area. When mining operations encroached on the townsite, the company moved the town to Leadville. In 1982 full-scale mining stopped, with only a small workforce remaining to manage environmental reclamation of former mine sites. Interpretive signs at the summit explain the significance of the mineral and provide some history about mining operations and the former town.

Details: *About 12 miles north of Leadville on Hwy. 91. Interpretive exhibits available in summer. No tours of the mine facility. (1 hour)*

★★ **Healy House and Dexter Cabin**—These two examples of Leadville's 1880s architecture provide an interesting contrast. The three-storied Healy House boasts an uninhibited view of the Continental Divide on top of Harrison Avenue. The home's builder, August Meyer, was one of the first men in town to own a smelter. Meyer went to great lengths to please his new bride, Emma, filling the home with only the finest Victorian furnishings. The house is named Healy, after a later owner who donated it to the town of Leadville in the mid-1900s.

Next door to the Healy House is a curious two-room log structure, the Dexter Cabin, that at first glance appears to be a rudely constructed miner's cabin. It actually belonged to a learned and wealthy man, James Dexter, who maintained an elegant home for his family in Denver but used this cabin when on business in Leadville. Decorations of his "bachelor" digs (often used for late-night poker parties) included English wall coverings and a matched black walnut and white oak floor. A Persian rug and zinc-lined bathtub completed the lavish appointments. Both the Healy House and Dexter Cabin are operated by the Colorado Historical Society, which offers tours conducted by guides in period costume.

Details: *912 Harrison Ave.; 719/486-0487. Memorial Day–Labor Day 10–4:30, Sept on weekends only. $3 adults, $2.50 seniors, $2 ages 6–12. (1 hour)*

★★ **Ski Cooper**—During World War II, the present site of the Ski Cooper downhill ski area was Camp Hale, the center of active training for U.S. troops specializing in mountain and winter warfare. Thousands of men dubbed Soldiers of the Summit formed the famous Tenth Mountain Division, the only one of its kind in the country. The recruits mastered the arts of alpine skiing, snowshoeing, technical climbing, and alpine survival and rescue skills to effectively deter Hitler's army in the mountains of Europe. Serving in Italy in 1944, almost a thousand men from the Tenth Mountain Division were killed in active fighting and are memorialized today in a granite monument at the entrance to Ski Cooper.

After the war, many Tenth Mountain Division veterans returned to Colorado and pioneered the state's recreational ski industry at places like Ski Cooper, Vail, and Aspen. Ski Cooper is an affordable and challenging ski area, peaking at an elevation of 11,700 feet above Tennessee Pass. The facility includes a ski school, equipment rental, and a nursery. Lift tickets are less expensive than those at the slopes on I-70. Note the Tenth Mountain Division artifacts in the lodge.

Details: 10 miles north of Leadville on Hwy. 24; 719/486-3684. Usually open Thanksgiving—April. (full day)

✭ **Matchless Mine**—The final chapter in the odyssey of Horace Tabor and his second wife, the beautiful Elizabeth (better known as Baby Doe), is intertwined with the Matchless Mine. When Horace Tabor purchased sole title to this silver claim in 1879, he turned a questionable sale into an overnight success and became known throughout the country as the "Silver King of Colorado." The profits from this mine (over $7 million) kept him rolling in dough throughout the 1880s. But the 1893 silver crash rendered it worthless, and Tabor lost his entire fortune.

Tabor died in 1899, leaving Baby Doe penniless. A legend is told that on his deathbed he clutched Baby Doe and whispered, "Hang on to the Matchless. It will make millions again." Dramatic, isn't it? Well, yes, but Tabor never actually said it. Regardless, Baby Doe did spend the rest of her life and energy holding on to the Matchless. She moved into a shack at the Matchless Mine, sold her jewels, and borrowed money from influential friends to hold on to her "last chance." But the Matchless never again produced anything of value, and Baby Doe never regained her former status. In March 1935, at the age of 80, she froze to death in her cabin. Thousands of people have visited Baby Doe's lonely shack at the Matchless Mine to steal a quick glimpse of her extraordinary life.

Details: 414 E. Seventh St., Leadville; 719/486-0371. Memorial
Day–Labor Day daily. $3 adults, $1 ages 6–12. (30 minutes)

✷ **Heritage Museum**—Leadville's municipal museum exhibits mining
artifacts, ore samples, and other artifacts donated by early pioneers.
One of the most interesting is a quarter-inch scale replica of Leadville's
Ice Palace. To raise morale during the interminable winter of 1895,
Leadville businessmen concocted a fantastic Winter Carnival, including
a massive timber palace surrounded by five thousand tons of ice.
Opening on January 1, 1896, it included an indoor skating rink, ball-
room, taxidermy displays, and intricately carved ice statues. But to
everyone's chagrin, unseasonable chinook winds caused an early melt-
down by the end of March. Still, the palace helped raise the spirits of
Leadville residents after the dreadful Panic of 1893.
    Details: 102 E. Ninth St., Leadville; 719/486-1878. May–Oct daily
10–6. $2.50 adults, $1.50 children. (30 minutes)

FITNESS AND RECREATION

The **Arkansas Headwaters Recreation Area**, encompassing 150
miles of numerous recreational possibilities, begins north of Leadville.
Along this high stretch, the Arkansas is a gentle stream spooling
through meadows and forested areas. Fishing is possible at **Turquoise
Lake** and at the petite **Crystal Lakes**, in a scenic overlook south of
Leadville. It isn't until below Granite that the river begins to change,
crashing through narrow canyons ideal for white-water rafting. For
more information on raft trips in the lower sections of the river, refer
to the Salida chapter of this book. Lands in the **San Isabel National
Forest** have multitudes of trails for hiking, mountain biking, and backcountry camping. One of the more difficult mountain biking trails in the
area ascends to the summit of **Mosquito Pass**, east of Leadville. Hiking
trails around **Twin Lakes** (see the "Scenic Route" section at the end of
this chapter) make for moderate outings. Contact the **Leadville Ranger
District**, San Isabel Forest, 2015 Poplar; 719/486-0749.

FOOD

For an authentic Leadville experience, stop at the **Silver Dollar
Saloon**, 315 Harrison Avenue, 719/486-9914, which has been serving
libations since 1879 (during Prohibition, the moonshine was concealed

underneath the bar). An original silver dollar marquee manufactured by silver titan Horace Tabor has an honored place here. The bar serves only personal pizzas, so plan to eat somewhere else.

Authentic Mexican food is prepared at **The Grill**, 715 Elm, 719/486-9930. À la carte items might look alluring, but the real temptations are the dinners, such as stuffed sopapillas smothered in green chile, and other authentic dishes from $10 to $20. Prepared with homemade bread, the French toast ($3) at the **Golden Burro**, 710 Harrison Avenue, 719/486-1239, is truly delightful. Breakfast is served all day, in addition to lunch (try a Monte Cristo sandwich with fries, $5.50, or a cheeseburger on a homemade bun with fries, $4.75) and dinner (rainbow trout, baked half-chicken, baby back ribs, or chicken-fried steak, $6.50 to $12.95).

Also downtown is the **Old Glory Café**, 222 Harrison Avenue, 719/486-8432, specializing in breakfast and lunch, with good Mexican food and tasty burgers. Prices range from $5 to $10.

The **Prospector Restaurant**, three miles north of Leadville on Highway 91, 719/486-3955 or 800/844-2828, is one of the area's best restaurants. It's open for dinner Tuesday through Saturday during winter and also on Sunday during summer. The menu features steaks, seafood, and pasta, with specials such as prime rib, New York strip steak, and 24-ounce sirloin. All meals include soup and salad.

In the historic Twin Lakes village is the **Twin Lakes Nordic Inn**, a restored 120-year old lodge and restaurant specializing in German and American cuisine. With traditional German specialties such as *Rinderrouladen*, tenderly roasted Colorado beef stuffed with onions and pickles, and other dishes featuring chicken and pork, this is truly a dining experience. Entrees range about $13 to $15. Also serving breakfast and lunch, the restaurant is a great place to visit after exploring Twin Lakes or hiking in the area.

LODGING

Leadville is becoming more popular in both the summer and winter, especially as an alternative to the pricier ski resorts nearby. Reservations are often needed during the peak months of December through February and June through August. Most of the lodging rates listed here are for the high season, unless noted. Off-season rates are generally 10 to 20 percent less.

Located near the small community of Twin Lakes is a comfortable country lodge that makes for a relaxing getaway. Just west of Twin

LEADVILLE

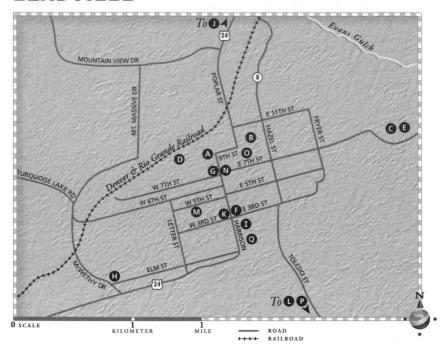

Sights

- **A** Dexter Cabin
- **A** Healy House
- **B** Heritage Museum
- **C** Matchless Mine
- **D** National Mining Hall of Fame and Museum
- **E** Route of the Silver Kings
- **F** Tabor Opera House

Food

- **G** Golden Burro
- **H** The Grill

Food (continued)

- **I** Old Glory Café
- **J** Prospector Restaurant
- **K** Silver Dollar Saloon
- **L** Twin Lakes Nordic Inn

Lodging

- **M** Apple Blossom Inn
- **N** Delaware Hotel
- **O** Leadville Country Inn
- **P** Mt. Elbert Lodge
- **Q** Timberline Motel
- **L** Twin Lakes Nordic Inn

Note: Items with the same letter are located in the same place.

Lakes, the **Mt. Elbert Lodge**, 10764 Highway 82, 719/486-0594, is on Independence Pass. Situated below its towering namesake, the lodge allows you good access to the back route up Mount Elbert. After you complete your hike up Colorado's tallest mountain, you can enjoy a relaxing night in comfort at the lodge. Year-round rates for a double with a shared bath are $59; for a private bath with jet tub, $84.

In Twin Lakes is the historic **Twin Lakes Nordic Inn**, a comfortable lodge that formerly hosted "ladies of the night" in a mountain bordello. The lodge has been completely restored. Its 17 rooms ($48 to $70 for two people) each have featherbeds and either a private or European (shared) bath.

In downtown Leadville, the **Apple Blossom Inn**, 120 West Fourth Street, 719/486-2141 or 800/982-9279, is housed in a restored Victorian built by a wealthy banker in 1879. The inn's gigantic featherbeds make for an untroubled night's sleep. Rates, including breakfast, are $64 to $128. Another place to treat yourself is the **Leadville Country Inn**, 127 East Eighth Street, 719/486-2354 or 800/748-2354, where attention to details, such as complementary mountain bikes for guests, a hot tub in the gazebo, a first-class gourmet breakfast, and freshly baked goods, make this a special getaway. Rates begin at $57, going up to $152.

The **Delaware Hotel**, 700 Harrison Avenue, 800/748-2004, built in 1886, has long been a favored stopping place for travelers passing through Leadville. The hotel is restored in high-Victorian splendor, and the owners often feature theme packages, such as murder mystery weekends or ski and golf packages that include tickets to nearby resorts. Rates range from $60 to $120.

One of the most affordable lodging options, and the only motel in downtown Leadville, is the **Timberline Motel**, 216 Harrison Avenue, 719/486-1876 or 800/352-1876, where doubles range from $39 to $63, depending on the season (August is the busiest month).

CAMPING

The **San Isabel National Forest** hosts 500 campsites, including those at **Twin Lakes**, near the town of the same name, **Halfmoon Campground**, and **Elbert Creek Campground**, near the trailhead for Mount Massive and Mount Elbert. **Turquoise Reservoir**, west of Leadville on Turquoise Lake Road, is another good spot. For reservations in national forest campgrounds, call 800/280-2267 or contact the San Isabel National Forest, 2015 Poplar Street; 719/486-0749.

Sugar Loafin' Campground, 719/486-1031 (summer) and 719/486-1613 (winter), can be found off Highway 24 south of Leadville, at milepost 177. Drive three and a half miles down the county road to the site. The campground is open from late May to late September. It has marvelous views of Mount Elbert and Mount Massive, large pull-through RV sites, water, and electricity.

Scenic Route: Leadville to Aspen

The 59-mile trip over Independence Pass between these two legendary mining towns is steeped in gorgeous scenery and history. It's especially breathtaking during autumn, when the quaking aspens make their annual debut in shades of russet, gold, and orange. The Independence Pass road (Highway 82) is open only during the summer and usually closes by mid-September, after the first heavy snowfall. Perched precariously on the slopes of Independence Mountain, this paved road tests the skills of even the most experienced mountain drivers. If you have a long recreational vehicle, I wouldn't recommend you tempt fate by taking this drive.

Head south on Highway 24 through Leadville, past the remaining buildings of the **American Smelting and Refining Company**, which closed its doors in 1961. This smelter is only one example of the area's many refineries that once flourished by converting raw carbonate ores into valuable silver. Continuing south on Highway 24, follow the dips and bends of the Arkansas River until you reach the junction of Highway 82; turn west (right).

Approximately six miles up the road is the village of **Twin Lakes**,

LEADVILLE TO ASPEN OVER INDEPENDENCE PASS

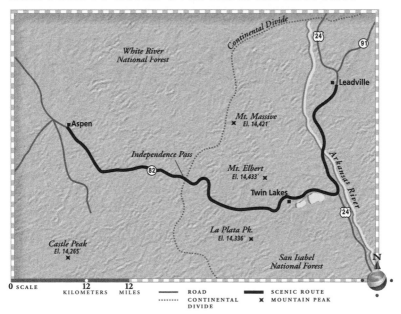

White River National Forest

Aspen

Leadville

Mt. Massive
El. 14,421'

Independence Pass

Mt. Elbert
El. 14,433'

Twin Lakes

La Plata Pk.
El. 14,336'

Castle Peak
El. 14,265'

San Isabel National Forest

Continental Divide

Arkansas River

0 SCALE
KILOMETERS 12
MILES 12

ROAD
CONTINENTAL DIVIDE

SCENIC ROUTE
MOUNTAIN PEAK

N

a National Historic District, where several Forest Service hiking trails depart into the surrounding wilderness. Twin Lakes began as a mining town and later became a resort destination. Many people came to stay at the famous **Interlaken Hotel**, built in 1890, on the southern shore of the upper lake. The remains of this once-glamorous hotel can be visited along a hiking trail that loops around the lake.

After leaving Twin Lakes, the road begins to climb toward Independence Pass, scaling to a height of 12,095 feet at the top of the Continental Divide. Hacked out as a toll road between the boom towns of Leadville and Aspen in the 1880s, the road received a lot of use year-round, as sleighs could travel easily over the snow that traps today's automobiles.

Four miles west of the summit of the pass is the ghost town of Independence, where gold was first discovered on July 4, 1879. While Independence did enjoy some prosperity, Aspen eclipsed it in importance during the 1880s. Several lonely buildings remain. This is a nice spot to pull off for a picnic before reaching Aspen, another 16 miles west. ◼

6

ROARING FORK VALLEY

The Roaring Fork Valley, including the communities of Aspen, Glenwood Springs, and Carbondale and their neighbors in the Crystal River Valley, Redstone and Marble, can easily be called the heart of Colorado's arts and culture scene. A diverse offering of dance, music, culture, lectures, art exhibits, and theater thrives here. Aspen leads the way with a boggling array of talent for a community its size. Beginning in the 1940s, several influential Aspen residents began transforming the depressed mining town into a haven for the world's artists and intellectuals. When teamed with a fascinating regional history, plentiful recreational opportunities, and first-class restaurants and lodging options, it is easy to see why this area is already popular. However, if you prefer to avoid crowds, don't worry—you can still find places and times in which to appreciate this region without having to fight the masses.

The area hosts several music festivals during summer. The Glenwood Springs Summer of Jazz is a free concert held every Wednesday night from mid-June to mid-August at 6:30 in Two Rivers Park. Snowmass hosts a free Summer of Music Concert Series during July and August weekends. Aspen also has its fair share of festivals throughout the year. By far, the most popular and renowned is the Aspen Music Festival, which includes more than 150 annual events featuring some of the world's most talented and innovative musicians. ◼

ROARING FORK VALLEY

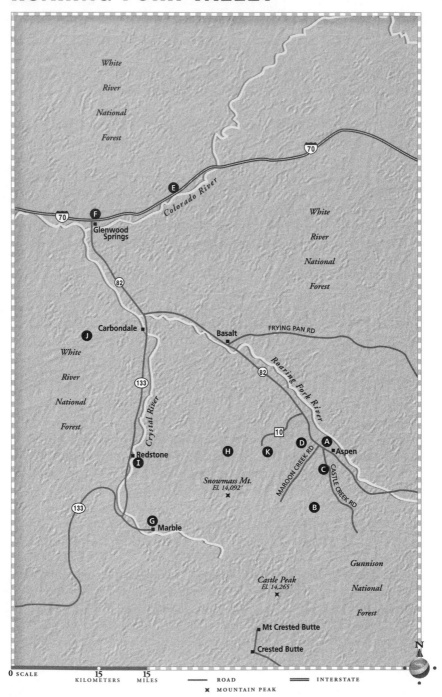

White
River
National
Forest

E

Colorado River

70

F
Glenwood
Springs

White
River
National
Forest

82

Carbondale

J

White
River
National
Forest

Basalt

FRYING PAN RD

82

Roaring Fork River

133

Crystal River

10

H

K

D

A
Aspen

MAROON CREEK RD

Redstone

I

C

CASTLE CREEK RD

Snowmass Mt.
El. 14,092'
✕

133

B

G
Marble

Castle Peak
El. 14,265'
✕

Gunnison

National

Forest

Mt Crested Butte

Crested Butte

N

0 SCALE
15
KILOMETERS
15
MILES
ROAD
✕ MOUNTAIN PEAK
INTERSTATE

Sights

- Ⓐ Aspen Art Museum
- Ⓐ Aspen Center for Environmental Studies
- Ⓑ Aspen Highlands
- Ⓐ Aspen Historical Society
- Ⓒ Aspen Mountain
- Ⓒ Aspen Mountain Gondola
- Ⓐ Aspen Music Festival
- Ⓓ Buttermilk/Tiehack
- Ⓔ Glenwood Canyon
- Ⓕ Glenwood Hot Springs
- Ⓕ Glenwood Springs Center for the Arts
- Ⓔ Hanging Lake Trailhead
- Ⓖ Marble National Historic District
- Ⓗ Maroon Bells-Snowmass Wilderness
- Ⓘ Redstone Castle
- Ⓘ Redstone National Historic District
- Ⓙ Ski Sunlight
- Ⓚ Snowmass
- Ⓕ Yampah Spa and Vapor Caves

Note: Items with the same letter are located in the same town or area.

A PERFECT DAY IN THE ROARING FORK VALLEY

Take time to explore the National Historic Districts of Redstone and Marble. In Redstone, tour the opulent Redstone Castle, visit the art galleries along Main Street, and walk over to see the coke ovens across the road. Then drive to Marble down Highway 133, view the historic marble quarry, and see the work of local sculptors. Seek out a bubbling hot springs or hot tub before setting out for dinner, live music, or other entertainment.

SIGHTSEEING HIGHLIGHTS

☆☆☆ **Aspen Music Festival**—Launched during Aspen's renaissance in the late 1940s, this internationally renowned music festival is connected with the Aspen Music School. This extremely competitive summer school for younger musicians is taught by faculty from major symphonies, orchestras, and universities throughout the world. From June through August, the school offers more than 150 performances, a quarter of which are free. Between November and April, the Winter

Music Festival features 15 or more performances from some of the most talented musicians in the country. Reservations are needed for many of the special benefits, but otherwise, you can usually find performance tickets when you arrive.

Details: *Box office located in the gondola building at the foot of Aspen Mountain; 970/925-3254. Tickets average $40, but lower prices are available for some shows.*

★★★ **Glenwood Hot Springs**—This has always been—and probably always will be—the most popular attraction in Glenwood Springs. The Utes describe how their ancestors used the soothing mineral waters to heal ailments, aches, and pains. Miners from nearby coal mines soaked in the hot springs after a hard day's digging. Today's visitors are no different, except now they relax in two huge outdoor pools maintained at constant temperatures, while the kids keep busy with the water slide.

The pools rent towels and even swimsuits if you've forgotten yours, and the modern locker rooms have showers, hair dryers, and other amenities. For an additional fee, you can use the Hot Springs Athletic Club, with weight machines, aerobics, racquetball, and an indoor Jacuzzi.

Details: *I-70 exit 116, Glenwood Springs; 800/537-SWIM or 970/945-7131. Summer 7:30–10, winter 9–10. Pool admission $7.25 adults, $4.75 ages 3–12. Four water slide rides $3, eight rides $4. (2 hours)*

★★★ **Marble National Historic District**—The marble quarry for which this small town is named once yielded the largest block of marble ever quarried, used for the Tomb of the Unknown Soldier in Arlington National Cemetery. The Colorado Yule Marble Company began extracting marble from this area in 1892, halted in 1942, and began again in 1990. Today the marble is hauled by truck to Glenwood Springs and then shipped to points all over the world. Artisans come here to work on the marble and display their sculptures in town. You can also take a four-mile hike from town to the original Yule Quarry site. The free **Marble Museum**, 412 West Main Street, is open daily May to Labor Day, 2 to 4 p.m. (half day)

★★★ **Redstone National Historic District**—In the late 1880s, the Colorado Fuel and Iron Company built Redstone as part of its extensive coal mining operations in this part of the West Elk Mountains. The company's president, John C. Osgood, an industrialist with humanitarian interests, created a unique environment for the miners and their families.

Unlike other company coal towns known for their poor living conditions, Osgood built Swiss chalet–style homes for the family men and an inn (today known as the **Redstone Inn**) for the bachelors, all equipped with indoor plumbing and electricity. Osgood believed, correctly as it turned out, that if he provided his workers with clean and modern homes, they would return his investment in productivity. He applied his experiment at Redstone to other areas of his business.

Osgood built his own lavish residence, Cleveholm Manor (now called **Redstone Castle**), about a mile south of town. This Tudor-style mansion, completed in 1902, still has many of its exquisite original furnishings. His second wife, Alma, was a favorite with Redstone's children for her generosity and kindness. You can tour this incredible home by purchasing a ticket at the Redstone Country Store, $10 for adults, $5 for ages 5–12. Call 970/963-3408 for more information.

Across the highway from the entrance to Redstone stands a row of beehive ovens that once burned the high-grade coal extracted from this region into coke, used to make steel. The **Redstone Historical Museum** exhibits artifacts from the coal industry in this area, and is open daily from Memorial Day to Labor Day, in the village of Redstone. (half day)

★★ **Aspen Center for Environmental Studies** (ACES)—This innovative naturalist center provides a wonderful opportunity to learn about the environment of the Roaring Fork Valley. Located on the 25-acre Hallam Lake Preserve, the center offers a wide variety of programs for people of all ages. A self-guided nature trail is open year-round. The nature center is home to non-releasable birds of prey, including a golden eagle, red-tailed hawk, western screech owl, ferruginous hawk, and great horned owls. Special programs provide a terrific opportunity to observe these magnificent creatures.

In winter, naturalists lead two-hour snowshoe excursions departing from Aspen Mountain or Snowmass that cost $39 per person, including the ride on the gondola. There are also evening snowshoe programs and a lecture series. During summer, guided walks are led in Aspen and the Maroon Bells Wilderness.

Details: 100 Puppy Smith St., Aspen; 970/925-5756. Summer Mon–Sat 9–5, rest of the year Mon–Fri 9–4:30. (1–2 hours)

★★ **Glenwood Canyon**—In 1887 the Denver & Rio Grande Railroad blasted a standard-gauge railway through the stunning Glenwood

Canyon of the Colorado River. The steepest portions of the canyon had never been entered by humans prior to the opening of the railroad. An automobile road followed in 1902, and the two kinds of vehicles squeezed into narrow corridors on opposite sides of the river. Eventually, traffic accidents on the highway escalated, and for many decades Coloradans clamored for a solution to improving the road through Glenwood Canyon.

A massive highway project to upgrade the two-lane highway into a four-lane interstate without ruining the surrounding environment took more than 20 years and cost roughly $180 million. Road builders took pains to preserve the magnificence of the canyon by contouring the roadway to the existing canyon walls and avoiding existing boulders and trees. The result, the final link of I-70 from coast to coast, has won numerous engineering and design awards.

Glenwood Canyon also is the center for many recreational activities, and has four recreational rest areas along the canyon. An 18-mile recreational path runs east from the Yampah Vapor Caves in Glenwood Canyon to the town of Dotsero. It is completely paved and suited for long bike rides, walks, and in-line skating. To rent a bike, contact Canyon Bikes in the Hotel Colorado, 970/945-8904. They also offer a shuttle service to the end of the canyon for folks who want to travel it just one way. Another great way to experience the beauty of Glenwood Canyon is from a raft. Whitewater Rafting, P.O. Box 2462, Glenwood, CO 81602, 970/945-8477, offers guided tours on the Colorado and Roaring Fork rivers, with short, half-day, and full-day trips. A half-day guided trip costs $35 for adults and $25 for kids.

Hanging Lake Trail, one of Colorado's most popular hiking trails, can be accessed at the Hanging Lake Rest Area in Glenwood Canyon. Even though traffic on this trail is always heavy, seeing the remarkably beautiful Hanging Lake still makes the trip worthwhile. The hike climbs a steep 900 feet in 1.2 miles. There are plenty of places to rest along the way, but remember to bring some water. The best way to access the trail is to start from Glenwood Springs, traveling east through the canyon, as there is no westbound access to the rest area. If you're traveling west on I-70, exit at Grizzly Lake, then get back on the interstate heading east to Hanging Lake. (1 hour–half day)

★★ **Maroon Bells-Snowmass Wilderness**—The distinctive Maroon Bells are perhaps the most photographed mountains in Colorado. The entrance to the wilderness area is usually crowded during summer, but most people don't venture beyond the actual wilderness boundary. One of the best ways to appreciate the area is to take a free summer tour with a naturalist from the Aspen Center for Environmental Studies. Tours last about 45 minutes. Afterward, you can take a longer hike into the wilderness. Cars are not allowed in the Maroon Bells area because of congestion and environmental concerns. Buses depart from the Ruby Park Transit Center on Durant and Mill Streets in Aspen.

Details: *For tour information, contact the Aspen Center for Environmental Studies, 970/925-5756. Tours offered mid-June–Labor Day 10–2 hourly. (3–4 hours)*

✰✰ **Skiing**—Before you dig deep into your pocket for the expensive lift ticket at Aspen, look into **Ski Sunlight** (800/445-7931 or 970/945-7491), only 10 miles from Glenwood Springs. Sunlight has both downhill and Nordic skiing with trails for all abilities, a rental shop, and ski school. To reach the resort take Grand Avenue south in Glenwood Springs to Four Mile Road.

If you are looking for premier skiing at one of Colorado's finest ski areas, you will love the four different ski areas at Aspen and Snowmass.

© Jack Olson

Maroon Bells-Snowmass Wilderness

Aspen Mountain and **Aspen Highlands** appeal to intermediate and advanced skiers, while **Snowmass** and **Buttermilk/Tiehack** are more popular with those just learning.

Details: All mountains use the same lift ticket. For more information, call the Aspen Skiing Company, 800/525-6200 or 970/925-1220. For information on back country ski trails, contact White River National Forest, 900 Grand Avenue, Glenwood Springs, 970/945-2521. (full day)

✷✷ **Yampah Spa and Vapor Caves**—These caves are actually natural underground steam baths, where hot mineral waters keep the floors at 125 degrees Fahrenheit. For the ultimate in pampering, get a massage or facial, sink into an herbal Jacuzzi bath, or luxuriate in a variety of body treatments. To really splurge, try the European Body Wrap.

Details: 709 E. Sixth St., Glenwood Springs; 970/945-0667. Daily 9–9. Vapor cave: $8.75, partial or full massages: $32–$74, European Body Wrap: $99. (1½ hours)

✷ **Aspen Art Museum**—Housed in an historic hydroelectric plant, this museum was founded by local artists and patrons in 1979. The museum provides changing exhibits, lectures, and classes.

Contemporary art is the focus, but other periods and cultures are also represented. There is a free reception every Thursday from 6 to 8 with refreshments and gallery tours.

Details: 590 N. Mill St., Aspen; 970/925-8050. Tue–Sat 10–6, Sun noon–6. $3 adults, $2 students and seniors.

✷ **Aspen Historical Society tours**—On Monday and Friday from mid-June to mid-September, the Aspen Historical Society offers a guided walking tour of downtown Aspen. Costumed tour guides lead visitors through Aspen's Victorian past, covering the town's mining history, its people, and architectural landmarks such as the Wheeler Opera House, Wheeler-Stallard House Museum, and Hotel Jerome. Tours last two hours, covering about a mile in distance.

Details: Aspen Historical Society; 970/925-3721. Tours mid-June–mid-Sept Mon and Fri 9:30 a.m. $10 per person. (2 hours)

✷ **Aspen Mountain Gondola**—The gondola will take you two and a half miles to the glorious summit of Aspen Mountain in just 18 minutes. The Aspen Center for Environmental Studies runs nature hikes at the summit from mid-June to Labor Day, every hour on the hour from 10 to 2.

Details: *Base of Aspen Moutain; 970/925-1220, ext. 3598. Daily June–Sept, weekends only late May and late Sept. $15 adults weekdays, $18 adults weekends; $12 for seniors 65-69, $6 for ages 7–12 and seniors over 70. $19 joint Gondola/Maroon Bells bus tour ticket. (2 hours)*

✯ **Glenwood Springs Center for the Arts**—This center, adjacent to the Hot Springs Pool, supports the Glenwood Springs art community with poetry readings, dance classes, and gallery exhibits.

Details: *601 E. Sixth St.; 970/945-2414. Tue–Fri 11–5, Sat and Sun noon–4. (1 hour)*

FITNESS AND RECREATION

With scenery this beautiful, it's easy to find a form of outdoor recreation here to suit you. The **Crystal River** and **Dinkle Lake** are well-known fishing spots. A wide variety of trails for hiking and mountain biking are scattered throughout the valley. Contact **White River National Forest**, 900 Grand Avenue, Glenwood Springs, 970/945-2521, for more information. The bicycle/pedestrian trail in **Glenwood Canyon** is a perfect way to exercise and see the canyon at the same time. A short hike in Glenwood Springs is the **Boy Scout Trail**, which begins at Eighth Street. A half-mile trail at **Linwood Cemetery** takes visitors to the grave of Doc Holliday, the legendary gambler and outlaw who died in Glenwood Springs of tuberculosis in 1887. The trail begins at 12th Street and Palmer Avenue.

FOOD

Most eateries in the Roaring Fork Valley offer a high standard in cuisine, service, and atmosphere. In Aspen, the choices are multiplied, so I have given you a few options in a variety of price ranges. For a great stuffed croissant, muffin, or pastry with a cappuccino, all under $5, try the **Paradise Bakery**, 320 South Galena Street, on the corner of Cooper Avenue, 970/925-7585. The bakery also has homemade ice cream. Open daily from 6:30 a.m. to midnight. **La Cocina**, 308 East Hopkins Avenue, 970/925-9714, has been serving healthy and tasty New Mexican food in Aspen for many years, a good sign in a town with revolving restaurants. Dinner ranges from $6 to $12, featuring

ROARING FORK VALLEY

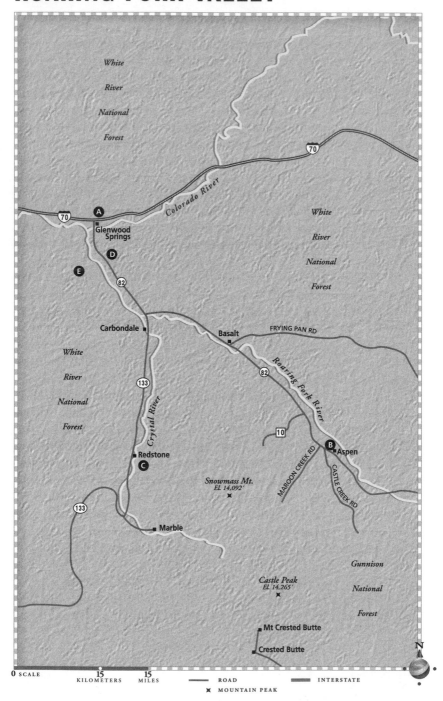

White
River
National
Forest

Colorado River

70

70

Ⓐ
Glenwood
Springs
Ⓓ
Ⓔ
82

White
River
National
Forest

Carbondale

Basalt

FRYING PAN RD

Roaring Fork River

82

133

Crystal River

White
River
National
Forest

10

Ⓑ Aspen

Redstone
Ⓒ

MAROON CREEK RD

CASTLE CREEK RD

133

Snowmass Mt.
El. 14,092'
✕

Marble

Gunnison

National

Forest

Castle Peak
El. 14,265'
✕

Mt Crested Butte

Crested Butte

N

0 SCALE   15   15
         KILOMETERS   MILES   ■■■ ROAD   ═══ INTERSTATE
                              ✕ MOUNTAIN PEAK

Food

- Ⓐ The Bayou
- Ⓑ Caché Caché
- Ⓑ Crystal Palace
- Ⓐ Daily Bread Cafe and Bakery
- Ⓑ La Cocina
- Ⓑ Paradise Bakery
- Ⓒ Redstone Inn
- Ⓓ Sopris Restaurant and Lounge

Lodging

- Ⓒ Redstone Castle
- Ⓐ Hotel Colorado

Lodging *(continued)*

- Ⓐ Hotel Denver
- Ⓑ Hotel Jerome
- Ⓑ Limelight
- Ⓑ Molly Gibson Lodge
- Ⓒ Redstone Inn

Camping

- Ⓔ Hideout Cabins and Campground

Note: Items with the same letter are located in the same town or area.

several varieties of enchiladas, seafood specials, taco plates, and salads. **Caché Caché,** 205 South Mill Street, 888/511-3835, specializes in Provençal cuisine, with entrées such as osso bucco, lamb ratatouille, Chilean sea bass, and well-prepared vegetarian and pasta dishes for $14 to $28.

For an evening of dinner and entertainment, treat yourself to the **Crystal Palace**, 300 East Hyman Avenue, 970/925-1455. The rate of $49.50 per person includes dinner, dessert, and a comedy act that spoofs politics, social events, and famous people. There is one seating during summer and two during winter. Reservations are recommended.

In Glenwood Springs, try a treasured institution, the **Daily Bread Cafe and Bakery**, 729 Grand Avenue, 970/945-6253. This restaurant is prized for its healthy menu, enormous breakfasts, and delicious bakery sweets. The daily quiche is usually great, as are several of the sandwiches on the low-fat menu. Sometimes the wait is long, but it's always worth it.

Local Glenwood Springs residents love the relaxed atmosphere at the **Bayou**, a Cajun restaurant featuring fresh seafood, po' boys, blackened everything, and other New Orleans specialities. The sun deck is a great place for a drink when the weather turns warm, and with specialties like Hurricanes and Woo Woos, a good time will be had by all.

South of Glenwood Springs five miles is **Sopris Restaurant and Lounge**, open daily for dinner, 970/945-7771. This is a great place to treat yourself to a carefully selected wine list and well-prepared entrees including veal, seafood, steak, and lamb, as well as vegetarian options. Call ahead for reservations. Prices range from $8.95 to $20.

The **Redstone Inn** has two excellent restaurants. The Grill is more casual and serves light entrees, soups, and sandwiches for under $10. Breakfast here is also good, with the standard two eggs-and-hash browns dish as well as fresh muffins, omelets, and other healthy fare. The Dining Room is classy, formal, and well known as one of the best restaurants in this area, serving dinner nightly and Sunday brunch. Specials might include Colorado prime rib, Samurai salmon, or elk meat wrapped in phyllo pastry. Dinner entrées average $15 to $25.

LODGING

Even though lodging rates in the Roaring Fork Valley prices fluctuate according to season (with additional highs and lows in each season), you will be able to find something to fit your budget. In Aspen, winter rates are at least 20 to 30 percent higher than in summer, while Glenwood Springs rates are higher in the summer. Expect rate hikes during festivals and holiday weekends, but otherwise look for deals mid-April to early June, late September, and mid-November to mid-December.

In Aspen, there are many options to suit several tastes, from extravagant to budget. Let's start with extravagant. The landmark **Hotel Jerome**, 330 E. Main St., 800/331-7213, is often the first place people think of when they think of Aspen. Built in 1889, this restored hotel is a monument to Aspen's former mining glory days. Restored in 1985, the four-star hotel features luxurious accommodations such as king size beds, restored antiques, and fluffy robes in the closets. Best of all, dogs are welcome at this luxurious hotel. Summer rates start at $295, winter at $465.

The **Molly Gibson Lodge**, 101 West Main Street, 888/271-2304, has a variety of lodging options, including standard hotel rooms, rooms with wood-burning fireplaces and private Jacuzzis, studios, and one- and two-bedroom apartments. The lodge has a healthy European breakfast in the morning with fruit, juice, pastries, and cereal. Summer high-season rates range from $125 to $260 and winter from $165 to

$369. The **Limelite** offers standard hotel rooms in a family-style lodge with two pools, Jacuzzis, 24-hour coffee, tea, and hot chocolate service, and Continental breakfast. During summer, rates range from $74 to $120, winter is $79 to $225.

The main streets of Glenwood Springs are lined with any number of standard chain motels and hotels. Two unique options stand apart. One is the classic **Hotel Colorado**, 526 Pine Street, 800/544-3998 or 970/945-6511, built in 1893 and an imposing presence on the main corner of Glenwood Springs. The hotel is in the process of renovation, with upgrades planned for all the rooms. Rates begin at $80 for a double with two beds. The hotel is located on Grand Avenue and Sixth Street, directly across from Hot Springs Pool. The hotel also has a restaurant, lounge, and exterior courtyard with a stately European atmosphere. Another option is the **Hotel Denver**, 402 Seventh Street, 800/826-8820 or 970/945-6565, located across the river from the hot springs with a hard-to-miss red neon sign. The standard rooms in the hotel are adequate, ranging from $55 to $145. On the first floor is the Brewpub, operated by the Glenwood Canyon Brewing Company, a good place to relax with burgers and beers.

Redstone boasts two exceptional places to stay. The **Redstone Inn**, 82 Redstone Boulevard, 970/963-2526, has a range of prices ($40–$195) depending on the day of the week, season, and type of room. At the **Redstone Castle**, 58 Redstone Boulevard, 970/963-3463, rooms start at $95 for a shared bath and go up to $225 for elegant private suites. See Sightseeing Highlights for descriptions of both the inn and the castle.

CAMPING

Contact the **White River National Forest**, 900 Grand Avenue, Glenwood Springs, 970/945-2521, for information on campgrounds and primitive camping within national forest boundaries. **Hideout Cabins and Campground**, outside Glenwood Springs at 1293 Road 117, Four Mile Road, 970/945-5621 or 800/987-0779, has RV sites and rustic cabins and is open year-round.

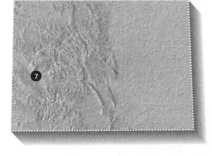

7

GRAND JUNCTION AND THE GRAND VALLEY

With attractions such as dinosaurs, mountain biking, wine tasting, and scenic driving, Grand Junction really does have something for everyone. Named for the junction of the Gunnison and Colorado Rivers, for many years Grand Junction has been the largest town on Colorado's Western Slope. Experiencing phenomenal growth for a city of its size, Grand Junction has a revitalized downtown Main Street district with boutiques and restaurants, several golf courses, interesting museums, and many recreational opportunities. Several great day trips, to Colorado National Monument, the Grand Mesa, and the remote Unaweep Canyon, can be done from here, making Grand Junction a perfect addition to itineraries in eastern Utah and western Colorado.

The Grand Valley, including the towns of Grand Junction, Palisade, and Fruita, is blessed with warm days, cool nights, low precipitation, and plenty of irrigable land. These favorable conditions are perfect for raising fruits and vegetables. Stands with top-quality fresh produce line the secondary highway near Palisade, and the vineyard industry has recently become popular. Mountain biking has found a new capital in Fruita, with challenging rides that include miles of trails in slickrock terrain. The Fruita Fat Tire Festival, held the last weekend in April, is helping to spread the word about the terrific mountain biking in the entire Grand Valley. ◼

COLORADO RIVER VALLEY

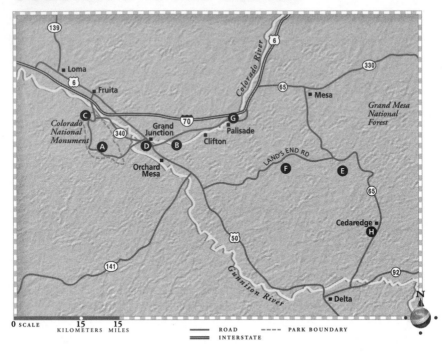

Sights

Ⓐ Colorado National Monument

Ⓑ Cross Orchards Living History Farm

Ⓒ Dinosaur Discovery Museum

Ⓓ Dinosaur Valley Museum

Ⓔ Grand Mesa

Ⓕ Lands End Observatory

Ⓓ Museum of Western Colorado

Ⓖ Palisade Vineyards

Ⓗ Pioneer Town

Ⓓ Western Colorado Botanical Garden

Camping

Ⓗ Aspen Trails Campground

Ⓒ Monument RV Park

Ⓔ Grand Mesa

Ⓐ Saddlehorn Campground

Note: Items with the same letter are located in the same town or area.

A PERFECT DAY IN GRAND JUNCTION AND THE GRAND VALLEY

Take the scenic Rim Rock Drive through Colorado National Monument and hike one of the park's many trails. Then visit Enstrom's Candies downtown, and Palisade, where you can taste Colorado wines and purchase fresh produce from stands along the highway. Before dinner, take a relaxing walk along the Colorado Riverfront Trail.

SIGHTSEEING HIGHLIGHTS

★★★ **Colorado National Monument**—These 32 square miles feature some of Colorado's most exquisite and unspoiled wilderness. Here you will find a maze of colorful sandstone canyons, arches, and monoliths sculpted by the forces of wind and water.

Part of the geologic province known as the Colorado Plateau, this region receives only 10 to 12 inches of rainfall per year. Drought-resistant plants living here include piñon pine and juniper shrubs, several species of cacti, and the Mormon tea plant, which resembles a cluster of green sticks that can grow up to three feet tall.

Both motorists and cyclists enjoy the 23-mile **Rim Rock Drive** ($4 per car) through the monument. You can stop and savor the dramatic views at its numerous scenic overlooks. Forty-two miles of trails exist for hiking or horseback riding through the canyons and on the mesa tops. Some of the best hiking and views are possible from **Serpent's Trail** (the first road in the monument, now converted into a hiking trail), and **Monument Canyon Trail**, which travels to the base of the park's most impressive monolith, Independence Monument.
Details: Colorado Hwy. 340; 970/858-3617. Monument open year-round; visitor center open June–Labor Day 8–8, otherwise 8–4:30. (3 hours–2 days)

★★★ **Dinosaur Discovery Museum**—This learning center at Fruita has interactive robotic displays and video presentations about dinosaurs, as well as an earthquake simulator. Dinamation's Discovery Expeditions offers trips with professional paleontologists to hunt dinosaur fossils. For information on digs, call 800/DIG-DINO.
Details: I-70 exit 19 (Fruita exit); 970/858-7282. Memorial Day–Labor Day daily 8:30–7, rest of year Mon–Sat 9–5, Sun 10–5. $5 adults, $3.50 seniors over 54 and children 3–12. (1–2 hours)

✰✰✰ **Grand Mesa**—The flat-topped Grand Mesa stands a commanding 11,000 feet above the arid valleys of the Colorado, Uncompahgre, and Gunnison Rivers in western Colorado. The mesa has one of the highest annual precipitation levels in Colorado, and its voluminous snowmelt, retained in some 300 lakes and reservoirs on its surface, supports the water consumption and irrigation needs of surrounding communities, farms, and ranches. During the dog days of summer, the mesa provides relief from soaring temperatures in the valleys below and some of the best fishing in the state. In fall, the thick stands of quaking aspens and narrow-leaf cottonwoods proudly display their golden hues, making this an ideal time to visit. Winter is a snow lover's paradise, with miles of trails for cross-country skiing, snowshoeing, and snowmobiling, as well as downhill skiing at **Powderhorn Resort**, 970/268-5700, which boasts low ticket prices and nonexistent lift lines. Springtime on the mesa, while beautiful, is also the time of snowmelt and mud, so hiking and camping usually have to wait until late May or early June. Also, beware the mesa's ferocious mosquitos from spring to July.

By far the most popular activity on Grand Mesa is scenic driving. Starting and ending in Grand Junction, a 150-mile tour climbs more than 6,000 feet, from the arid desert valley to a cool subalpine forest. Begin by driving south of Grand Junction on Highway 50 to the town of Delta. Just east of Delta, take Highway 65 up the southern flank of the mesa to the town of Cedaredge. Behind the Cedaredge Welcome Center is **Pioneer Town** (970/856-7554), a labor of love created by the Surface Creek Historical Society. Marked by the Surface Creek Livestock Company Bar I Silos, Pioneer Town is a collection of historic structures carefully outfitted with period artifacts and staffed by knowledgeable local volunteers. It is open Memorial Day through the third weekend in September.

Continuing north from Cedaredge, the road ascends though stands of Engelmann spruce, firs, and quaking aspens and passes numerous lakes, campgrounds, and picnic areas. One of the best hikes in Colorado is the **Crag Crest National Recreation Trail**, which travels along a high mesa top through open meadows with acres of bobbing wildflowers. To reach the trailhead, pass the Grand Mesa Visitor Center on Highway 65 and look for Crag Crest signs.

Spectacular views are possible all over Grand Mesa, and they just get better at **Lands End Observatory**. Accessible to cars only during the warmer months, the observatory was built by the Works Progress Administration in the 1930s. To the west you can see Grand Junction and all the way to the La Sal Mountains in Utah. The northern view reveals the dramatic Book Cliffs running from Colorado to Utah. On the way to the observatory, the road passes the **Raber Cow Camp,** a collection of cabins used by the extended Raber family when tending to their cattle on summer pasture. Elsewhere on the mesa, you'll see the San Juan Mountains to the south, at the far end of the Uncompahgre River Valley, and the majestic Elks to the east.

It is possible to descend the western side of Grand Mesa from the steep Lands End Road, but I only recommend this to those who are used to driving on steep roads with tight switchbacks. Otherwise, retrace your route back to Highway 65 and continue north to the other side of the mesa. Along the way you will pass Powderhorn Resort, the town of Mesa, and the scenic Plateau Canyon before joining I-70 back to Grand Junction.

Details: Cedaredge Welcome Center, Hwy. 65 and Second St., 970/856-6961; U.S. Forest Service Grand Mesa Visitor Center, Lake Ward, 970/856-4153. Visitor Centers open summer only. (3 hours–full day)

✯✯ **Cross Orchards Living History Farm**—Early settlers diverted the Colorado and Gunnison Rivers in the Grand Valley and planted orchards, quickly establishing a thriving fruit industry. The Cross Orchards Living History Farm re-creates the daily activities of a prosperous turn-of-the-century apple orchard. The old ranch house, packing shed, bunkhouse, carpentry shop, and barn contain authentic equipment and artifacts from the early days. An apple grove is cultivated here, and the fall harvest yields freshly picked apples, cider, and other products.

Details: 3073 F (Patterson) Rd. Grand Junction; 970/434-9814. Memorial Day–Labor Day Tue–Sun 9–4, off-season Tue–Sat 10–4. $4 adults, $3.50 seniors, $2 children. (1 hour)

✯✯ **Dinosaur Valley Museum**—The pastel and buff-colored shales, silts, and mudstones of northwestern Colorado and northeastern Utah are practically littered with dinosaur fossils, remnants of the inland seas and giant forests that blanketed this region millions of years ago. Many fossils discovered here have contributed significantly to modern paleontological research, and several recent discoveries have brought new attention to the region. Dinosaur Valley Museum demonstrates how dinosaurs still touch our lives today. Dinosaur robots, such as stegosaurs, apatosaurs, and triceratops, are the main attraction, with dino skeletons, tracks, and other fossils also featured.

Details: *362 Main St., Grand Junction; 970/241-9210. Memorial Day–Labor Day daily 9–5:30, otherwise Tue–Sat 10–4, with last admission at 3. $5 adults, $3 children. (1 hour)*

★★ **Museum of Western Colorado**—This municipal museum operates several sites, including the Cross Orchards Living History Farm and Dinosaur Valley. Exhibits at the main downtown facility focus on how mining and agriculture shaped the region's settlement. Also featured is the story of Alfred Packer, Colorado's infamous cannibal (see Chapter 10).

Details: *248 S. Fourth St., Grand Junction; 970/242-0971. Memorial Day–Labor Day Mon–Sat 10–4:30, otherwise Tue–Sat 10–4:30. $2 adults, $1 ages 2–12 (1 hour)*

★★ **Palisade Vineyards**—Vineyards flourished in this fertile river valley prior to Prohibition, when they were replaced with fruit orchards. The cultivation of wine grapes has recently made a comeback in the Grand Valley, and vineyards produce a variety of wines, including distinctive fruit wines from plums and peaches. Several wineries operate tasting rooms to sell their products, and many people take leisurely bicycle tours of the vineyards surrounding Palisade.

Details: *For a brochure about Colorado's vineyards, including tasting rooms' addresses, and hours, call 970/523-1232. (2 hours)*

★ **Western Colorado Botanical Garden**—Started in 1997, this innovative botanical garden is located at the site of the city's first greenhouse. Filled with lush and colorful tropical plants and a small succulent cactus garden, the facility also hosts 50 to 100 species of domestic butterflies. Outside are miniature exhibits of the geology and plant zones of the Grand Valley, representing Grand Mesa, Mount Garfield (the prominent peak on the east end of the Book Cliffs), and Colorado National Monument.

Details: *655 Struthers St., Grand Junction; 970/245-8565. Thu–Sat 10–5, Sun noon–5. $3 adults, $2 seniors and students, $1.50 ages 5–12. (1 hour)*

FITNESS AND RECREATION

The low elevations and warm weather of this region make it a year-round destination for bicyclists. The **Colorado Plateau Mountain Bike**

Trail Association (COPMOBA) is a great source for trail recommendations. Contact them at P.O. Box 4603, Grand Junction, CO 81502; 970/241-9561. Or stop in at **Tompkin's Cycle Sports**, 301 Main, 970/241-0141, for ideas on trails. **Kokopelli's Trail**, an intermediate to advanced mountain bike trail roughly 128 miles long, stretches between Loma (east of Grand Junction) and Moab, Utah. Most of the trail is on unpatrolled Bureau of Land Management land.

Beautiful canyon hiking can be found near Grand Junction on the **Pollack Bench Trail**. For more information, contact the Bureau of Land Management office, 2815 H Road, Grand Junction, CO 81506; 970/244-3000.

The **Colorado Riverfront Trail** is a series of interconnecting bicycle and pedestrian trails resulting from a project to clean up urban blight along the Colorado River in Grand Junction. Good access points are found across from Mesa Mall on Redlands Parkway and at the Western Colorado Botanical Garden on Seventh Street.

FOOD

While Grand Junction tends to be a meat-and-potatoes town, it also has several unique eateries. It is the home of the world-famous **Enstrom's Candy**, 200 South Seventh Street, 970/242-1655, where an addictive almond toffee and other sinful confections are prepared. Be sure to stop here for gifts to bring back home.

The best restaurant in town is the **Crystal Café and Bake Shop**, 314 Main, 970/242-8843, open for breakfast and lunch. Fresh and well-prepared menu items include many vegetarian options, pasta dishes, sandwiches, and omelets, from $5 to $7. Another excellent place for breakfast and lunch is **Jitters**, 504 Main Street, 970/245-5194. This tastefully decorated art deco diner serves waffles, eggs Benedict, muffins, homemade soups, creative sandwiches, and salads, and has a complete espresso bar.

Pomidori's Italian Deli, 319 Main Street, 970/242-5272, serves authentic pasta dishes, calzones, and sandwiches on freshly baked bread Monday through Friday 11 a.m. to 2 p.m., Saturday 11 to 3. Takeout items and sandwiches are available until 6 p.m.

At the **Blue Moon Café**, 120 North Seventh Street, 970/242-4506, a bar and restaurant, lunch runs $4 to $6.50, dinner from $10 to $16. The bar has 12 beers on tap. Several tempting appetizers include fried calamari, flaming Greek cheese, and spicy buffalo wings. The **Rock**

GRAND JUNCTION

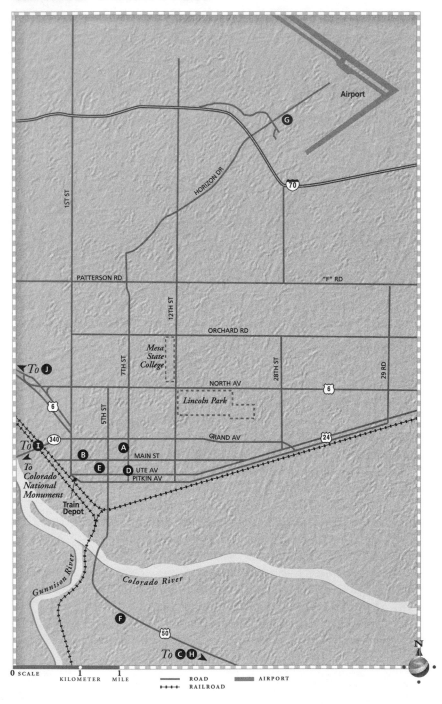

Airport

G

HORIZON DR

1ST ST

70

PATTERSON RD

"F" RD

12TH ST

ORCHARD RD

Mesa State College

7TH ST

28TH ST

29 RD

To J

NORTH AV

6

5TH ST

Lincoln Park

6

340

GRAND AV

24

To I

A

MAIN ST

B

To
Colorado
National
Monument

E

D UTE AV

PITKIN AV

Train
Depot

Gunnison River

Colorado River

F

50

To C H

N

0 SCALE   1   1
KILOMETER   MILE   ROAD   AIRPORT
                  RAILROAD

Food

Ⓐ Blue Moon Café

Ⓑ Crystal Café

Ⓒ The Divot/Berardi's

Ⓓ Enstrom's

Ⓔ Jitters

Ⓕ Mali Thai

Ⓖ Pomidori's Italian Deli

Ⓗ Rock Slide Brewery and Restaurant

Ⓖ W. W. Peppers

Lodging

Ⓗ Cedar's Edge Llama Ranch

Ⓔ Historic Hotel Melrose and International Hostel

Ⓘ Los Altos Bed and Breakfast

Ⓙ Stonehaven Bed and Breakfast

Note: Items with the same letter are located in the same area.

Slide Brewery and Restaurant, 401 Main Street, 970/245-2111, serves its own flavorful brews and brewpub fare of pizzas, burgers, plus prime rib or pasta entrees from $6 to $13. Its happy hour deals (half-price appetizers and $1.50 pints) attract a crowd at 4 p.m.

Mali Thai Restaurant, 757 U.S. Highway 50 South on Orchard Mesa, 970/255-8444, provides a nice switch from standard restaurant fare. Sumptuous dishes are served in this unassuming "hole-in-the-wall," such as *pad Thai omeetee* (ground peanuts, shrimp, rice noodles, and bean sprouts) or *pa nang* curry with coconut milk, Thai basil, and pork, chicken or beef.

For a terrific dinner, head to W. W. Peppers, 753 Horizon Court, across from the Grand Vista Hotel, 970/245-9251. Creative Southwestern entrees ($10–$15), such as crab meat enchiladas or stuffed sopaipillas smothered in green chile and cream sauces, are tasty and different. Be prepared to wait, especially for dinner on weekends.

In Cedaredge, the Divot, at the Deer Creek Golf Course south of town, 970/856-7782, offers a traditional lunch from 11 to 4:30. At 5, the restaurant turns into Berardi's and begins serving mouth-watering Italian food, such as Caesar salad, minestrone, eggplant Parmesan, or tortellini covered with a red sauce, fresh basil, and tomatoes. Prices for dinner range from $8.75 to $14.

LODGING

There is no shortage of chain hotels along Horizon Drive in Grand Junction. Be aware that at the end of June, the area hosts **Country Jam**, a music festival that features top-notch country acts. This popular event also jams all of the hotel rooms in Grand Junction, so plan accordingly. For a list of performers, call 800/530-3020.

As an alternative to the corporate hotels on Horizon Drive, Grand Valley also has some unique lodgings. The **Historic Hotel Melrose and International Hostel**, 337 Colorado Avenue, 970/242-9636, is popular with international guests visiting the national monuments and parks in this region. Accommodations include rooms with private baths. It can get a little noisy because of younger travelers, but if you're on a tight budget or looking for out-of-the-ordinary lodging, this restored historic hotel has period antiques and is very clean.

In a neighborhood closer to Colorado National Monument is a new bed-and-breakfast, **Los Altos**, 375 Hillview Drive, 970/256-0964 or 888/774-0982. With a commanding view of the entire valley, this is a special place. The innkeepers treat guests to afternoon tea, a full breakfast, and plenty of comforts in each of their rooms. Rates range from $80 to $150.

The **Stonehaven Bed and Breakfast**, 798 North Mesa Street, 970/858-0898, is a restored Victorian mansion in Fruita with five rooms; prices range from $65 to $135 in the summer and are discounted heavily during fall and winter. The master bedroom features a Jacuzzi and queen-size bed; the Cherry Suite, perfect for families, has two connecting rooms with a private bath. A new hot tub and homemade gourmet breakfast round out the amenities at this historic property.

If you've never been to a working llama ranch, here's your chance to enjoy one on the slopes of Grand Mesa. **Cedar's Edge Llama Ranch**, 2169 Highway 65, 970/856-6836, is about six miles north of Cedaredge, with comfortable and peaceful rooms ranging from $60 to $85. The owners of this bed-and-breakfast gladly show off their llamas and ranch, where 10 new babies are born each year.

CAMPING

The first-come, first-served **Saddlehorn Campground** in Colorado National Monument, 970/858-3617, gets crowded in the summertime. Amenities include picnic tables, charcoal grills, restrooms, and water.

The fee is $10 for this year-round campground. For backcountry camping, obtain a permit at the visitor center.

Numerous campgrounds on the **Grand Mesa** have water and fishing access or primitive camping. For more information, contact Grand Mesa Forest Headquarters, 2250 Highway 50, Delta, CO 81416; 970/874-6600. Nine of the campgrounds charge a fee.

For RV camping in the Grand Valley, try the **Monument RV Park**, I-70 exit 19, across from Dinosaur Discovery Museum; 970/858-3155. Three miles north of Cedaredge is the **Aspen Trails Campground**, 1997 Highway 65, 970/856-6321, with 30 RV sites open in the warmer months.

Scenic Route:
Unaweep Tabeguache Byway

This remote part of western Colorado has remained a secret for years. Ranching has been the mainstay since the 1880s, but the ups and downs of mining a powdery yellow mineral called carnotite (that contains radium, vanadium, and uranium) have greatly affected this area's economy. This route is longer than Highway 50 between Grand Junction and Telluride but much more beautiful and interesting. Start with a full tank of gas because you won't find more until Naturita or Norwood, a distance of 100–120 miles.

Travel south of Grand Junction on Highway 50 until you come to **Whitewater** and take Highway 141 south. After traveling through East Creek Canyon, you will enter the dramatic **Unaweep Canyon**, sculpted by the ancestral Gunnison River. No improved road penetrated this canyon until the 1940s, although stagecoaches and wagons began negotiating crude trails to transport ore as early as the 1890s. At the far end of Unaweep Canyon, you will come to **Gateway,** a commercial and social center since 1881.

After Gateway, the road enters the **Dolores River Canyon**, a beautiful maze of red-rock sandstone canyons. Farther down the Dolores

UNAWEEP TABEGUACHE BYWAY

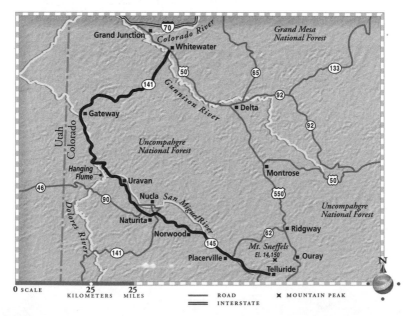

River Canyon is the **Hanging Flume**, the remains of a wooden trough clinging to the eastern wall of the canyon. A gold mining company built this structure to transport water to its placer mine on Mesa Creek in the 1890s. Building it cost five times more than estimated, and to make matters worse, the gold proved too fine to recover. The mine owner abandoned the mine after he went bankrupt. Be sure to pull off at the Hanging Flume for a terrific view of the structure and the Delores River Canyon.

During World War II, large conglomerates such as Union Carbide began to tap this region's significant stores of uranium for nuclear bombs developed in the supersecretive Manhattan Project. The Atomic Energy Commission encouraged uranium production in the 1950s, and a swarm of prospectors descended on the area. Million-dollar deals changed hands daily, and a few lucky desert rats made their fortunes in the rim rock country. At the end of the Cold War, changes in international policy caused a decrease in production. Past Hanging Flume, look up on the canyon walls for tannish heaps of waste rock and dilapidated structures that mark the locations of small uranium mines.

Farther down on Highway 141 you will come to **Uravan**, a company town and uranium mill operated by Umetco Minerals Corp., which once housed more than 600 people. Today almost nothing remains of this once-bustling community. Umetco began a massive remediation project to clean up the area in 1987. They left two historic buildings standing, the boarding house and community hall, as reminders of Uravan's role in the region's mining industry. Both buildings are visible from Highway 141.

Past Uravan the highway follows the scenic **San Miguel River Canyon** all the way to Telluride. Portions of the river are owned by the Nature Conservancy and the Bureau of Land Management. Before you reach the historic oasis of Telluride, you will come to the towns of **Naturita, Norwood**, and **Placerville**. Be sure to spend some time in these friendly ranching communities before heading down deeper into the majestic San Juans. ◼

8

THE NORTHERN SAN JUAN MOUNTAINS

The San Juan Mountains, a massive range stretching through southwestern Colorado, feature some of the state's most impressive and rugged scenery. They are also richly laden with a variety of minerals that sparked a major mineral rush in the 1870s. For centuries, these venerable mountains belonged to the Ute tribe. As early as the 1760s, Spaniards knew that gold lay in these mountains, but it wasn't until the 1870s that Coloradans began clamoring for the right to enter Ute lands and exploit the precious minerals. The Utes lost their mountain homeland to Colorado Territory in 1874. Immediately thereafter, the area became a hotbed of feverish bonanzas and get-rich-quick schemes.

While many gold seekers never intended to put down roots, others immediately set to work putting their infant settlements on the map. Wealthy businessmen in the more populous mining camps soon built permanent homes and commercial buildings, in only the finest Victorian tradition. Today these buildings and homes are preserved in the National Historic Districts of Telluride, Ouray, and Silverton.

Many people think of this area as the "Wild West," the place of great Western legends and shoot-'em-ups. In fact, the San Juans have been the set for many famous Hollywood Westerns, such as *True Grit* and *How the West Was Won*. Both the mythical and historical West still lurk here, in frontier mining towns and forgotten ghost towns, but today these mountain communities are also modern in every sense of the word. ◤

NORTHERN SAN JUAN MOUNTAINS

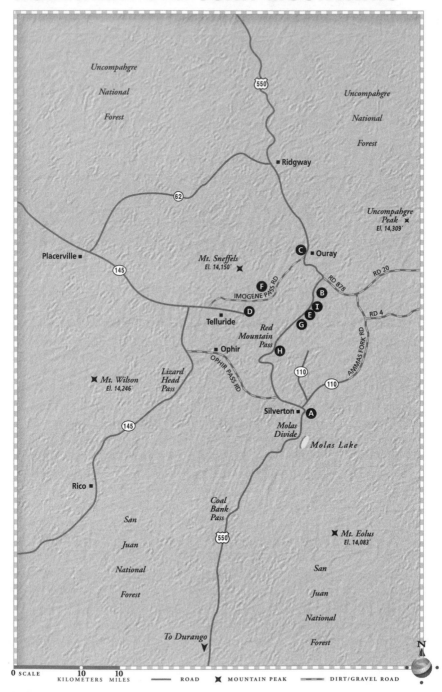

Uncompahgre National Forest

Uncompahgre National Forest

550

■ Ridgway

62

Uncompahgre Peak ✖
El. 14,309'

Placerville ■

145

Mt. Sneffels
El. 14,150' ✖

C ■ Ouray

RD 878

RD 20

F
IMOGENE PASS RD

RD 4

B

I
E

D
■ Telluride

G

Red Mountain Pass

AMMAS FORK RD

H

■ Ophir

OPHIR PASS RD

Lizard Head Pass

110

✖ Mt. Wilson
El. 14,246'

110

145

Silverton ■ **A**

Molas Divide

Molas Lake

Rico ■

Coal Bank Pass

San Juan National Forest

550

✖ Mt. Eolus
El. 14,083'

San Juan National Forest

To Durango
⌄

N

0 SCALE 10 10
KILOMETERS MILES   ━━━ ROAD   ✖ MOUNTAIN PEAK   ━━━ DIRT/GRAVEL ROAD

Sights

Ⓐ A Theater Group

Ⓑ Bear Creek National Recreation Trail

Ⓒ Box Canyon Falls

Ⓓ Bridal Veil Falls

Ⓔ Chattanooga

Ⓓ Galloping Goose

Ⓕ Imogene Pass

Ⓖ Ironton

Ⓐ Mayflower Mill

Ⓗ Million Dollar Highway

Ⓐ One Hundred Gold Mine Tour

Ⓒ Ouray Hot Springs Pool

Ⓘ Riverside Slide

Note: Items with the same letter are located in the same town or area.

A PERFECT DAY IN THE NORTHERN SAN JUANS

Experience the beauty of the San Juans on a jeep tour, long hike, or mountain bike ride. Although there is a lot to see from the main highways, much more awaits visitors who take to one of the many backcountry roads. After a long day of sightseeing and using your muscles, head to the Ouray Hot Springs Pool (or the hot tub of your choice) for a soak. Afterwards, walk the streets of the National Districts in either Ouray, Telluride, or Silverton, then take in a great bar or restaurant.

HISTORIC SAN JUAN FREIGHTING AND TOLL ROADS

Most early explorers thought that crossing this precipitous range was simply impossible, winter or summer, but the lure of riches in the mountains proved these early travelers wrong. Starting in the 1870s, men hacked and blasted freighting roads, and later railroads, from the sheer mountains and canyons. The promise of profit led to the necessity for transportation, even during the worst storms or the most desperate of circumstances. Lacing the country today are such early roads as the Million Dollar Highway between Ouray and Silverton, and dozens of backcountry roads accessible to four-wheel-drive vehicles, adventurous mountain bikers, and hardy hikers.

The options for exploring these historical routes are many. Some of the roads follow scenic state highways, such as the San Juan Skyway, an All-American Road, National Byway, and Colorado Scenic Byway, called by some the most beautiful drive in America. The 236-mile route tours southwestern Colorado along major roads beginning on Highway 145 from Cortez to Telluride and Placerville, then east on Highway 62 to Ridgway. From Ridgway, the road turns south on Highway 550 to Ouray, Silverton, and Durango, where it heads west on Highway 160 to return to Cortez. In addition to this well-traveled route, dozens of backcountry roads take intrepid travelers deep into the San Juans' dramatic geology and mining history.

San Juan roads aren't ordinary. They follow steep switchbacks, hairpin turns, and narrow curves along the sides of mountains and canyons, all requiring careful attention. Numerous roadside pull-offs usually exist so that you can enjoy the marvelous views. You will want to take it slow, not only to savor the views, but because speed limits are posted low. Please be considerate of other drivers behind you and pull into an overlook to let faster vehicles pass. Also remember that frequent snowstorms and summer rainstorms can turn a dry road into a slick ribbon in a matter of minutes. Call the local State Patrol for road condition updates.

Some unimproved roads, if in good condition, are navigable by a regular passenger car. But when a road gets rough, it can be negotiated only by a four-wheel-drive vehicle, preferably with a manual transmission and high clearance. If you aren't used to driving on rough mountain roads, or don't have an adequate vehicle, you can always take a guided jeep tour or rent a vehicle in a nearby town. Ouray, Silverton, and Telluride all have jeep touring companies that specialize in eventful trips into the mountains.

SIGHTSEEING HIGHLIGHTS

✩✩✩ **Million Dollar Highway**— Many stories have been told about the naming of the Million Dollar Highway. Some say that when builders constructed the road after World War I, costs soared to more than $1 million, a huge sum in those days. Others say the road is named for the value of its views.

Otto Mears, an early road builder and promoter, built the first toll road connecting Ouray and Silverton in the early 1880s. Mears blasted almost half of his toll road from solid rock on precipices hundreds of feet above the canyon floor. Today Highway 550 follows Mears's original road, although it is generally higher.

Just two miles south of Ouray, you will come to the **Bear Creek National Recreation Trail**, a moderate hiking trail that takes you past several former mine sites. The trail continues on to American Flats and Engineer Mountain, returning on Horsethief Trail back to Ouray. For trip distances and the difficulties of this trail, consult the Forest Service, 2740 Highway 145, Telluride; 970/728-4211.

The **Riverside Slide** is three miles from the Bear Creek trailhead at milepost 87. A snowshed here protects the highway from frequent avalanches. This stretch is subject to more slides than any other highway in the country and has claimed many lives throughout the years. A monument at the base of Red Mountain Pass is dedicated to those who have died in avalanches here.

You will continue your drive past several former mines and towns, such as **Ironton** (milepost 82) and **Chattanooga** (milepost 78, on the other side of Red Mountain Pass). Ironton is the first of several settlements stacked like dominos in this cramped gulch. During its heyday, this mining district produced over $1 billion worth of minerals.

Chattanooga served as a staging point for freighters and mule skinners traveling between Silverton and the outlying mining camps. This bare patch of ground once held more than 75 buildings.

After Chattanooga, you will drive more than 10 miles before beginning your descent into **Silverton**. You will first see the town hundreds of feet below you, at about milepost 68. Even though it is only 23 miles between Ouray and Silverton, this drive will take at least an hour, depending on how many times you stop.

Details: Hwy. 550 between Ouray and Silverton. (1 hour minimum)

★★ **Imogene Pass**—Not for beginning mountain drivers, this extremely rough road requires a four-wheel-drive vehicle. Imogene Pass, the high road between Telluride and Ouray, is usually passable only from late July to mid-September. The road summits at an amazing 13,114 feet, making it the second highest automobile pass in North America for four-wheel-drive vehicles (the highest is near Leadville).

To take this drive, start on North Oak Street in Telluride. Turn right on the Imogene Pass Road, marked as Forest Road 869. You will climb out of Telluride and soon see breathtaking views of the town and valley. Continuing on Road 869, you will encounter the remains of the massive **Tomboy Mine**. This area once contained a mill, numerous houses, a boarding house, a store, and even a bowling alley for the men working the mine. The Rothschilds bought this property in 1897 for a mere $2 million. A famous book, *Tomboy Bride*, by Harriet Backus, is partly about a housewife who lived in this small settlement during harsh winter conditions.

Imogene Pass is just over two miles from the Tomboy. Fort Peabody once sat on the summit of this pass and played a significant role during turn-of-the-century labor disputes in the mines. The fort kept union supporters from sneaking into Telluride to cause more labor unrest. After descending the other side of the pass, you'll come upon the famous **Camp Bird Mine**, continuously operated since the late 1890s. From here you will take Forest Road 853 and descend into the town of Ouray at Box Canyon Falls

Details: *Imogene Pass Rd. (Forest Rd. 869) between Telluride and Ouray. Open late July–mid-Sept. (full day)*

★★ **Ouray**—Rimmed on all sides by the Uncompahgre (Un-come-pah-gray) Mountains, Ouray was first known as Uncompahgre City, established in 1876 to supply the many mines of the San Juan Mountains above town. Founders later changed the name to honor Chief Ouray, a great Ute leader and friend of the whites, who died in 1880. Ouray quickly became a respectable community, as seen in the quality and splendor of buildings constructed from 1880 to 1900. The whole town is a National Historic District, and residents have done a great job preserving many of the older structures. The downtown district is a pleasant street of restored buildings, with shops and restaurants.

The Ouray Recreation Association opened the **Ouray Hot Springs Pool** (Main Street; 970/325-4638) in 1926. Today the facilities include a fitness center and a pool separated into three sections. The outdoor hot springs are especially inviting during winter, when snowflakes gently fall into the soothing waters..

Box Canyon Falls, a narrow gorge created by a pounding waterfall, can be seen from several vantage points in Ouray. To view the falls, you can take three different pathways: One travels beneath the falls, another climbs up to a steel bridge spanning a gap above the falls, and a third fairly steep and rocky trail takes you to the top of the falls, for a stunning view of the surrounding mountains. The falls are open year-round and are located south of Ouray off Highway 550 near the Box Canyon Motel. Call 970/325-4464 for information.

Details: *Ouray Visitor Information Center, 1000 Main St., 970/325-4746 or 800/228-1876. (1–2 days)*

★★ **Silverton**—The story of Silverton, one of the earliest centers of mining activity in the San Juans, is one of a hardy community continually overcoming adversity. Known as "the Treasury Chest of the San Juans," Silverton has at times faced severe depressions, as when silver prices plunged after the great 1893 Silver Panic. Still, the town has managed to survive, relying on its fascinating history and beautiful setting to attract visitors.

The **One Hundred Gold Mine** (970/387-5444 or 800/872-3009), built and operated by hardrock miners, gives you the rare chance to explore a mine burrowed a third of a mile into Galena Mountain. Miners demonstrate drilling with working equipment and point out gold and other mineral veins, as well as several mineshafts and tunnels, within the mountain. Wear warm clothes and shoes as temperatures inside the mountain are chilly. Tours are offered mid-May to October 15, weather permitting. To get to the mine from Silverton, head east on Highway 110 to Howardsville, today a ghost town. Turn right on County Road 4, then left on County Road 4-A.

On the way to the Old Hundred Mine, you'll pass **Mayflower Mill** (970/387-0294), which shut down in August 1991 when Silverton's last mine, the Sunnyside, closed. The mill, a National

© Jack Olson

14,150-foot Mt. Sneffels

Historic Landmark, has been preserved with its machinery intact and offers a rare opportunity to tour one of the last remaining precious-metal mills in the West. A property of the San Juan County Historical Society, it offers tours daily from mid-May to the end of September.

Each summer, Silverton's **A Theatre Group,** a company of volunteer actors, hosts a George Bernard Shaw festival, in addition to several other American plays. During December the company offers a special holiday production. Productions are staged at the Miners Union Theatre, 1069 Greene St.; 970/387-5337 or 800/752-4494.

Details: Silverton Chamber of Commerce, Hwy. 550 at Greene St., 970/387-5654 or 800/752-4494. (full day)

★★ **Telluride**—Telluride is situated in a heavenly valley at the base of the San Sophia Mountains. This robust little ski town is crawling with celebrities and socialites, who have raised Telluride's status to that of an international resort, with lodging and restaurant prices to match. Telluride's modern, pleasant streets are a far cry from the dusty, crowded streets of yore, often clogged with long wagon trains, lines of gruff oxen, and braying burros laden with supplies. This noisy scene was enacted each morning, as Telluride once was a major shipping and freighting center between the mountain mining camps and the train depot at Ridgway. Incorporated in 1878, the town enjoyed relative prosperity until the Great Depression crippled most mining in the area.

But no one would have predicted a tough future for Telluride when the Rio Grande & Southern Railroad arrived in the fall of 1891. Telluride was finally connected directly to points east and west. Freight prices became more affordable overnight, and the heavy machinery hauled by the railroad helped miners dig more efficiently for the ore. But eventually the railroad also fell on hard times. As automobile roads were developed throughout the area, the Rio Grande & Southern struggled to compete. A last-ditch effort to save the railroad came with the **Galloping Goose**, a bizarre hybrid of freight car and passenger car, actually a Pierce-Arrow automobile fitted to the rails and refashioned to carry six to seven tons of freight along with passengers. Today you can see a preserved Galloping Goose in Telluride's Town Park next to the county courthouse.

Telluride Ski Area, 800/525-3455, is one of the best in the state for advanced skiers, with almost half of its runs rated intermediate, a snowboard park, and several high-speed lifts. Cross-country skiers enjoy several regional options. The **Telluride Nordic Center** in Town Park, 970/728-6265, offers lessons and many ideas for routes, in addition to a groomed three-kilometer trail that connects to a ten-kilometer loop along the San Miguel Valley.

Bridal Veil Falls, visible east of town in the high mountain cliffs, boasts the longest waterfall in Colorado, at 365 feet. The private home that sits at the top of the falls was once a hydroelectric power plant for the Smuggler-Union Mine, Telluride's most famous. One of the first discovered in the district, it proved to be one of the greatest. A hike from downtown up to the falls affords a spectacular view. Just head east up Colorado Avenue toward the falls and walk up the rough road to the top, about two miles one way. The hike continues on past the falls through beautiful fields of wildflowers.

Telluride is known for its festivals. The **Telluride Bluegrass Festival** started in 1973 and has grown more popular every year. Held the third weekend in June in Telluride Town Park, it is one of the best ways to experience innovative bluegrass music. During the rest of the summer, festivals devoted to theater, art, music, dance, and culture abound.

Details: *Telluride Visitor Services, 700 W. Colorado, 1/88-TELLURIDE or 800/525-3455. (1–3 days)*

FITNESS AND RECREATION

In Telluride, the **San Miguel River Trail** winds through town for walking, biking, and Rollerblading. Backcountry opportunities for hiking, mountain biking, and backpacking abound in the northern San Juans. The **San Juan Hut System** features a trail stretching 205 miles from Telluride to Moab, a paradise for hikers and mountain bikers in the summer and skiers in the winter. For more information, contact P.O. Box 1663, Telluride, CO 81435; 970/728-6935. **Lizard Head Wilderness Area**, southwest of Telluride (accessible from Lizard Head Pass on Highway 145), is great for cross-country skiing in the winter, hiking and backpacking in the summer. The **Weminuche Wilderness** (accessible from Highway 550 near the Purgatory Ski Resort or from the Durango & Silverton Narrow Gauge Railroad and Colorado Trail) and the **Mount Sneffels Wilderness** (north of Telluride) also provide ample opportunity for day hikes or extended backpacking trips. Mountain biking is not allowed in wilderness areas, but the variety of trails that wind

NORTHERN SAN JUAN MOUNTAINS

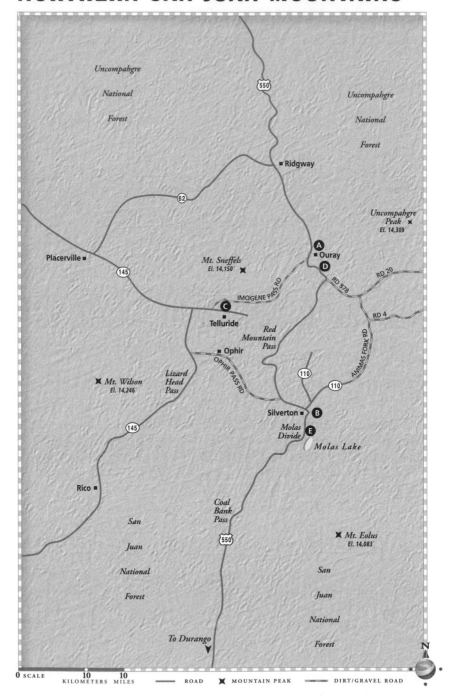

Uncompahgre National Forest

Uncompahgre National Forest

550

■ Ridgway

Uncompahgre Peak
El. 14,309'

62

Placerville ■

145

Mt. Sneffels
El. 14,150'

Ⓐ
■ Ouray
Ⓓ

RD 20

RD 978

IMOGENE PASS RD

Ⓒ
■ Telluride

RD 4

Red Mountain Pass

ANIMAS FORK RD

■ Ophir

OPHIR PASS RD

✖ Mt. Wilson
El. 14,246'

Lizard Head Pass

110

110

145

Silverton ■   Ⓑ

Molas Divide   Ⓔ

Molas Lake

Rico ■

Coal Bank Pass

San Juan National Forest

550

✖ Mt. Eolus
El. 14,083'

San Juan National Forest

To Durango ▾

N

0 SCALE   10   10
KILOMETERS MILES   —— ROAD   ✖ MOUNTAIN PEAK   ⋯⋯ DIRT/GRAVEL ROAD

Food

Ⓐ Bon Ton Restaurant

Ⓑ Brown Bear Inn

Ⓒ Campagna

Ⓐ Piñon Restaurant & Tavern

Ⓑ Pickle Barrel

Ⓒ Sofio's

Ⓒ Wildflour Cooking Company

Lodging

Ⓒ Bear Creek Bed and Breakfast

Ⓐ China Clipper

Lodging *(continued)*

Ⓒ New Sheridan Hotel

Ⓐ St. Elmo Hotel

Ⓑ Teller House Hotel

Ⓑ Wyman Hotel and Inn

Camping

Ⓓ Amphitheatre Campground

Ⓔ Molas Lake Park

Ⓑ Town Park Campground

Note: Items with the same letter are located in the same town or area.

through former mining districts will keep any rider busy. Outdoor equipment stores in Silverton, Ouray, and Telluride can suggest trails and provide detailed topographic maps.

Fishing in high alpine lakes is excellent, accessible from the many four-wheel-drive routes described in this chapter. Don't forget a fishing license in addition to rod and reel.

FOOD

You could probably blow your whole trip budget on one meal in Telluride. Below is a bare sampling of restaurants here, encompassing a range of prices and meals. **Wildflour Cooking Co.**, near the chair gondola at 250 West San Juan, 970/728-8887, prepares homemade soups, fresh baked goods, sandwiches, and light meals from 7:30 a.m. to 8 p.m. **Sofio's**, 110 East Colorado Avenue, 970/728-4882, serves excellent Mexican food and margaritas. Prices range from $10 to $15, for dinner from 5:30 to 10 p.m. For a special night out, visit **Campagna**, 435 West Pacific, 970/728-6190, a premier restaurant serving wonderful Tuscan Italian dishes. Dinner starts at 6 daily; closed from mid-April to June.

In Ouray, the **Bon Ton Restaurant**, in the St. Elmo Hotel, 426 Main, 970/325-4951, specializes in rich and flavorful Italian cuisine and continental specials, with menu items such as beef Wellington, veal marsala, tortellini carbonara, and chicken Bolognese. Dinners range from $11 to $20. **Piñon Restaurant and Tavern**, 737 Main Street, 970/325-4334, serves premium meals downstairs, including beef, salmon, tuna, pasta, and chicken. The upstairs tavern offers bar food such as barbecued ribs, burgers, and fries.

For a great sandwich or dinner in Silverton, go to the **Pickle Barrel**, 1304 Greene Street, 970/387-5713, open May through October. Hot and cold sandwiches of every stripe run no more than $6, and the evening menu varies to include fresh, seasonal ingredients. In Silverton, the **Brown Bear Inn**, 1129 Greene Street, 970/387-5630, offers full egg breakfasts as well as lunch and dinner, with fresh home-made soups, sandwiches, burgers, steaks, and pasta.

LODGING

The northern San Juans host a variety of lodging options. At any time of the year, rooms in Telluride will be more expensive than those in Ouray or Silverton. But Telluride's rates drop in the summer, except during major festival weekends, and rooms in Ouray are pricier in summer. Most of the region's accommodations offer special deals, sometimes including half-price or free lift tickets. Several lovingly restored historic hotels on the National Register of Historic Places are choice lodging options listed below.

In Telluride, check with Telluride Resort Accommodations, 800/538-7754, which lists rooms starting as low as $60 during the summer. The **New Sheridan Hotel**, 231 West Colorado Avenue, 970/728-4351, offers moderate rates in a beautifully restored hotel. When it was built in 1895, it rivaled the Brown Palace, Denver's finest establishment. Today guests are pampered with many in-room amenities and a full breakfast. Rates for a double with a private bath range from $80 to $145, depending on the season and weekend, including a full breakfast in the restaurant downstairs. The **Bear Creek Bed and Breakfast**, 221 East Colorado Avenue, 970/728-6681 or 800/338-7064, offers comfortable European lodging in 10 rooms, each with a private bathroom. Other amenities are a hot tub on the rooftop, a sauna, and steam room. Rates range from $70 to $227.

In Silverton, the **Teller House Hotel**, 1304 Greene Street,

970/387-5423 or 800/342-4338, is a restored Victorian hotel built in the late 1890s and decorated with period furnishings. Priced very reasonably year-round, this hotel's summer rates are $48 for a room with a shared bath, $68 with a private bath. The **Wyman Hotel and Inn**, 1371 Greene Street, 970/387-5372 or 800/609-7845, has 18 rooms in a 1902 building with large arched windows that reveal wonderful views of the surrounding mountains. The guest rooms ($85 to $150) contain a private bath, VCRs, telephones, and queen or king beds. Some have two-person whirlpool tubs, for the ultimate in pampering.

The **St. Elmo**, 426 Main Street, Ouray, 970/325-4951, is tastefully decorated with luxurious antiques and furnishings from its beginnings in 1898. Rooms with a private bath start at $84 in summer, $65 winter. The **China Clipper**, 525 Second Street, 970/325-0565 or 800/315-0565, is a new bed-and-breakfast built in the style of a gracious Southern home, filled with antiques and art. Some of the rooms have private Jacuzzis, with another Jacuzzi in the outside garden. Winter rates range from $65 to $160; summer, from $85 to $160.

CAMPING

The **Amphitheatre Campground** in the Uncompahgre National Forest sits just outside of Ouray. The 30 units here, $10 per night, must be reserved in advance. Telluride's **Town Park Campground** is often full, but give it a try if you're traveling on a weekday or during off-season. **Molas Lake Park** is five miles south of Silverton on Highway 550, with 60 campsites, trout fishing, a store, showers, fishing licenses, and horseback rides.

Scenic Route: Alpine Loop

This route covers 78 miles of former mining roads between Ouray, Silverton, and Lake City, and crosses Engineer Pass and Cinnamon Pass, both of which summit well over 12,000 feet. You can negotiate the route's lower sections in a passenger car but definitely need a four-wheel drive with high clearance to travel the high mountain passes. You can also mountain bike or walk part of the route to experience the high-altitude country. Several campgrounds, picnic areas, and ghost towns can be explored along the way. Alpine lakes and streams offer great fishing, so don't forget your pole and license if so inclined. If you don't have a four-wheel-drive vehicle, rent one or take a four-wheel-drive jeep tour and let someone else do the driving.

Freighters hacked out these rough roads to haul ore and supplies to and from mines in the San Juan Mountains. These former mines and forgotten settlements tell many stories. The roads were used for hauling, regardless of winter snow depths or treacherous conditions.

ALPINE LOOP

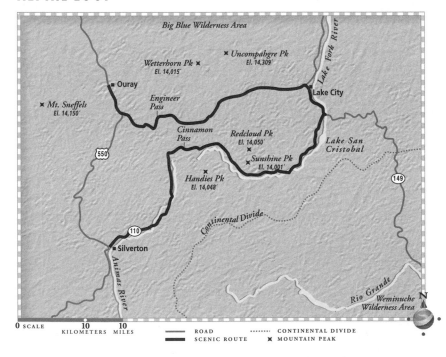

Men, women, and children lived in these high-mountain mining settlements year-round, carrying out their day-to-day activities at dizzying altitudes.

This trip will also take you past incomparable vistas of numerous 14,000-foot peaks, such as the view from Engineer Pass, where Mount Sneffels (14,150 feet) lies to the west and the craggy Mount Uncompahgre (14,309 feet), to the northeast. Backcountry access from the Alpine Loop is tremendous. The **Big Blue Wildernesses** and two other wilderness study areas are readily accessible and laced with hiking trails and backcountry camping spots. On the other side of the mountains, Alpine Loop travelers are welcomed by the village of Lake City, on the Silver Thread Scenic and Historic Byway (see the Upper Rio Grande River chapter). ◼

9

DURANGO AND CORTEZ

Ancient and modern cultures have shaped the unique heritage of the Durango-Cortez region. Between A.D. 1000 and 1300, the population in the region now known as the Mancos River Valley was double what it is today. The valley's early residents, called the Ancestral Pueblo peoples, abruptly disappeared from their homes in the year 1300. While several plausible explanations for their disappearance exist, no one knows for sure why they left. Remains left behind, such as cliff houses, baskets, and pottery, give us scant clues as to their way of life.

The Utes, who once claimed all of Colorado's mountains as their homeland, have probably lived in this area since at least 1300 but are not related to the early Pueblos. The Utes began losing portions of their lands in 1849, with the first of several controversial government treaties. Eventually they lost almost all of it. Today they inhabit two small areas in the southwest corner of Colorado, the Ute Mountain Ute and the Southern Ute Reservations. Of the many native peoples who once lived in present-day Colorado, the Utes are the only tribe to retain land holdings in the state.

Southwest of Cortez lies the legendary Sleeping Ute Mountain. One Ute legend says the landform is a sleeping god. His headdress flows to the north, his arms are folded on his chest, and his legs and knees stretch toward the south. When clouds collect over Sleeping Ute, the god is said to be changing his blankets for the new season. ◼

DURANGO AND CORTEZ

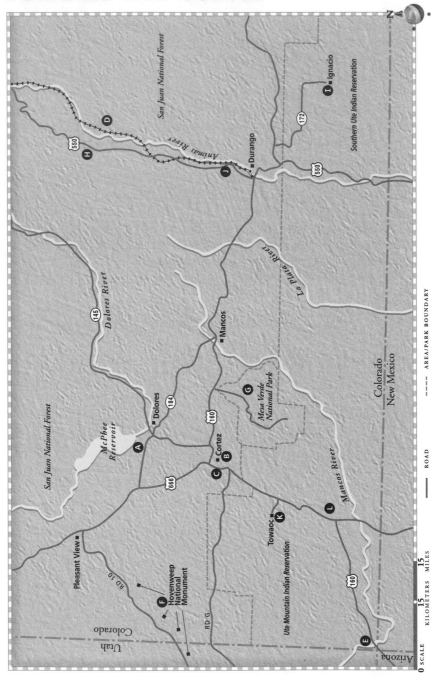

Sights

Ⓐ Anasazi Heritage Center

Ⓑ Cortez Center

Ⓒ Crow Canyon Archaeological Center

Ⓓ Durango-Silverton Narrow Gauge Railroad

Ⓔ Four Corners Monument

Ⓕ Hovenweep National Monument

Ⓖ Mesa Verde National Park

Ⓗ Purgatory Ski Resort

Ⓘ Southern Ute Reservation

Ⓙ Trimble Hot Springs

Ⓚ Ute Mountain Ute Reservation

Ⓛ Ute Mountain Ute Tribal Park

A PERFECT DAY IN DURANGO AND CORTEZ

Spend the day exploring the cliff dwellings at either Mesa Verde National Park, Ute Mountain Tribal Park, or Hovenweep National Monument. Mesa Verde is the most accessible but also the most crowded. The Ute Mountain Tribal Park and Hovenweep will be appreciated by adventurous travelers wanting to see more remote dwellings without a crowd. In the evening, attend one of the excellent programs at the Cortez Center to learn more about Native cultures of the Southwest.

THE ANCESTRAL PUEBLOS

The people we call the Ancestral Pueblos (formerly known as the Anasazi, which means "ancient enemies" in Navajo) lived in the Mancos and Dolores River Valleys from approximately A.D. 1 to 1300. Over the centuries, they slowly changed their mesa-top village sites to homes built under rock overhangs. Although the Ancestral Pueblos are usually associated with cliff dwellings, the time they spent in them accounts for only about 10 percent of the entire time they lived in the region.

After they moved to the cliff houses, the Pueblos became more sedentary, developing advanced horticultural and food storage technologies to support a larger population. They planted terraced crops, built canals and dams, grew corns, beans, and squash, and hunted wild turkey and other game. Traveling on established trade routes, they traded these goods with larger pueblos to the south. Their descendants are the Pueblo and Hopi Indians living in what is now New Mexico and Arizona.

The Pueblo cliff dwellings were multistoried and made of stone. The complexes included towers, large plazas surrounded by "apartments" with windows, and underground structures known as kivas, used for sacred ceremonies. The rock overhangs protected the homes from the wind, and the dwellings' openings all faced south to soak up the sun's rays. The people collected water from seeps and springs in the canyon walls.

Why did these people leave their cliff homes and the Mancos River Canyon? Perhaps they had to move because of changing environmental conditions, such as a long drought, or cooler weather which shortened the growing season. They might have been overpowered by the stronger pueblos to the south, or had to abandon their homes because they became too crowded and had used all available natural resources. Whatever the reason, they never returned, but they left behind intriguing archaeological clues for us to examine. Throughout this region are many locations where you can examine the remnants of this once-thriving civilization.

SIGHTSEEING HIGHLIGHTS

★★★ **Cortez Center**—If you're interested in learning more about the diverse peoples of this area, attend one or several of the cultural events held at the Cortez Center. The summer Native American Culture Series includes concerts, dance, art, lectures, sandpainting demonstrations, and storytellers who evoke the history and culture of Native peoples. The Octubre Fiesta in the fall focuses on all regional ethnic groups and may include cowboy poetry or a classical music concert. *Details: 25 N. Market; 970/565-1151. Summer programs run nightly Mon–Sat 7:30.*

★★★ **Durango & Silverton Narrow Gauge Railroad**—This historic railroad line, today Durango's most popular attraction, fittingly tributes the town's reason for existence. In 1882 the Denver & Rio Grande Railroad built a narrow-gauge line through the Animas River Valley to reach the San Juans' rich mines to the north. Platted by the railroad, the town of Durango blossomed overnight, becoming a commercial supply center for the mining camps. Like many Western towns, Durango aggressively promoted itself, struggling to become the biggest and best city in southwestern Colorado. The railroad quickly saw the value of advertising the San Juans' stunning scenic views on the Durango & Silverton line and ran special excursion trains for visitors.

Today the Durango & Silverton Narrow Gauge Railroad continues to carry thousands of passengers through the Animas River Valley on the original Denver & Rio Grande route. The restored steam engines are fired by coal, and the railroad uses only authentic turn-of-the-century railroad equipment. The train runs 45 miles (90 miles round-trip) between Durango and Silverton daily, from May to October, with several different departure times. Special winter excursions run from late November through April. These trips offer an incomparable way to experience the beauty and high elevations of the San Juans.

The round trip between Durango and Silverton takes a full day. You can also spend the night in Silverton and return the next day (see the Northern San Juans chapter for Silverton specifics). Many people like to disembark midway and go hiking or backpacking in the Weminuche Wilderness of the San Juans, then return on the railroad the same day or several days later.

Details: 479 Main St., Durango; 970/247-2733. Round-trip fares $49.10 adults, $24.65 children under 12. Advance reservations are advisable. (full day)

★★★ **Mesa Verde National Park**—First photographed in 1874 by pioneer photographer William Henry Jackson, the cliff dwellings preserved in Mesa Verde have long been a source of wonder and amazement for both archaeologists and lay people. You will understand why when you explore them for yourself. Take at least one of the tours guided by park rangers who do a great job of explaining the dwellings and the culture of their inhabitants.

Start your visit at the **Far View Visitor Center** (open spring, summer, and fall, 8–5), 15 miles inside the park. From here you can get tickets to see Cliff Palace and Balcony House. These are two of the more popular dwellings, and free tickets are distributed on a first-come, first-served basis.

Hiking is allowed only in designated areas, and hikers must register at Park Headquarters at **Chapin Mesa**, located five miles from Far View Visitor Center. Two trails run from Spruce Tree House: **Petroglyph Point Trail** (2.8 miles round trip), which ends at a wall of petroglyphs, and **Spruce Canyon Trail** (2.1 miles round trip), which takes you along the lush canyon bottom. Chapin Mesa is home to a fascinating archaeological museum.

While the park is open year-round, some of the cliff dwellings are closed to public access during winter. Still, many visitors prefer this season because they usually have the park to themselves. The beauty of snow gracing the mesa tops and dwellings is an incomparable sight. The Cliff Palace and Balcony House Loop are open during the winter from 9 a.m. to sunset for cross-country skiing.

Details: Enter the park nine miles east of Cortez on Highway 160, or 36 miles west of Durango; 970/529-4461. $10 for a week's pass. (1–2 days)

★★★ **Ute Mountain Ute Tribal Park**—This secluded park is twice the size of Mesa Verde National Park—and much less crowded. Ute Mountain Ute guides give interpretive tours of the park's cliff dwellings and petroglyph sites, a terrific opportunity to explore seldom-seen ruins and to learn about the Ute Mountain Ute tribe. You can take a half-day or full-day tour, bringing your own lunch and vehicle with a full tank of gas. Two-day guided backpacking trips are also available.

Details: Tribal Park Visitor Center, 20 miles south of Cortez at the junction of Hwys 666 and 160. Call ahead to reserve: 970/565-9653 or 800/847-5485. $17 half-day tour; $30 full-day tour. (half–full day)

★★ **Anasazi Heritage Center**—This Bureau of Land Management museum is devoted to understanding and preserving Ancestral Pueblo artifacts. Archaeologists worked for eight years to unearth and record

© Jack Olson

Mesa Verde National Park

artifacts from several significant archaeological sites before the Dolores River was dammed to create McPhee Reservoir.

The center offers several nice hands-on experiences, such as learning to weave on a loom, grind corn with a metate, and handle actual artifacts. You can also take short hikes to the remains of two twelfth-century settlements.

Details: 27501 Hwy. 184; 970/882-4811. Mar–Oct daily 9–5, Nov–Feb daily 9–4. Free. (2 hours)

★★ **Crow Canyon Archaeological Center**—If you're itching to work at a dig with a professional archaeologist, here is your chance. This hands-on experience can be hot, dirty, and exhilarating. In addition to digging, the center offers several other programs, including lectures and Native American artists' workshops on weaving or ceramics. Either day trips or weeklong seminars are possible.

Details: 23390 County Rd. K, Cortez; 970/565-8975 or 800/422-8975. Advance reservations required. (full day minimum)

★★ **Purgatory Ski Resort**—Just 25 miles north of Durango, Purgatory receives a ton of snow and is typically less crowded than most ski areas. Purgatory's terrain is varied, with beginning trails at the base village and more expert runs farthest back on the mountain. A shuttle bus departs from Durango during winter.

Details: 1 Skier Place. Snow report: 800/525-0892. Lodging: 800/525-0892. (full day)

★★ **Southern Ute Reservation**—The Southern Utes operate the **Sky Ute Lodge** in Ignacio, 970/563-3000, a casino with limited-stakes gaming. The **Southern Ute Cultural Center**, 970/563-9583, displays Ute and other Native artifacts, offering guided tours on advance request and a gift shop. Rodeos and other happenings are held at the Event Center, so check local events when you get to town.

Details: Hwy. 172, Ignacio. Call Southern Ute Cultural Center for more information, 970/563-9583. (1–2 hours)

★★ **Ute Mountain Ute Reservation**—In addition to the **Ute Mountain Ute Tribal Park**, this reservation operates the **Ute Mountain Casino** just outside of Towaoc. The Ute Mountain **Pottery Plant** (*970/565-8548*), which is open to the public, blends ancient and Ute styles with original hand-painted designs.

Details: *East side of Highway 666, just before the turnoff to Towaoc, roughly 12 miles south of Cortez. (1 hour)*

✻ **Hovenweep National Monument**—This remote monument straddles the Colorado/Utah border and is open year-round. Although a ranger is always on duty, other services are limited, and you can usually appreciate these impressive stone villages from around A.D. 1200 in solitude. The Square Tower Ruins are easy to get to, but the other five villages in the monument can be reached only from hiking trails varying in length. Before leaving for Hovenweep, inquire about road conditions, as dirt roads leading to the monument can be impassable when wet.

Details: *From Cortez, head north on Highway 666 about 20 miles to Pleasant View. Take County Road CC a little more than six miles to County Road 10, then head south approximately 20 miles to the monument access road. $6/vehicle. Call Mesa Verde National Park, 970/529-4461, for more information. (1–2 days)*

✻ **Trimble Hot Springs**—First discovered and promoted by the arthritic W. F. Trimble in 1874, this natural hot springs pool has been a local favorite for many years. The facility has several different pools and provides spa treatments such as massage therapy and acupuncture.

Details: *Trimble Ln. at 6475 County Rd. 203. Six miles north of Durango on Highway 550. 970/247-0111. Daily 8 a.m.–11 p.m. $7 adults, $5 children under 13. (half day)*

Four Corners Monument—This is the only place in the country where four states (Colorado, Utah, Arizona, and New Mexico) meet. It's worth a look to say you've been there.

Details: *Ute Mountain Ute Reservation, 38 miles southwest of Cortez off Highway 160. (10 minutes)*

FITNESS AND RECREATION

Numerous outfitters in this region provide a variety of adventure trips, such as rafting or kayaking on the **Dolores** and **Animas Rivers**, horseback rides in the **San Juan National Forest**, and jeep tours along bumpy mountain roads. Contact the Durango Chamber of Commerce, 800/525-8855, for more information. Durango has a thriving bicycle culture, and several maintained mountain bike trails are accessible right from town. Contact **Mountain Bike Specialists**, 949 Main Avenue, 970/247-4066, for information about tours, rentals, and area trails.

. Some of the best hiking in Colorado is found just outside of the Durango area. Because so many options exist, contact the Forest Service district office in Durango, 701 Camino Del Rio, 970/385-1286, for more information. Right in town, a short hike that begins on the east end of 10th Street takes you to the mesa top at Fort Lewis College, where you'll enjoy a great view of the La Plata Mountains and town.

Trophy-size rainbow trout are found in the **Dolores River below McPhee Dam**, just outside of Dolores. **McPhee Reservoir** is considered one of the best fishing spots in the whole San Juan Basin. **Vallecito Lake**, northeast of Durango, is another popular fishing hole. For advice on where to go or to schedule a guided trip, contact **Duranglers Flies and Supplies**, 801 Main Avenue, 970/385-4081.

FOOD

In Durango, **Carver's Bakery, Café and Brewery**, 1022 Main Avenue, 970/259-2545, is a moderately priced restaurant that specializes in healthier food. The menu includes wonderful breakfasts as well as vegetarian burgers, sandwiches, pizzas, and stews in bread bowls. Prices are in the $5 to $10 range. This hearty fare can be washed down with a range of house beers. For a wonderful fresh Mediterranean meal, with spanakopita, lamb, pasta, and tempting vegetarian options, visit the **Cyprus Café**, 725 East Second Avenue, 970/385-6884. It offers an outdoor patio and full bar; prices range $8 to $16. **Seasons Rotisserie & Grill**, 764 Main Avenue, 970/382-9790, serves upscale continental cuisine with mouth-watering appetizers and entrees from a wood-fired grill, such as rib-eye steak, lamb chops, and pork medallions. The tossed Caesar salad and homemade roasted garlic–mashed potatoes are first-rate.

The best breakfast place in the Cortez area is the **M & M Truck Stop and Family Restaurant**, one mile south of town on Highway 160, 970/565-6511, where a huge breakfast is served 24 hours a day. A friendly waitstaff pours an endless stream of coffee. You can also order from lunch and dinner menus. Also in Cortez, the **Main Street Brew Pub**, 21 East Main, 970/564-9112, serves several handcrafted beers in addition to a reasonably priced and inventive menu of specialty pizzas, salads, pastas, and excellent dinner entrees, such as chicken Florentine,

DURANGO AND CORTEZ

San Juan National Forest

550

Antonius River

Durango

A

550

172

Ignacio

Southern Ute Indian Reservation

La Plata River

Mancos

Dolores River

145

H

Dolores

184

E

McPhee Reservoir

San Juan National Forest

D

160

Mesa Verde National Park

F

B

Cortez

666

G

Mancos River

Colorado

New Mexico

Pleasant View

RD 10

Hovenweep National Monument

Towaoc

C

RD G

Ute Mountain Indian Reservation

160

Utah   Colorado

Arizona

N

0 SCALE   15 KILOMETERS   15 MILES

ROAD   AREA/PARK BOUNDARY

Food

Ⓐ Carver's Bakery, Café and Brewery

Ⓐ Cyprus Café

Ⓑ M & M Truck Stop and Family Restaurant

Ⓑ Main Street Brew Pub

Ⓑ Nero's Italian Restaurant

Ⓐ Seasons Rotisserie & Grill

Lodging

Ⓑ Maple Street Bed and Breakfast

Ⓒ Kelly Place

Ⓐ River House Bed and Breakfast

Lodging (continued)

Ⓐ Rochester Hotel/Leland House

Ⓑ Sand Canyon Inn

Ⓐ Strater Hotel

Camping

Ⓐ A & A Mesa Verde RV Resort Park

Ⓐ Cottonwood Camper Park

Ⓔ McPhee Reservoir

Ⓕ Morefield Campground

Ⓖ Ute Mountain Ute Tribal Park

Ⓗ West Fork Campgrounds

Note: Items with the same letter are located in the same town or area.

aged steaks, and Rocky Mountain trout, priced from $6.25 to $13. Pub appetizers are also delicious, including baked Brie, escargot, and marinated beef ribs, for $4 to $5. Open Monday through Saturday at 11:30 a.m., Sunday at 4:30 p.m.

Nero's Italian Restaurant, 303 West Main, 970/565-7366, has been a Cortez tradition for years. House specialties include wonderful pestos, grilled chicken in lime sauce, and steaks, ranging from $7 to 16.

LODGING

If you are planning a trip to this area during the summer, be sure to reserve lodgings beforehand. Accommodations in Durango and Cortez can be full during the summer, especially on the weekends, and rates increase as well. You'll be able to find all of the usual hotel chains in Durango and Cortez, in addition to a few out-of-the-ordinary options listed on the following page.

When the **Strater Hotel** opened its doors in 1888, Durango celebrated the addition of a high-class hotel to its railroad depot area, the center of the newly founded town. Since its opening, the Strater has operated continuously as a hotel. Its elegant hotel rooms are decorated in late-19th-century Victorian style, with an abundance of black walnut furniture and special touches. Standard room rates in summer are $159. Details: 699 Main; 970/247-4431 or 800/247-4431.

The **Leland House** and **Rochester Hotel**, 721 East Second Avenue, 800/664-1920 or 970/385-1920, are two carefully restored historic properties in downtown Durango that have revitalized a formerly dilapidated neighborhood. The Leland House, originally a 1927 apartment house, has been renovated into rooms with kitchen facilities and private baths. Rooms are named after historic figures associated with the hotel. The lobby features historical photographs and framed biographies. The Rochester Hotel, across the street, is a trip into Old West Americana, with theme rooms based on Hollywood Westerns filmed in and around Durango. If it sounds different, it is—and very comfortable and hospitable. Full breakfasts are included in summer rates that ranging from $95 to $145 at the Leland House and $125 to $185 at the Rochester.

The **River House Bed and Breakfast**, 495 Animas View Drive (north of Durango, just off Highway 550), 970/247-4775 or 800/254-4775, has seven rooms, all with private baths. Rates start at $65 during the summer. A hearty and healthy full breakfast is served.

In downtown Cortez, the **Sand Canyon Inn**, 301 West Main Street, 970/565-8562 or 800/257-3699, provides an excellent deal in a clean, well-kept motor court. Rates start at $42 in the summer, $25 in the winter. Also centrally located in Cortez is **Maple Street Bed and Breakfast**, 102 South Maple, 800/665-3906, an easy walk to the Cortez Center and downtown restaurants. This home has been renovated extensively, caters to guests with children, and has an outdoor Jacuzzi. Rates, starting at $59 for the loft and $79 for the queens, include a big breakfast.

Kelly Place, 14663 Road G (near Cortez), 800/745-4885, is a 100-acre ranch once owned by a horticulturalist, who planted mini orchards of apples and peaches as well as a variety of trees and plants. The 1960s adobe lodge has seven comfortable rooms, plus three cabins. You can visit several of the property's Ancestral Puebloan ruins on a self-guided tour. Kelly Place also offers seminars on weaving, pottery, and archaeology. Rates include breakfast and range from $69 to $110.

CAMPING

The 500 sites at **Morefield Campground** in Mesa Verde National Park, 970/529-4465, are open from spring to fall. Fees are $19 for full hookups and $10 for tent sites. Camping is available for $10 per vehicle at the **Ute Mountain Ute Tribal Park**, 970/565-3751, with a permit from the tribe. Several campsites at **McPhee Reservoir**, west of Dolores, 970/882-2257, have RV hookups. The **West Fork Campgrounds** in the San Juan National Forest are accessed from Highway 145. From Dolores, drive 13 miles northeast, then go north on Forest Service Road 535. Some campgrounds have RV pull-throughs and dump stations. Contact the Forest office at 701 Camino del Rio, Durango; 970/247-4874.

Cottonwood Camper Park, on Highway 160 a third of a mile west of Highway 550, 970/247-1977, is centrally located near downtown Durango and is open year-round. The **A & A Mesa Verde RV Resort Park**, 970/565-3517 or 800/972-6620, sits across from the entrance to Mesa Verde. The park offers a playground, basketball and volleyball courts, and a heated pool, plus horses for trail riding.

NIGHTLIFE

The students at Fort Lewis College in Durango frequent several watering holes, some with live music. The most popular, **Farquahrts**, 725 Main Avenue, 970/247-5442, serves pizza and nachos. **El Rancho**, 975 Main Avenue, 970/259-8111, is a great dive with pool tables and a cast of local characters. The **Diamond Belle Saloon**, in the Strater Hotel, 699 Main Avenue, 970/247-4431, is an Old West throwback, complete with honky-tonk piano, plush red velvet walls, and dance-hall girls—the kind of place where singing along and joining in the festivities is encouraged.

10

UPPER RIO GRANDE VALLEY

Lake City, Creede, and South Fork are three remote communities on the "other" side of the San Juan Mountains, in the pristine Rio Grande River Valley. The towns are connected by Highway 149, the Silver Thread Scenic Byway, which pays homage to this region's mining history. Silver was mined in Creede until the late 1980s, when operations halted due to plummeting values. Lake City boomed about the same time as its mountain neighbors Silverton and Ouray. These early San Juan mining communities were connected by rough wagon and toll roads, now traveled by the Alpine Loop Scenic and Historic Byway (see description in Northern San Juans).

Nowadays most residents have turned to tourism because the Rio Grande Valley is the perfect getaway for travelers avoiding resort town crowds and prices. Summer brings glorious sunny days, wildflowers, and plentiful fishing in Gold Medal waters, while in winter the region succumbs to a restful slumber, stirred only by an occasional cross-country skier or snowshoer. Most tourist services close during winter, but a few remain open for those who really want to get off the beaten path. Visitors often return here year after year, to stay in the same lodge or guest ranch until it begins to feel like a second home. Once you discover the beauty of this area for yourself, you may also want to return. It's just that kind of place. ◼

UPPER RIO GRANDE VALLEY

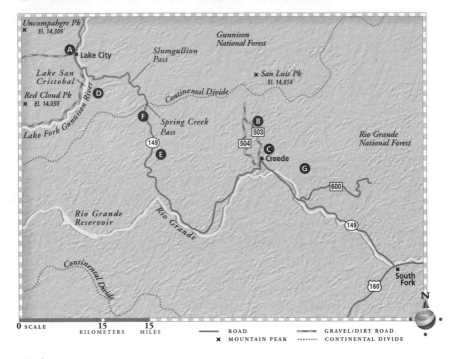

Sights

- **Ⓐ** Alfred Packer Massacre Site
- **Ⓑ** Bachelor Loop Driving Tour
- **Ⓒ** Creede Museum
- **Ⓒ** Creede Repertory Theatre
- **Ⓒ** Creede Underground Mining Museum
- **Ⓐ** Hinsdale County Historical Museum
- **Ⓓ** Lake San Cristobal
- **Ⓔ** North Clear Creek Falls
- **Ⓕ** Silver Thread Scenic and Historic Byway
- **Ⓒ** Underground Firehouse
- **Ⓖ** Wheeler Geologic Wilderness Area

Note: Items with the same letter are located in the same town or area.

A PERFECT DAY IN THE UPPER RIO GRANDE VALLEY

Spend the day exploring the vast wilderness between Lake City and South Fork on the Silver Thread Scenic and Historic Byway. Stop at North Clear Creek Falls, Creede, Slumgullion Earthflow, Lake San Cristobal, Alfred Packer's Massacre Site, and Lake City. Attend a performance at the Creede Repertory Theater in the evening, after feasting on a gourmet meal prepared in one of the area's friendly restaurants.

SIGHTSEEING HIGHLIGHTS

★★★ **Creede Repertory Theatre**—Housed in a prominent building on Creede's Main Street, this theater has earned its reputation as one of the best in the Southwest. It started as a struggling company in 1966 and has developed into a well-known playhouse, featuring actors from all over the country, who perform a different play each night, in true repertory style. Recent seasons have featured *Arsenic and Old Lace*, *Travels With my Aunt*, *A Streetcar Named Desire*, *You Can't Take It With You*, and *Steel Magnolias*.

Details: 124 N. Main St., Creede; 719/658-2540. Tickets $12–$15. (2 hours)

★★★ **Silver Thread Scenic and Historic Byway**—This 75-mile route links the communities of Lake City, Creede, and South Fork. The Rio Grande, which begins high in the Weminuche Wilderness, lazily meanders through the landscape. Paralleling the drive from South Fork to Creede are the former Denver & Rio Grande railroad tracks that carted many loads of ore extracted from Creede silver mines. Residents are currently trying to remove the rails and turn the railroad grade into a multi-use recreational trail.

Cattle ranching has proven profitable and certainly much more reliable than mining in this valley. Miners were known to be a transitory lot, but homesteaders and ranchers set up permanent ranches here in the last years of the 19th century. Several large family-owned spreads remain in the area, some of which have been converted into guest ranches.

One of the most beautiful places to stop along this route is **North Clear Creek Falls**, a little more than 20 miles from Creede. North Clear Creek is a quiet meadow stream until it comes to a steep basalt cliff, where it plummets more than 100 feet and travels through a narrow canyon before uniting with the mighty Rio Grande. The falls overlook is a nice place to stop for a picnic. From Highway 149, drive east on Forest Road 510 about a mile to the scenic overlook.

Six miles outside of Lake City is a creeping earthflow that started sliding down the landscape about 700 years ago. Called the **Slumgullion Earthflow** because it resembles the thick slumgullion stew favored by miners, this weak volcanic tuff and ash became oversaturated with water and succumbed to the force of gravity. You can tell where the slide begins by looking for trees precariously leaning on top of a yellowish mud. The slide is still moving—about a half-inch per day.

Along this spectacular drive you will cross the Continental Divide twice, at **Spring Creek Pass** and **Slumgullion Pass**, through a subalpine forest with an abundance of wildlife. I have happened upon a herd of bighorn sheep, two soaring bald eagles, more elk and antelope than I could count, and a couple of moose rummaging in the willow bottoms.

Details: *Hwy. 149 from Lake City to South Fork. (2 hours–half day)*

★★ **Bachelor Loop Driving Tour**—This 17-mile tour travels through Mineral County's rich mining history, starting at the south end of Creede. Although it traverses steep and narrow roads, it can be navigated, albeit carefully, by passenger cars. One highlight is seeing what remains of the Amethyst and Last Chance Mines, two of the greatest producers in the district. As the story goes, a prospector discovered the Amethyst while cursing his stubborn burros that refused to move from a nearby hill. In desperation, he began to flail his pick at the mountainside, finding a rich vein that he quickly laid claim to. While it is fun to explore this former mining country, please remember to be careful near mine sites. Never climb on the unstable structures and watch for shafts sunken in the cliffs.

Details: *North of Creede on Hwy 503. For more information, contact Creede's Chamber of Commerce, 1207 N. Main St., 719/658-2374 or 800/327-2102. (2 hours)*

★★ **Lake San Cristobal**—The three-mile-long Slumgullion Earthflow dammed the Lake Fork of the Gunnison River, forming this natural lake. Located three and a half miles from Lake City, Lake San Cristobal is known for its boating, fishing, scenic views, and picnic spots.

Details: *Hinsdale County Rd. 30. (2 hours)*

★★ **Wheeler Geologic Wilderness Area**—This 640-acre wilderness area encompasses a maze of volcanic tuff eroded into fantastic formations. The volcanic debris settled here after a violent episode 30 million years ago. Exploring the area requires a full day, or even two if you want to camp overnight. You can also mountain bike, horseback ride, or simply hike on Forest Service Trail 790, an eight-mile trip one way. Plan to go in either late May or June, after the snow has melted and the mud has dried. You'll need a four-wheel-drive vehicle to access the area.

Details: From Creede, drive 7.3 miles southeast on Highway 149 to Pool Table Road (County Rd. 600) and head northeast about 27 miles. For more information contact Rio Grande National Forest, Del Norte; 719/657-3321. (1–2 days)

★ **Alfred Packer Massacre Site**—The story of Alfred Packer began when a party of six eager prospectors foolishly entered the San Juan Mountains during the harsh winter of 1873. They hoped to reach the Los Piños Indian Agency to the south, then get a jump start on the goldfields recently opened in Breckenridge. The following April, only Alfred Packer made it to Los Piños, looking surprisingly fit and supple for someone who had just survived several months in one of the worst winters ever recorded. He was observed with a large amount of money, causing a great deal of suspicion as to the whereabouts of his fellow travelers. When questioned, Packer revealed that the men resorted to cannibalism, as several members of the party isolated in a winter camp began to die from starvation and illness. When just Packer and a man named Bell remained, Packer claimed, Bell went mad and attacked him, forcing him to kill Bell in self-defense. Packer then gathered the men's possessions and headed out of the mountains to civilization. However, no one believed his story.

A *Harper's Weekly* reporter stumbled upon the bodies of Packer's companions northeast of Lake San Cristobal in August 1874, increasing the outrage at Packer for such a brutal act of cannibalism and murder. Coloradans demanded a trial and anticipated an execution. But before it could begin, Packer escaped from the Saguache jail. When reapprehended in 1883, his infamous trial took place in Lake City. Dubbed "the Maneater," Packer spent the next 18 years in the state penitentiary for his crime but all the while proclaimed his innocence. Lake City likes to toast poor Alfie by sponsoring an annual rib dinner Memorial Day weekend.

Details: *From Lake City, head south on Highway 149 for a little over two miles. The Cannibal Plateau grave site is well marked as the Alfred Packer Massacre Site. (1 hour)*

✤ **Creede**—With the discovery of an enormous silver vein in Willow Creek Canyon in 1889, the full-scale rush to these remote mountains began. The tent town of Creede quickly gained a wild reputation as a place where revelers partied day and night. The railroad line entered town two years later to capitalize on shipping ore, freight, and passengers, and Creede's population soon soared to 10,000 people. The free **Creede Museum** contains early mining tools, photos, and other pioneer artifacts housed in the 1891 Denver & Rio Grande depot on Main Street. It is open Memorial Day to Labor Day.

After the last hard-rock mine pulled out of Mineral County in the mid-1980s, Creede lost 32 percent of its population and its economic mainstay. Several miners built the **Creede Underground Mining Museum** as a tribute to hard-rock mining in Mineral County. Dug into the side of a mountain, the museum replicates a working mine, with exhibits depicting mining here from the 1890s to the 1980s. Silver still lies waiting in many local mines, but because of its current low value, it isn't profitable to extract it.

Creede's **Underground Firehouse** (719/658-0811), next to the mining museum, is still used. The fire department volunteers, all miners, decided to blast underneath a mountain rather than build a new structure for their firehouse. This firehouse is well known as one of the most unusual in the country.

Details: *Creede Chamber of Commerce, 1207 N. Main St., 719/658-2374 or 800/327-2102. (full day)*

✤ **Lake City**—In an era known for its rough-and-tumble mining towns, Lake City was a breed apart. In 1874 a road builder discovered a rich vein of gold while surveying this area near Lake San Cristobal. His discovery spawned Lake City, one of the first incorporated towns on the Western Slope. While miners hastily threw together ramshackle log cabins and tents when they first came here, other forward-thinking residents constructed homes and commercial buildings in Greek, Gothic, Italianate Revival, and Queen Anne Victorian styles.

In keeping with its sophisticated architecture, late 19th-century Lake City residents enjoyed the refinements of a respectable town, with residents regularly attending socials, recitals, church gatherings, and concerts. Many original buildings from the late 1870s and 1880s still stand in this National Historic District, one of the largest in Colorado.

During the summer and fall, the Hinsdale County Historical Society sponsors house tours. The **Hinsdale County Historical Museum** (130 Silver St.) is located in a mercantile building that dates from 1877. Changing exhibits on the Utes, early mining history, and the geology of the Upper Rio Grande River Valley are featured.

Details: Lake City Chamber of Commerce, Silver St., 970/944-2527 or 800/569-1874. (full day)

FITNESS AND RECREATION

Fishing is the preferred summer activity on the **Rio Grande**, known for its 16- to 18-inch rainbow trout. The best stretch on the river starts from the bridge on Highway 149 in South Fork and goes downstream toward Del Norte at the Rio Grande Canal diversion structure. This area has been designated one of Colorado's Gold Medal Waters. Although much of it is privately owned, several public access spots do exist. For fishing information, contact the **Division of Wildlife**, 1035 Park Avenue, Monte Vista; 719/852-2731.

During the cold months, pull on a pair of cross-country skis or snowshoes and experience the glorious winter landscape. Trails exist for every ability in this region, and several beginner trails are groomed periodically. The **Bachelor Loop/East West Willow Trail**, starting from Creede, features levels for every type of skier. The first three miles are suitable for beginners; the trail then becomes progressively more difficult.

FOOD

The **Lake City Bakery**, 922 Highway 149, 970/944-2613, is open during the summer daily from 7 a.m. to 6 p.m. The deck is a great place to enjoy their freshly baked breads, pastries, cookies, and other treats. The restaurant at the **Crystal Lodge**, two miles south of Lake City, 970/944-2201, is a year-round gourmet's delight. Breakfast, lunch, and dinner all feature unusual and delicious entrees that incorporate seasonal ingredients. Some specials include a spicy jumbo shrimp with a special Cajun seasoning, New York steak, macadamia nut–encrusted halibut served with green chile cilantro sauce, or a roasted stuffed chicken breast.

UPPER RIO GRANDE VALLEY

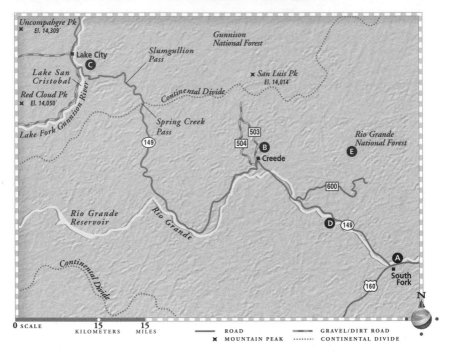

Food

- Ⓐ Brown's Country Store
- Ⓐ La Casita
- Ⓑ Creede Hotel
- Ⓒ Crystal Lodge
- Ⓒ Lake City Bakery
- Ⓑ Mucker's Bucket Saloon

Lodging

- Ⓒ Cinnamon Inn
- Ⓓ Cottonwood Cove

Lodging (continued)

- Ⓑ Creede Hotel
- Ⓒ Crystal Lodge
- Ⓓ Old Firehouse Bed and Breakfast

Camping

- Ⓑ Broadacres Guest Ranch
- Ⓓ Cottonwood Cove
- Ⓒ Lake City Campground
- Ⓔ Rio Grande National Forest

Note: Items with the same letter are located in the same town or area.

Vegetarian specials vary from a Mediterranean torte to penne pasta with a basil cream sauce. Breakfast and lunch run $5 to $7; dinner, $9 to $19.

Creede Hotel, 719/658-2608, serves fresh and well-prepared meals and homemade baked goods. Breakfast starts with big cinnamon rolls or other pastries and includes traditional egg dishes. Lunch features homemade soups, salads, and burgers, from $3 to $7. The dinner menu is more elegant, with entrees such as tamari honey chicken, salmon, prime rib, and several vegetarian pasta dishes, from $10 to $15. The **Mucker's Bucket Saloon**, on Highway 149 in Creede, 719/658-9997, stays open daily year-round, from 7 a.m. to 9 p.m. The saloon serves delicious and inexpensive meals, such as fried chicken, burgers, and french fries. The unusual name comes from the miners who shoveled "muck" into buckets, thus becoming known as muckers.

At **La Casita**, 76 West Highway 149, South Fork, 719/873-5556, the owner makes every dish from scratch. Specialties include tacos, enchiladas, and chile rellenos, all accompanied with rice and beans for about $8. À la carte options start at $2. For a quick sandwich, go to **Brown's Country Store**, 29411 U.S. Highway 160, South Fork; 719/873-5582.

LODGING

The most common local lodgings are guest cabins, usually a cottage with one or two bedrooms and a small kitchenette. Most are open only in the summer, but a few are available year-round. **Cottonwood Cove**, at the historic Wagon Wheel Gap about 10 miles southeast of Creede, 719/658-2242, continues to uphold a long-standing tradition of guest ranches in this region. Accommodations include small cabins with one, two, or three bedrooms, and an RV park. Cabin rates range from $55 to $140; RV sites are $17.50, with the seventh night free.

Each of the rooms at Creede's **Old Firehouse Bed and Breakfast**, 719/658-0212, is filled with interesting antiques and collectibles. The owner did a remarkable job converting this former firehouse into a bed-and-breakfast. The **Creede Hotel**, on Main Street, 719/658-2608, has four comfortable rooms with private baths for $70 to $85. The hotel also has an annex, with a kitchen, that can sleep up to 11 people. It's usually open from mid-March to mid-October.

The **Crystal Lodge**, two miles south of Lake City, has rooms starting from $55 in the summer, $45 in the winter. Also available are suites starting at $75 and cottages starting at $105. Rooms are rustic but have modern conveniences and beautiful bay windows revealing the view. Rates do not include breakfast.

In Lake City is the **Cinnamon Inn Bed and Breakfast**, 426 Gunnison Avenue, 970/944-2641 or 800/337-2335. The home is centrally located in town, in a beautiful 1878 Victorian home with a large, meditative garden. A particular amenity is that the innkeeper, a jazz pianist, plays during breakfast. Five rooms range from $75 to $120. Open year-round.

CAMPING

For rustic camping, several good campgrounds are situated in the **Rio Grande National Forest**: Marshall Park, North Clear Creek, and Silver Thread. The forest charges a nominal fee for each site. Rio Grande National Forest, Third and Creede Avenues, Creede; 719/658-2556.

Several guest ranches near Creede also have RV sites, such as **Cottonwood Cove**, 719/658-2242, and **Broadacres Guest Ranch**, 719/658-2291. The **Lake City Campground**, at Eighth and Bluff Streets, 970/944-2920, is centrally located, close to the downtown district, shops, and restaurants.

11

UPPER ARKANSAS RIVER VALLEY

The Arkansas River begins its 1,400-mile journey to the Mississippi in the high reaches of the Sawatch Range, a broad swath of mountains that start near Leadville and ends just southwest of Salida. This range is home to 15 mountains above 14,000 feet, including Colorado's highest, Mount Elbert, 14,433 feet. Framing the southern border of the Arkansas Valley are the Sangre de Cristo Mountains. Named by Spanish explorers, Sangre de Cristo means blood of Christ. During sensational sunsets, when these mountains are bathed in crimson hues, the reason for its name is quite clear. The mountainous setting of the upper Arkansas River Valley is something to behold, a place people fall in love with the first time they see it.

What's even nicer about this region is that the Sawatch Mountains shelter this broad valley from harsh winters, which is why it is known locally as the Banana Belt. Most outdoor activities are possible here year-round, and locals still hike or mountain bike on many trails at lower elevations during the winter months. The bodies of water rarely ice over, even during January and February, and year-round fishing in creeks, streams, lakes, and beaver ponds is usually possible. And most surprising of all, while the surrounding mountains receive dozens of inches of snow annually, the valley receives only a scant 10 to 12 inches. ◼

UPPER ARKANSAS RIVER VALLEY

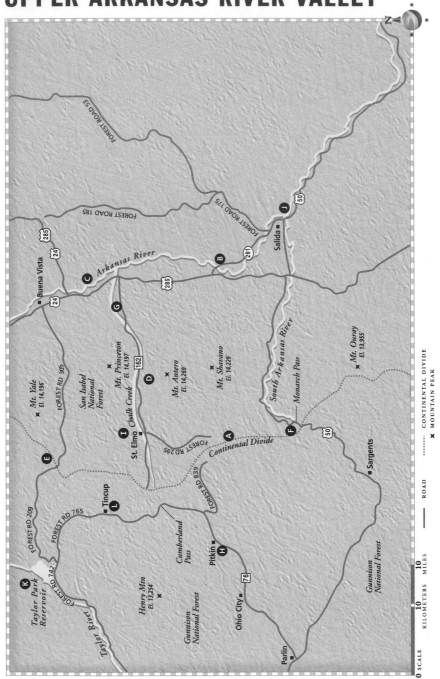

N

Buena Vista

Salida

Arkansas River

South Arkansas River

Mt. Ouray
El. 13,955'

Mt. Shavano
El. 14,229'

Mt. Antero
El. 14,269'

Mt. Princeton
El. 14,197'

Mt. Yale
El. 14,196'

Chalk Creek

St. Elmo

San Isabel
National
Forest

Monarch Pass

Sargents

Continental Divide

Tincup

Cumberland
Pass

Henry Mtn
El. 13,254'

Pittkin

Ohio City

Parlin

Gunnison
National Forest

Gunnison
National Forest

Taylor Park
Reservoir

Taylor River

FOREST ROAD 53

FOREST ROAD 185

FOREST ROAD 175

FOREST RD 305

FOREST RD 295

FOREST RD 839

FOREST RD 765

FOREST RD 209

FOREST RD 742

285

24

24

285

291

50

291

162

76

50

A B C D E F G H I J K L

SCALE

0

10 KILOMETERS

10 MILES

······· CONTINENTAL DIVIDE

✖ MOUNTAIN PEAK

—— ROAD

Sights

- Ⓐ Alpine Tunnel at Alpine Pass
- Ⓑ Arkansas Headwaters
  Recreation Area
- Ⓒ Arkansas River
- Ⓓ Chalk Creek Canyon
- Ⓔ Cottonwood Pass
- Ⓕ Monarch Ski Area
- Ⓖ Mount Princeton
  Hot Springs Resort
- Ⓗ Pitkin
- Ⓘ St. Elmo
- Ⓙ Salida Aquatic
  Hot Springs Pool
- Ⓙ Salida Steam Plant
- Ⓚ Taylor Park
- Ⓛ Tincup

Note: Items with the same letter are located in the same town or area.

A PERFECT DAY IN THE UPPER ARKANSAS RIVER VALLEY

Sign up for a river-rafting trip for a half day and spend the other half exploring Chalk Creek Canyon, where you can take a dip in the Mount Princeton Hot Springs, visit St. Elmo, a remarkably well-preserved ghost town, and hike or drive to the historic Alpine Tunnel. In the evening browse through Salida's downtown National Historic District, which hosts galleries, bookstores, and restaurants.

GHOST TOWNS

Several mute ghost towns remain in this mountain range, as reminders of the booming gold rush that once took place here. Places like **Tincup**, **St. Elmo**, and **Pitkin** originally aspired to be the county seat—if not the state capital—but the decline of the mines and their isolation eventually buried those dreams under the thick winter snows.

A wonderful way to explore these ghost towns is to take a scenic drive on the backcountry roads. Most can be negotiated by a two-wheel-drive vehicle, but I've noted where four-wheel drive is necessary. Take your time to explore the beautiful and serene alpine environment, the tremendous vistas, and the interesting historical attractions along the way.

SIGHTSEEING HIGHLIGHTS

★★★ **Arkansas River**—From its inauspicious beginnings high in Colorado's Rocky Mountains, the Arkansas River is a major drainage coursing through Kansas, Oklahoma, and Arkansas, which joins the Mississippi River before reaching the Gulf of Mexico. But at its headwaters the Arkansas is a spirited mountain river, rushing through beautiful granite canyons and open valleys and supporting numerous fun-filled water sports, such as river rafting, kayaking, and fishing.

As many outfitters in this area will tell you, this river offers more excitement per mile than any other in the West. A raft trip could be the highlight of your stay here. The season usually runs from May to September but peaks in June, when the rivers are at their highest. A variety of trips are possible, from exciting adrenaline rushes on the boiling white-water rapids to gentle floats down the milder sections. Brown's Canyon, eight miles south of Buena Vista, is known as the ultimate in white-water rafting because of the number of rapids encountered along the route. At least 20 local companies run trips (half day, full day, and multiday trips available).

Headquartered in Salida, the **Arkansas Headwaters Recreation Area** begins in Leadville and ends in Pueblo, encompassing 150 miles of state parks, campgrounds, picnic areas, boat ramps, and fishing access along the Arkansas River. The Bureau of Land Management and the Colorado Department of Parks and Outdoor Recreation teamed up to create this unique recreation area and to protect the riparian environment.

Details: *Arkansas Headwaters Recreation Area, P.O. Box 126, Salida, CO 81201; 719/539-7289. (full day)*

★★★ **Chalk Creek Canyon**—This backcountry drive takes you through some of Colorado's richest mining and railroad history. About 15 miles north of Salida on Highway 285 is County Road 162, just south of the town of Nathrop. Head west on this road. After about five miles you will come to the **Mount Princeton Hot Springs Resort**, a great place to start or finish your trip to the canyon with a dip in the hot springs ($6).

Twelve miles west is **St. Elmo**, one of Colorado's best-known and best-preserved ghost towns. In the 1880s St. Elmo served as the major transportation and supply hub for mining camps in the district, but today it is isolated from the busy highways and towns of the Arkansas

Valley. Miners from all over the area flocked here on weekends to kick up their heels in the town's saloons. Yet, as the demand for silver decreased, St. Elmo slowly withered, and by 1950 only two people lived there.

The Denver, South Park & Pacific Railroad built a narrow-gauge line to service the mines in this area in 1880. The owners optimistically planned for their railroad to stretch all the way to the Pacific, but first they had to conquer the Continental Divide and the impenetrable Rockies. The owners came up with an ingenious plan. Instead of attempting to build the tracks over the Divide, they would bore a tunnel beneath it. This resulted in the 1,772-foot Alpine Tunnel, the first ever burrowed under the Continental Divide. While constructing the tunnel at such high elevations was a feat of tremendous significance, harsh winter conditions caused too many fatal accidents, and the tunnel closed in 1910.

You can see the eastern portal of the **Alpine Tunnel at Alpine Pass**. Head south of St. Elmo about four and a half miles on Forest Road 295 until you reach the former railroad station of Hancock. From here, head west, then take the right fork in the road to the tunnel. This road is very rough. You can drive it if you have a four-wheel drive with high clearance, or you can hike up the road about three miles to see the tunnel. A short trail from the east portal will take you over the divide to the western portal, viewable from the scenic drive over Cumberland Pass.

Details: *County Rd. 162 (half–full day)*

☆☆ **Cottonwood Pass, Taylor Park, and Pitkin**—A well-maintained paved road takes you over the Continental Divide, summiting at 12,126 feet at Cottonwood Pass. You can access several trailheads to climb Fourteeners and a beautiful portion of the Colorado Trail from the Cottonwood Pass Road. From the stoplight in Buena Vista, head west 20 miles on Forest Road 306 to Cottonwood Pass. The road is paved until just before the top, but you can drive the gravel portions with a two-wheel-drive passenger car.

At the summit of Cottonwood Pass, a moderate hike starts at an elevation of 12,100 feet and gains about 1,000 feet. Walking at this elevation will be much harder than down in the valley, so don't overdo it and bring along water and snacks. This short walk will take you south along the Continental Divide to higher views of the surrounding region. Taylor Park is on the western slope of the divide, while to the north is the majestic Sawatch Range.

After hiking or enjoying the views from the pass, get back in the car to descend into Taylor Park and toward Taylor Park Reservoir. From the reservoir, head south on Forest Road 742 until you reach Forest Road 765, which takes you into **Tincup**. The town probably was named after a miner who carried out his earnings in a tin cup. During this area's mining boom in the late 19th century, Tincup's major thoroughfare to the outside world was through St. Elmo, over the treacherous Tincup Pass. Be sure to visit the cemetery just outside of town and take time to read the inscriptions on the headstones, poignant reminders of the bygone mining era.

For a longer trip from Tincup, continue south on Forest Road 765 over Cumberland Pass (12,000 feet) to the small historic community of Pitkin on Quartz Creek. You can camp in one of the many campgrounds along the way or spend the night at a hostel or bed-and-breakfast in Pitkin. Just outside of town, Forest Road 839 will take you to the western portal of the historic narrow-gauge Alpine Tunnel, described in the Chalk Creek Canyon entry.

Details: Forest Rds. 306, 742, and 765 from Buena Vista to Pitkin. (1–2 days)

★★ **Monarch Ski Area**—This ski area is tremendously popular because of its reasonable prices and volumes of snow: almost 36 feet dumped annually. The slope offers both alpine and Nordic skiing, catering to expert and intermediate skiers, but several beginner trails and a ski school also exist. Monarch also grooms three kilometers of Nordic trails on Old Monarch Pass, over the top of the Continental Divide. The trail begins just west of the ski area.

Details: 22 miles west of Salida on Hwy. 50; 719/539-3573. (full day)

★ **Salida**—This revitalized National Register Historic District contains several interesting art galleries, antique stores, restaurants, and bookshops, perfect for leisurely window shopping and people-watching. The **Salida Steam Plant** (312 W. Sackett Street) first brought electricity to the streets of Salida in 1887. This historic landmark is now an innovative community space for theater, dance, lectures, or whatever else comes to town during spring and summer. An outdoor sculpture garden sits next to the building. Look for community notices or posters announcing current events or contact the Salida Chamber of Commerce for more information (719/539-2068).

Beginning in mid-July, Salida brings musicians from the Aspen

Music Festival to town for six Saturday evening performances known as the **Salida-Aspen Music Festival**. Performances start at 8 p.m. at the John Held Auditorium, 10th and D Streets. Look for posters announcing any concerts during your stay or call the Chamber of Commerce.

If you visit Salida in mid-June, you will encounter a crazy festival known as the **FIBArk** (First in Boating on the Arkansas) **Boat Race Weekend**. The weekend event centers around a 26-mile kayak race from Salida to Cotopaxi. Festival activities include a bed race, parade, live music, and art booths. Billed as the most prestigious downriver kayak race in North America, this event is lots of fun to watch.

The water in the **Salida Aquatic Hot Springs,** 410 W. Highway 50 (Rainbow Street), 719/539-6738, is actually piped in from eight miles away, near Poncha Springs. The Works Progress Administration constructed the hot springs building and pool facilities during the 1930s. An Olympic-size pool offers lap swimming, aerobics, and water games. There's also a soaking pool and a child's pool.

Details: Salida Chamber of Commerce, 406 W. Hwy. 50; 719/539-2068. (full day)

FITNESS AND RECREATION

Eighty percent of Chaffee County is public land. The **San Isabel National Forest, Collegiate Peaks Wilderness, Sangre de Cristo Wilderness, Buffalo Peaks Wilderness** northeast of Buena Vista, and sections of the **Colorado Trail** all offer an unlimited variety of hiking and backpacking trails. Maps and information about these areas can be purchased from several wilderness equipment stores in Salida, Buena Vista, or Poncha Springs. The **San Isabel National Forest** office, 325 West Rainbow Boulevard, Salida, 719/539-3591, also has detailed maps of the National Forest, including trails and campgrounds.

When recreating in this area, remember that summer afternoons in the mountains usually bring thunder and lightning storms. Always be aware of changing weather conditions when staying outdoors for an extended period of time. Pack a raincoat and several layers of clothing to keep you comfortable if there is a severe weather change. Even if you are only going for a day hike, carry extra water and food in case of an emergency. When camping, stay off the trail and at least 200 feet from any water sources to avoid damaging these fragile areas.

Hikers who are in good physical condition and accustomed to

UPPER ARKANSAS RIVER VALLEY

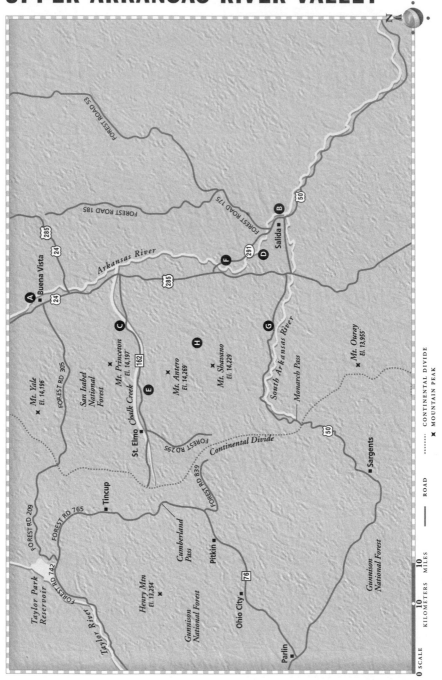

Taylor Park Reservoir

Taylor River

FOREST RD 742

FOREST RD 209

FOREST RD 765

Tincup

FOREST RD 305

Mt. Yale
El. 14,196'

San Isabel National Forest

Mt. Princeton
El. 14,197'

St. Elmo

Chalk Creek

162

Mt. Antero
El. 14,269'

Mt. Shavano
El. 14,229

FOREST RD 295

FOREST RD 839

Continental Divide

Cumberland Pass

Henry Mtn
El. 13,254'

Gunnison National Forest

Pitkin

Ohio City

76

Parlin

Gunnison National Forest

Sargents

50

Monarch Pass

South Arkansas River

Mt. Ouray
El. 13,955'

Buena Vista

24

285

24

Arkansas River

285

291

Salida

50

FOREST ROAD 175

FOREST ROAD 185

FOREST ROAD 53

N

SCALE
0   10
KILOMETERS

0   10
MILES

—— ROAD   ‥‥‥‥ CONTINENTAL DIVIDE
✕ MOUNTAIN PEAK

A   B   C   D   E   F   G   H

Food

Ⓐ Casa del Sol

Ⓑ First Street Café

Ⓑ Il Vicino

Ⓒ Mt. Princeton Restaurant

Lodging

Ⓐ Adobe Inn

Ⓐ Meister House

Ⓓ River Run Inn

Ⓔ Streamside Bed and Breakfast

Camping

Ⓕ Arkansas Headwaters Recreation Area

Ⓖ Heart of the Rockies Campground

Ⓗ San Isabel National Forest

Note: Items with the same letter are located in the same town or area.

the altitude will be challenged by the many Fourteeners in this region, such as **Mount Yale** and **Mount Princeton**, both strenuous day hikes. There are also countless number of mountain bike trails in the Salida/Buena Vista area, thanks to the many former railroad beds and rocky roads to the mountain mining districts. The **Monarch Crest Trail** from the crest of Monarch Pass to Marshall Pass has been called the best mountain bike ride in the state. Stop in at **Otero Cyclery**, 108 F Street, 719/539-6704, for recommendations on other great rides.

FOOD

The **First Street Café**, 137 East First Street, Salida, 719/539-4759, has an excellent and varied menu, including many vegetarian dishes. Huevos rancheros, breakfast enchiladas, and other standard breakfasts run up to $5.95; Mexican specials, quiche, or sandwiches for lunch range from $5 to $9; and New York strip steak, stuffed chicken, and trout dinners run $10 to $18. Closed Sunday. **Il Vicino**, 136 East Second Street, Salida, 719/539-5219, fires pizzas in a wood oven and brews its own beer. It also serves calzones and *paninos* (sort of like pizza sandwiches). Lunch and dinner, $5 to $7.

The unique recipes at **Casa del Sol**, 303 North Highway 24, Buena Vista, 719/395-8810, are inspired by regional recipes from Mexico and New Mexico. Popular dishes include the *pechega suiza*, a folded flour tortilla sautéed in butter with chicken and green chiles, and enchiladas in a carefully prepared red sauce from homegrown New Mexican chiles. The restaurant is open every day in summer for lunch and dinner. Winter hours are erratic, so call ahead. Lunch ranges from $5 to $10; dinner, $8.50 to $15.

The **Mount Princeton Restaurant** is located at the Mount Princeton Hot Springs Resort, 15870 County Road 162, five miles from Nathrop, 719/395-2361. It's open for breakfast, lunch, and dinner. For dinner, the chef prepares an assortment of pasta entrees, in addition to several excellent cuts of meat and other Southwestern dishes. The dining room is open from 7 a.m. to 9 p.m. in summer. Breakfast runs $2 to $7; lunch, $5 to $7; dinner, $9 to $20.

LODGING

There is no shortage of standard motels in Salida and Buena Vista. However, plenty of out-of-the-ordinary lodging options with friendly hosts can also be found. The **River Run Inn**, 8495 County Road 160, 719/539-3818 or 800/385-6925, is a Victorian mansion on five acres of riverfront property outside of Salida. The house has a huge front porch, 12-foot ceilings, and four-poster beds in each room. The inn contains seven private rooms ($60–$80) and a coed dorm ($30) for large groups or families.

The historic **Meister House**, 414 East Main Street, Buena Vista, 719/395-9220 or 888/395-9220, has six nicely decorated Western-style rooms. Rates, including a full breakfast, are $65 to $125. The owners also have a romantic room on the Arkansas River with a hot tub. The **Adobe Inn**, 303 North Highway 24, next to the Casa del Sol Restaurant in Buena Vista, 719/395-6340, has five rooms with distinct and tasteful furnishings. Prices range from $59 to $89, including a complete breakfast.

Streamside Bed and Breakfast, 18820 County Road 162, eight miles west of Nathrop, 719/395-2553, with three guest rooms, has as its backdrop the magnificent Mount Princeton, Mount Antero, and Chalk Cliffs. The owners enjoy suggesting trails for hiking, skiing, wildlife viewing, and other nonmotorized recreation. The year-round range is $64 to $76.

CAMPING

Campgrounds located along this section of the **Arkansas Headwaters Recreation Area**, 719/539-7289, include Five Points, east of Salida; and Hecla Junction and Ruby Mountain, both north of Salida. To enter all Arkansas Headwater recreation sites, you must obtain a Colorado State Parks Pass and pay a nominal camping fee per night.

Some campgrounds in the **San Isabel National Forest** may be reserved by calling 800/280-CAMP (2267). Backcountry campsites also exist within national forest boundaries. For more information on camping, contact the San Isabel National Forest, 325 West Rainbow Boulevard, Salida; 719/539-3591.

The **Heart of the Rockies Campground**, 16105 Highway 50 West, 11 miles east of Monarch Pass and five miles west of Poncha Springs, 719/539-4051 or 800/496-2245, has 45 RV sites with picnic tables, grills, and campfire rings. An arcade room, swimming pool, evening movies, and scenic horseback rides will keep the kids busy.

NIGHTLIFE

About the only thing going on in Salida after 9 p.m. is at "The Vic," or the **Victoria Hotel and Tavern**, 143 North F Street, 719/539-4891. It's open daily from noon to 2 a.m. On weekend nights the tavern hosts live bands—usually rock 'n' roll or rhythm and blues.

12

SAN LUIS VALLEY

In 1598 the kingdom of Spain laid claim to all lands drained by the Rio Grande River in the present southwestern United States. This claim included the San Luis Valley, even though several Native American tribes had held this region for thousands of years. The Spanish harshly subjugated the Pueblo peoples of New Mexico, but several other tribes, such as the Utes and Apaches, remained free from Spanish control. These tribes eventually acquired Spanish horses, allowing them to travel greater distances in larger groups and accumulate more possessions and goods. With their status and fighting power heightened dramatically, they roamed the San Luis Valley freely.

Extended families from northern New Mexico began moving permanently to the San Luis Valley during the first part of the 19th century, predating white homesteaders and gold seekers in other parts of Colorado. They settled along waterways, growing crops and tending flocks of sheep. Their homes, called *plazas*, were self-enclosed structures that helped defend against Indian raids, dreaded occurrences that decimated many families. The geographic isolation of this area insulated these early Hispanic settlers from outside influences, even after the area became part of the United States in 1848.

Today many of the older residents of the San Luis Valley still remain somewhat isolated, preferring to follow their longstanding traditions. Anglo homesteaders began moving to the valley in the 1860s. These two cultures now live side-by-side in the valley, each utilizing its abundant and diverse resources. ◣

SAN LUIS VALLEY

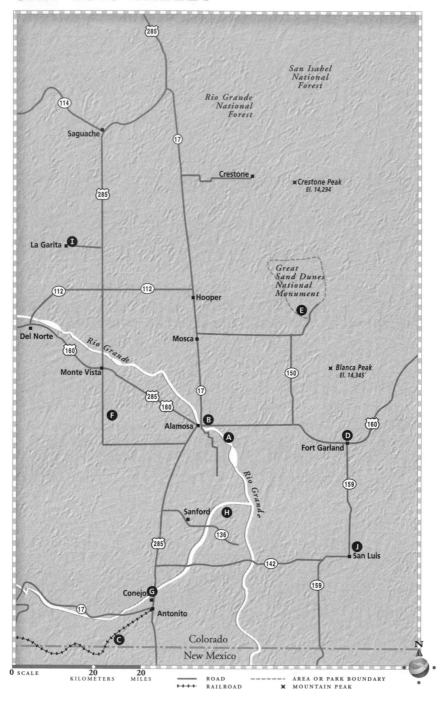

Sights

Ⓐ Alamosa National
    Wildlife Refuge

Ⓑ Luther Bean Museum

Ⓒ Cumbres & Toltec Narrow-
    gauge Railroad

Ⓓ Fort Garland Museum

Ⓔ Great Sand Dunes National
    Monument

Ⓕ Monte-Vista National
    Wildlife Refuge

Ⓖ Our Lady of Guadalupe Church

Ⓗ Pike's Stockade

Ⓘ San Juan Art Center

Ⓙ San Luis Museum and
    Cultural Center

Ⓚ Splashland

Ⓛ Stations of the
    Cross Shrine

Note: Items with the same letter are located in the same town or area.

A PERFECT DAY IN THE SAN LUIS VALLEY

Discover the San Luis Valley by spending the morning at the Great
Sand Dunes National Monument, and enjoying the views of the valley
and Sangre de Cristos from the park. Afterwards, tour the Fort
Garland Museum, a reconstructed frontier military post from the early
1860s. Then take a short drive to San Luis and visit the Stations of the
Cross Shrine and the Cultural Center to get a sense of the valley's history and rich artistic tradition.

ART OF THE SAN LUIS VALLEY

Much of the traditional art produced in the valley today reflects
the area's rich Hispanic heritage, a blend of early Spanish and
Native American influences. The weaving style of the San Luis
Valley and northern New Mexico, known as the Rio Grande style,
can be found in San Luis, La Garita, and other local galleries, along
with murals, *santos*, *milagros*, and other representations of Hispanic
religious art.

A new generation of artists has chosen the inspirational San Luis
Valley as home, resulting in more modern influences in photography,
pottery, paintings, watercolors, and sculpture. If you are interested in

the work of a certain local artist, you can usually make an appointment to visit his or her studio. Inquire at art galleries in Alamosa, San Luis, and La Garita.

SIGHTSEEING HIGHLIGHTS

★★★ **Cumbres & Toltec Narrow-gauge Railroad**—Take a trip back in time on this steam-powered narrow-gauge railroad line between Antonito, Colorado, and Chama, New Mexico. Today the railroad carries only passengers, but the Denver & Rio Grande originally built this narrow-gauge extension to haul minerals extracted from the San Juan Mountains. The line also picked up chiles from northern New Mexico villages, giving it the nickname "The Chile Line." The trip runs 64 miles through the San Juans, over trestles, curves, and bridges, offering incredible scenic vistas.

Details: 719/376-5483. Train runs Memorial Day weekend–mid-October, with various morning departure times. Prices range from $17–$27 for children, $34–$52 for adults. Seniors receive a 10 percent discount—notify the agent when making a reservation. (full day)

★★★ **Great Sand Dunes National Monument**—For centuries, high winds crossing the San Luis Valley have deposited millions of grains of sands to create these 700-foot-high sand dunes at the base of the Sangre de Cristo Mountains. The dunes actually cover an area of 39 square miles. Exploring this stark environment evokes an African desert experience—without the camels, turbans, and oases. Hiking to the summit takes about two hours uphill and an hour downhill. For a fun and fast way down, try "skitching" on a plastic sled or windbreaker.

Details: 1150 Hwy. 150, Mosca; 719/378-2312. From Alamosa, head east on Hwy. 160 about 20 miles to Hwy. 150. Turn north and drive about 18 miles. $3 per person. (3 hours–full day)

★★★ **Stations of the Cross Shrine**—Built by the Sangre de Cristo Parish, this shrine sits atop a bluff on the northern side of the town of San Luis. Religion is the glue for many communities of the San Luis Valley, as seen in the huge volunteer effort that went into constructing this sanctuary for prayer and solace. Fifteen dramatic bronze sculptures depicting the last hours of Christ's life, sculpted by local artist Huberto Maestas, are positioned at intervals along a half-mile trail to the top of the bluff. At the top is the **Capilla de Todos Santos**, a beautifully constructed adobe chapel, amidst a backdrop of the Sangre de Cristos, San Juans, and the valley below. Try to go just before the sun goes down—you may be rewarded with a legendary San Luis Valley sunset.

Details: Junction of Hwys. 159 and 142, San Luis (1 hour)

★★ **Alamosa and Monte Vista National Wildlife Refuges**—In spring, more than 20,000 greater sandhill cranes and a handful of their cousins, the endangered whooping cranes, migrate through the San Luis Valley on their way north. Approximately 20 whooping cranes raised at these refuges return annually, usually between February and the beginning of April.

Details: Monte Vista Refuge is south of Monte Vista on Highway 15. Alamosa Refuge is east of Alamosa on Highway 160, then south on County Road S-116. Call 719/589-4021 for information. (half day)

★★ **Fort Garland Museum**—Established in 1858, this frontier military outpost protected Hispanic homesteaders in the San Luis Valley from attacks by Ute and Apache warriors retaliating against settlement in the area. From 1866 to 1867, the frontiersman Kit Carson commanded the post, in charge of largely Hispanic troops. For a short time, "Buffalo Soldiers," African Americans who enlisted in the frontier army, were also stationed here.

Recent archaeological excavations by the Colorado Historical Society have unearthed many artifacts that illuminate the daily activities of soldiers, officers, and their families. The museum has done an excellent job of recreating the frontier era, seen in Hollywood Westerns as a hair-raising and exciting existence. But life here was seldom exciting, more often a humdrum repetition of marching and orders. You can also find more information on other local attractions and browse the gift shop.

Details: U.S. Hwy. 159; 719/379-3512. Daily 9–5. $2.50 adults, $2 seniors, $1.50 ages 6–16. Children under 6 and Colorado Historical Society members admitted free. (1–2 hours)

★★ **San Juan Art Center**—Housed in the historic La Capilla de San Juan Bautista (Church of Saint John the Baptist), this women's art cooperative is dedicated to Hispanic folk art. The church can be seen from a rise northwest of town.

Details: *In La Garita, six miles from Highway 285 between Saguache and Monte Vista. Memorial Day–Labor Day Mon–Fri 10–5, weekends 1–5. (1 hour)*

★★ **Luther Bean Museum**—On the campus of Adams State College in Alamosa, this museum has a unique collection of regional Native American and Hispanic folk art, including a bronze sculpture by noted Apache artist Alan Houser; Rio Grande-style weavings; and an extensive anthropological collection.

Details: *208 Edgemont Blvd., Richardson Hall, Room 256, 719/587-7151. Weekday 1–4:30. Admission is free. (1 hour)*

★★ **San Luis Museum and Cultural Center**—This center's exhibits and artwork reflect the rich history of San Luis, Colorado's oldest town (1851), and that of the entire San Luis Valley. Recent exhibits have focused on the area's multicultural heritage, and a fascinating photo exhibit chronicles the town's history. The center also focuses on living arts, including music, storytelling, folklore, and performance arts. Upstairs is a recreated *morada*, or chapel of the Penitente brotherhood, with significant religious items including *retablos*, (Hispanic religious paintings on wood) and *bultos* (carved religious figures). For generations, this

© Unicorn/Dave Lyons

Great Sand Dunes National Monument

fraternal organization has played an important role in the daily and religious life of many small villages in the valley.

Details: *402 Church St.; 719/672-3611. Memorial Day–Labor Day Mon–Fri 8–4:30, Sat and Sun 10–4. (1 hour)*

☆☆ **Splashland**—Located north of Alamosa, Splashland is a geothermal swimming pool supplied by an artesian well maintained at a constant 94 degrees. There are smaller pools for soaking and a larger pool with diving boards.

Details: *One mile north of Alamosa on Hwy. 17 (look for the colorful 1950s marquee of a woman in a bathing suit); 719/589-6307. Memorial Day–Labor Day weekdays (except Wed) 10–6:30, weekends noon–6. $4 adults and teens, $3 children. (2 hours)*

☆ **Pike's Stockade**—In 1806 Thomas Jefferson sent Zebulon Pike to explore lands west of the Mississippi River acquired through the Louisiana Purchase. Pike traveled through the San Luis Valley, battling harsh winter storms, and crossed the Sangre de Cristos in January 1807. His party of 12 men camped along the Conejos River, where they built a stockade and hoisted an American flag in the northern reaches of Spanish territory. In late February, 100 Spanish soldiers traveled north from Santa Fe to the stockade to arrest Pike for trespassing. The soldiers imprisoned Pike and forced him to Chihuahua, Mexico, where he was held for roughly a year.

A property of the Colorado Historical Society, Pike's Stockade has the distinction of being the first U.S. fort built on Colorado soil.

Details: *From Alamosa, travel south on Hwy. 285 to La Jara. Turn east on Hwy. 136 and drive about four miles to Sanford. Take County Rd. 20 six miles northeast of Sanford and follow the signs. For more information about the stockade, inquire at the Fort Garland Museum; 719/379-3512. Memorial Day–Labor Day 9–5. (2 hours, including drive from Alamosa)*

Our Lady of Guadalupe Catholic Church—Before Catholic parishes and churches came to the valley, residents met informally on Sundays to recite the rosary, or gathered when a traveling priest came to the area to perform marriages, baptisms, and other holy rites. Our Lady of Guadalupe, in Conejos, formed in 1856, is the earliest congregation in both the San Luis Valley and in Colorado. The parish's original adobe church, blessed by the Bishop of Santa Fe in 1860, has been replaced by a modern structure that can be visited during daytime hours.

Details: From 285 at Conejos, follow signs for the Oldest Church in Colorado, 719/376-5985 (half hour)

FITNESS AND RECREATION

The stacked loop at **Zapata Falls** is a good mountain bike trail for beginners. The trail features four different loops winding through a piñon-juniper forest. From the trail you can see the San Luis Valley and the Great Sand Dunes and visit the nearby Zapata Falls. To get to the trailhead, head east from Alamosa on Highway 160. Turn left on Highway 150, the Great Sand Dunes Road, and drive 12 miles north to a gravel road. A sign here will direct you to Zapata Falls, four miles away. For bike rentals or suggestions on rides in the area, contact **Kristi Mountain Sports**, in Villa Mall on Highway 160, Alamosa; 719/589-9759.

Adams State College rents a variety of outdoor equipment, and you don't have to be a student or local resident to take advantage of the program. Available equipment includes bikes, backpacks, kayaks, rafts, life jackets, tents, sleeping bags, and more. Call ahead for reservations. The college also schedules trips to Creede, Taos, Santa Fe, and sites within the San Luis Valley. For more information, call 719/589-7813.

FOOD

Emma's Hacienda, in San Luis, 719/672-9902, is known far and wide for its tasty, authentic Mexican dishes. Emma's specialty consists of two cheese enchiladas, one smothered in green chile, the other in red, with beans, rice, a taco, and sopaipillas. The bowl of green chile with two sopaipillas is also a favorite, and other items such as the smothered burritos are excellent. The **R&R Grocery**, on the main street of San Luis, is the oldest grocery in Colorado. **Rosa Mistica**, across from the entrance to the Stations of the Cross, 719/672-3550, has a wonderful collection of flowers, gifts, art, pottery, and coffee. **Fabian's Café**, 123 Main, 719/672-0322, serves breakfast, lunch, and dinner, and is a great place to grab a sandwich before exploring the valley. Specialties are Southwestern and American dishes.

True Grits Steak House, at the junction of Highways 160 and 17 in Alamosa, 719/589-9954, is the best place in town for a steak. It also features lobster, crab legs, and shrimp. Lunch prices start at $4 to $5; dinner ranges from $7 to $25, for a steak and lobster combination. For authentic Mexican food and wonderful steak fajitas, go to **El Charro Café**, 421 Sixth Street, 719/589-2262. This small hole-in-the-wall serves delicious food.

LODGING

For standard chain motel lodging, Alamosa offers the most choices. But the nicest place to stay is the comfortable **Cottonwood Inn & Gallery**, 123 San Juan Avenue, Alamosa, 719/589-3882 or 800/955-2623. This creative inn features artwork by regional artists, many of whom are internationally known, and has a recently renovated professional kitchen with hand-painted cabinets by regional artists. The breakfasts, needless to say, are made from scratch and delicious, and fresh cookies often greet guests upon arrival. A room with a shared bath starts at $52, including breakfast, for two people. Rooms with private baths range from $62 to $95.

Between Walsenburg and Alamosa is the **Fort Garland Motor Inn**, 719/379-2993, known for being an exceptionally clean and modest place to stay before Alamosa. It is also within walking distance of the Fort Garland Museum. Prices range from $50 to $95, and some rooms have kitchenettes.

In San Luis is **El Convento Bed and Breakfast**, 512 Church Place, 719/672-4223, housed in a two-story adobe building that dates to 1905. Built by Father Jose Samuel, it was formerly a religious school. Four guest rooms, each with a private bath, are decorated with Mission-style handcrafted furniture and colorful Southwestern fabrics. Centro Artesano, a local artists' gallery, is on the first floor. Also in San Luis is **Fabian's Bed and Breakfast**, 719/672-0322, which has four rooms with a shared bath. Next to Fabian's Café, the B&B is housed in one of the oldest buildings in San Luis. Nightly rates in summer start at $65 without breakfast, $75 with breakfast.

The town of Monte Vista, on the west end of the San Luis Valley, sits along the way to South Fork and Creede (see the Upper Rio Grande Valley chapter). Monte Vista hosts the most original place to stay in the San Luis Valley and, for that matter, all of Colorado: **Movie Manor**, 2830 West Highway, 800/528-1234 or 800/771-9468. Motel rooms are wrapped around a drive-in movie screen. During the summer, currently released movies (none are R-rated) are shown nightly, and guests can watch from their rooms, with the sound piped in from outside. Rates range from $59 to $85.

SAN LUIS VALLEY

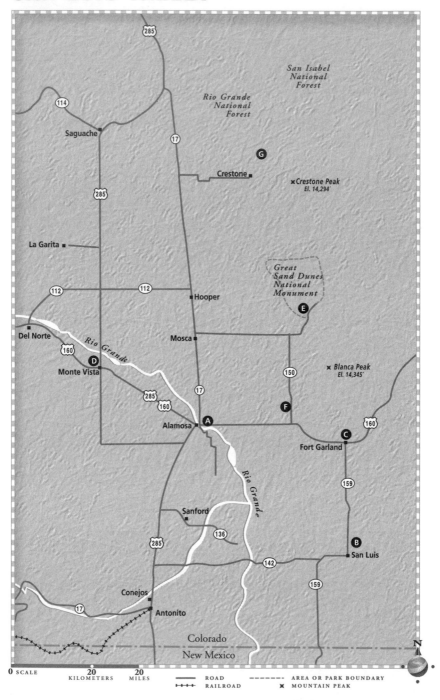

San Isabel National Forest

Rio Grande National Forest

285

114

Saguache

17

G

Crestone

×Crestone Peak
El. 14,294'

285

La Garita

112   112   Hooper

Great Sand Dunes National Monument

E

Del Norte

160   Rio Grande   Mosca

D
Monte Vista

285   160

17

150   × Blanca Peak
El. 14,345'

F

A
Alamosa

C   160
Fort Garland

Rio Grande

159

Sanford

285   136

B   San Luis

142

159

Conejos

17

Antonito

Colorado
New Mexico

0 SCALE   20   20
          KILOMETERS   MILES

——— ROAD   ------- AREA OR PARK BOUNDARY
++++ RAILROAD   × MOUNTAIN PEAK

N

Food

- Ⓐ El Charro
- Ⓑ Emma's Hacienda
- Ⓑ Fabian's Café
- Ⓑ R&R Grocery
- Ⓑ Rosa Mistica
- Ⓐ True Grits Steak House

Lodging

- Ⓐ Cottonwood Inn & Gallery
- Ⓑ El Convento Bed and Breakfast
- Ⓑ Fabian's Bed and Breakfast
- Ⓒ Fort Garland Motor Inn
- Ⓓ Movie Manor

Camping

- Ⓐ Alamosa KOA
- Ⓔ Great Sand Dunes National Monument
- Ⓕ Great Sand Dunes Oasis
- Ⓖ Rio Grande National Forest

Note: Items with the same letter are located in the same town or area.

CAMPING

Piñon Flats Campground in the **Great Sand Dunes National Monument**, 11500 Colorado State Highway 150, 719/378-2312, is open year-round. Fees are $10 per site, per night, or $3 per person in each group. April through October, it fills up quickly, on a first-come, first-served basis. Backcountry camping is allowed with a permit in designated sites, but fires are prohibited. An RV park close to the dunes is the **Great Sand Dunes Oasis**, 719/378-2222, which also has a grocery store and café. Or try the **Alamosa KOA**, 719/589-9757.

Many campgrounds in the **Rio Grande National Forest**, 1803 Highway 160, Monte Vista, 719/852-5941, have fishing access, space for travel trailers, and numerous camp units. They can be reserved through the National Campground Reservation System, 800/280-2267.

13

THE SANTA FE TRAIL

In the early 1820s the Santa Fe Trail linked the United States with Mexico in a vital commercial trading network, forever changing relations between the two countries. After Mexico gained independence from Spain in 1821, it decreed a policy of open trade with the United States. Missouri traders eagerly capitalized on this policy, commandeering caravans filled with cloth, kitchen utensils, knives, and firearms that slowly labored more than 1,200 miles to reach the New Mexico settlements of Taos and Santa Fe. They returned laden with silver coins, horses, burros, blankets, hides, and wool, commodities eagerly snatched up and shipped to merchandisers throughout the country.

Within present-day Colorado, the mountain route of the Santa Fe Trail followed the Arkansas River, the international boundary between the United States and Mexico until 1848. Today it's both a Colorado Scenic Byway and a National Historic Trail, and communities along the route preserve trail history through local museums and noted sites. While the southeastern plains of Colorado are not considered a major visitor destination, this area proves fascinating to travelers interested in history. Bent's Old Fort National Historic Site and the Trinidad History Museum are two official trail sites that interpret the trail's early significance. The area is less crowded and less expensive than Colorado's popular mountain resorts. ◣

THE SANTA FE TRAIL

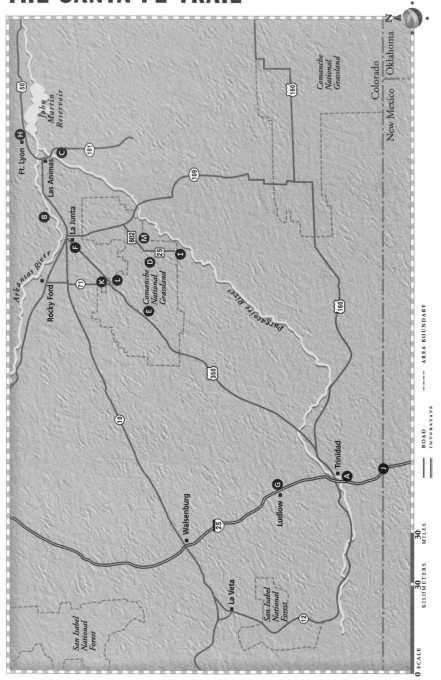

Sights

A A. R. Mitchell Museum
of Western Art

B Bent's Old Fort

C Boggsville

D Comanche National Grasslands

A Corazon de Trinidad
National Historic District

E Iron Springs Historic Area

A Kit Carson Park

F Koshare Indian Museum

G Ludlow Monument

H New Fort Lyon

I Picket Wire Canyonlands

J Raton Pass

L Sierra Vista Overlook

K Timpas Picnic Area

A Trinidad History Museum

M Vogel Canyon

Note: Items with the same letter are located in the same town or area.

A PERFECT DAY ALONG THE SANTA FE TRAIL

Don't miss Bent's Fort. You'll park your car about a half-mile from the fort and approach it on foot, as travelers did in the 1830s and 1840s. Afterward, explore the pristine canyons and prairies of the Comanche National Grasslands from several access points along Highway 350 between Trinidad and La Junta. Then continue on to Trinidad to explore El Corazon de Trinidad, a National Historic District with cobblestone streets and several wonderful museums.

SIGHTSEEING HIGHLIGHTS

★★★ **Bent's Old Fort**—Around 1834, the Missouri-based Bent, St. Vrain and Company established a fur-trading post in U.S. territory on the north side of the Arkansas River (today just east of La Junta, Colorado). The Southern Cheyennes promised William Bent, who operated the fort, that they would trade buffalo robes with him if he established the post in their hunting grounds along the river. Bent capitalized on this successful partnership with the Cheyennes and married into the tribe, fathering three sons and a daughter. He was well respected by the Plains Indians, which led to his success as a trader. As an Indian agent, he tried unsuccessfully to save Indian lands before they were usurped by the Colorado Territory.

Every Santa Fe Trail caravan on the Arkansas stopped at Bent's Old Fort to rest, catch up on the latest news, and conduct trade, making it the most important center for cultural exchange among Indians, Mexicans, and Americans between Missouri and New Mexico. The post flourished until 1849, when William Bent abandoned it. A cholera epidemic spread by trail travelers may have been the reason he left for a new site up the river. The National Park Service reconstructed the frontier trading post in the 1970s and now conducts living history activities featuring Santa Fe Trail customs, characters, and trivia.

Details: *35110 Hwy. 194 E., La Junta, CO 81050-9523; 719/384-2596. From La Junta on Hwy. 50, take Hwy. 194 eight miles to the site. Memorial Day–Labor Day 8–5:30, the rest of the year 9–4. $2 per person. (2–3 hours)*

★★ **Boggsville**—This early pioneer settlement, south of Las Animas, used to be the agricultural and commercial center for Bent County. In 1862 Thomas O. Boggs, following the example of Hispanic settlers who preceded him, built an adobe house for his family near the junction of the Purgatoire and Arkansas Rivers. William Bent had a ranch nearby, and other prominent local figures, such as Kit Carson and John Prowers, joined Boggs here. The site was a major stop for Santa Fe Trail travelers in the 1860s. The Boggsville Revitalization Committee has painstakingly restored several original buildings. Interpretive signs and a self-guided walking tour give detailed information about the site.

Details: *From Las Animas, go south on Highway 101 about two miles until you see the site to the east. 719/384-8113. (1 hour)*

★★ **Comanche National Grasslands**—This high plains prairie is home to grasses that seldom grow more than two feet tall but have broad root systems to consume large amounts of moisture and nutrients deep within the soil. Yucca and cholla, or candelabra cactus, thrive where the grasses have been disturbed because of overgrazing or other events.

Since 1954, the U.S. Forest Service has managed the Comanche National Grasslands as a legacy to the devastating Dust Bowl years of the 1930s. Management efforts focus on grazing, recreation, and preservation. More than 275 bird species migrate through here, including quail, pheasant, dove, prairie falcon, bald eagle, golden eagle, hawk, and the endangered lesser prairie chicken. While bison no longer blanket this prairie, several other species roam the area, including the rarely seen mountain lion, pronghorn antelope, fox, coyote, and bobcat.

Although primarily a grassland, the land is also crisscrossed with creek beds and river canyons studded with piñon and juniper trees. These canyons reveal some of the most lush and scenic portions of the Comanche National Grasslands. **Vogel Canyon** has loop trails, rock art, a stagecoach stop, and old structures from a former homestead. The canyon is about 13 miles south of La Junta on Highway 109. The access road lies just beyond the intersection of County Road 802 and Highway 109.

Another remarkable place in the grasslands is the **Picket Wire Canyonlands,** which contain several hiking trails, historical remnants, and a trail of dinosaur footprints from 150 million years ago. To reach the canyonlands, head south on Highway 109 to County Road 802. Turn right and drive southwest eight miles until you reach County Road 25. Head south on this road to the canyon access, a little over five miles.

From Highway 350 between La Junta and Trinidad several scenic pull-offs contain interpretive signs describing the Santa Fe Trail, local weather patterns, and the effect of the Dust Bowl on the grasslands. You will see these at **Iron Springs Historic Area, Sierra Vista Overlook,** and **Timpas Picnic Area.** If you don't have time to explore the grasslands for a full day, the pull-offs will help you better appreciate this area.

Details: Grassland Headquarters, 1321 E. Third St., La Junta; 719/384-2181. (2 hours–full day)

★★ **Corazon de Trinidad (Heart of Trinidad) National Historic District**—The long wagon trains and freighting caravans on the Mountain Branch of the Santa Fe Trail used to roll through what is now downtown Trinidad—literally right down Main Street—although the trail era preceded the town's founding by about 40 years. Incorporated in 1866, just before trundling wagon trains were replaced by more efficient railroads, Trinidad became the commercial center for sheep and cattle ranchers and several regional coal mines. The downtown area remains relatively unchanged, with many preserved historic structures and narrow, bricked streets. The Trinidad Historical Society has published an interesting walking guide to the history of downtown Trinidad.

The **Trinidad History Museum,** a museum complex managed by the Colorado Historical Society, includes the Baca House, Bloom House, and Santa Fe Trail Museum, all of which preserve vital links to the town's past. In the 1860s Don Felipe Baca encouraged several extended families from New Mexico to settle in the fertile river valleys surrounding Trinidad. Baca soon became a prominent sheep rancher and in 1873 moved into a two-story adobe house in the center of Trinidad. The **Baca House** is filled with elegant New Mexican furnishings, including colorful woven blankets, handcarved furniture, and religious folk art depicting the lifestyle of this prominent Hispanic family. Next door to the Baca House is the **Bloom House,** the home of Frank Bloom, a prominent Anglo cattle rancher. In contrast to the Baca House, the Bloom House exhibits period furnishings from the 1880s Victorian era, with ornate furniture, patterned wallpaper and carpets, and delicate china. Guides lead informative and interesting tours of both houses.

Behind the Baca and Bloom Houses is the **Santa Fe Trail Museum**, 300 East Main Street; 719/846-7217, recently opened as a interpretive site for the Mountain Branch of the trail. Included in the self-guided tour are exhibits with early trail and pioneer artifacts.

The **A. R. Mitchell Museum of Western Art,** 150 East Main; 719/846-4224, displays some of the oil paintings of Arthur Roy Mitchell, born on a homestead west of Trinidad in 1889. Mitchell illustrated early scenes of cowboy life from his own experiences on a cattle ranch in Las Animas County. His love for this region can be seen in his paintings and his efforts to preserve Trinidad's history for later generations. In addition to a rare collection of Hispanic and Native American art, the museum includes the Aultman Photography Collection, vintage photographs that encompass more than a century of Trinidad history.

Kit Carson Park sits at the corner of Kansas Avenue and San Pedro Street in Trinidad. The most prominent feature of this beautiful park is a striking bronze statue of Kit Carson and his horse, considered by many one of the finest equestrian statues ever made.

Details: *Trinidad Visitor and Convention Bureau, 309 Nevada, 719/846-9285. (1–2 days)*

✵ **La Junta**—Incorporated in the early 1870s, La Junta is a railroad town, conceived by the arrival of the Kansas Pacific Railroad. If you are interested in Native American art, visit the **Koshare Indian Museum** (115 W. 18th St., 719/384-4411) at Otero Junior College, which features a well-known and valuable collection of Native American art.

Details: *La Junta Chamber of Commerce, 110 Santa Fe Ave., 719/384-7411. (2 hours)*

✯ **Ludlow Monument**—Ludlow, a small coal town on the Colorado and Southern Railway, was the scene of a violent miners' strike in April 1914. The miners and their families had been evicted from their homes in town and were living in a tent colony. When the state militia attempted to disperse them, a fire swept through the tents, killing two women and 11 children.

Details: 10 miles north of Trinidad on I-25. Exit at milepost 27, heading west until you see a large United Mine Workers of America monument. (1 hour)

✯ **New Fort Lyon**—Visiting a Veterans Administration Hospital isn't usually high on many lists, but this site has a fascinating past. Built in 1867, it replaced the older Fort Lyon, which had been washed out by the Arkansas River. Troops stationed here protected white settlers and travelers during a turbulent period of conflict with Indians on Colorado's plains. The original officers' quarters, made from limestone blocks, still stand at Fort Lyon. In May 1868 Kit Carson died here in the post surgeon quarters, now the Kit Carson Chapel.

Details: East of Las Animas off Hwy. 50, 719/384-3100 (30 minutes)

✯ **Raton Pass**—If you'd like to travel an additional section of the trail from Trinidad (or are headed down to New Mexico), Raton Pass offers an interesting perspective on the rigors of early wagon travel. Dreaded and cursed by freighters, this pass was the major obstacle on the Mountain Branch of the Santa Fe Trail. It took over a week for heavily loaded wagons to make this leg of the trip, totaling less than 25 miles. In 1866 Richens "Uncle Dick" Wootton improved the road and opened a tollbooth on the pass. Although he charged an astronomical sum for those days—25 cents per wagon—he shortened the time needed for the trip and eased many problems. Today, thanks to an interstate highway and 75-mile-per-hour speed limit, travel time over the pass has been reduced to 15 minutes. On a clear day, views of the Spanish Peaks and the Sangre de Cristos to the northwest are simply breathtaking.

Details: Drive south from Trinidad on I-25 about 13 miles. Exit at the weigh-in station before the New Mexico/Colorado border and take the overpass to the other side of the road, where an interpretive sign placed by the Colorado Historical Society further describes the pass's history. (30 minutes)

THE SANTA FE TRAIL

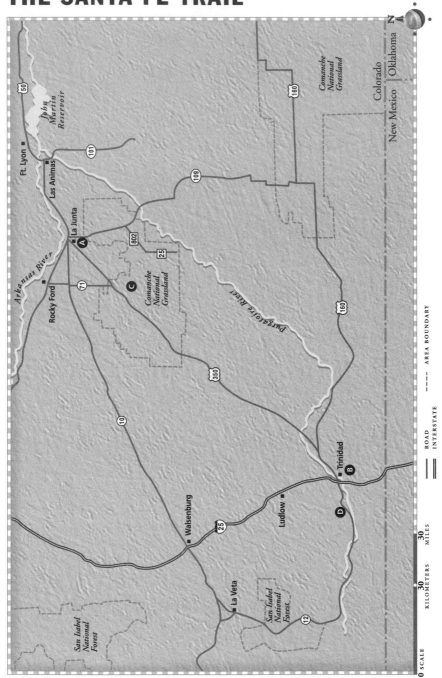

Food

- **A** Café Grandmere
- **B** Chef Liu's Chinese Restaurant and Lounge
- **A** Felisa's
- **A** Hickory House
- **B** Monteleone Deli
- **B** Nano & Nana's Pasta House

Lodging

- **B** Chicosa Canyon Bed and Breakfast
- **B** Inn on the Santa Fe Trail
- **A** Mid-Town Motel

Camping

- **C** Comanche National Grasslands
- **A** La Junta KOA
- **D** Trinidad State Park

Note: Items with the same letter are located in the same town or area.

FITNESS AND RECREATION

Southeastern Colorado has many reservoirs for a variety of outdoor recreation. Fishing, wildlife watching, and boating are all popular. **John Martin Reservoir**, 719/336-3476, east of La Junta, doesn't allow motorboats but is good for canoeing. Trinidad Lake State Park, west of Trinidad on Highway 12, 719/846-6951, is a great place for picnicking, boating, swimming, fishing, and hiking.

Comanche National Grasslands has numerous hiking trails. To pick up a map of the grasslands and obtain more information on outdoor activities, contact Comanche National Grasslands, 1321 East Third Street, La Junta; 719/384-2181.

FOOD

August through September, fresh produce stands line Highway 50 from Rocky Ford to Swink. This river valley is the home of the famous Rocky Ford cantaloupe, full of flavor and very sweet. Farmers also sell fresh asparagus, cucumbers, sweet corn, tomatoes, beans, and many other vegetables at the stands.

In La Junta, **Felisa's**, 27948 Frontage Road, 719/384-4814, serves traditional Mexican dishes, with combination and à la carte burritos, smothered enchiladas, and tacos. Open daily, Felisa's also includes a bar. For a little bit of everything, except Mexican, try the **Hickory House**, 1220 East Third, 719/384-9250, specializing in steaks, hickory burgers, beef ribs, and other stick-to-your-ribs meals.

Also in La Junta is the **Café Grandmere**, 408 West Third Street, 719/384-2711. Lunch is casual, with sandwiches, several chicken dishes, salmon, and steak, served Monday through Friday. Fixed-price dinners, served Thursday through Saturday, are a special treat: A five-course Greek meal, $21, is creatively prepared from locally grown products. The meal might include a baby greens salad, a seasonal soup, sorbet, and entrees such as Delmonico grilled steak or chicken Marsala, all finished by outstanding desserts.

Trinidad's variety of ethnic restaurants reflect the traditions of several cultural groups that have settled here over the years. **Chef Liu's Chinese Restaurant and Lounge**, 1423 Santa Fe Trail Drive, 719/846-3333, serves Chinese dishes that compete with those of restaurants in larger cities. Specials include vegetarian dishes and family dinners for about $10. For the best in traditional Italian food, with homemade sauces, macaroni, and lasagna, try **Nano & Nana's Pasta House**, 415 University, 719/846-2696. Prices range from $5 to $11. The **Monteleone Deli,** next door, is great for a quick sandwich ($5).

LODGING

In addition to plenty of standard motel options, places to stay include La Junta's **Mid-Town Motel**, 215 East Third, 719/384-7741, which is away from the noise of the highway and railroad tracks. A double room rents for $38 year-round. Although not fancy, it is clean, adequate, and close to the restaurants in town.

In Trinidad, the **Chicosa Canyon Bed and Breakfast**, 719/846-6199, is great for a relaxing getaway. The owners maintain three rooms in the main house and a lodge that sleeps four. Several hiking trails are accessible from the ranch, which sits on 64 acres of canyon country northwest of Trinidad. Rates vary but range from $75 to $95, including breakfast. The **Inn on the Santa Fe Trail**, 402 West Main Street, 719/846-4636, is in downtown Trinidad. The seven rooms in this circa-1900 Victorian rent for $70 in summer, including a three-course breakfast. The inn is not fancy but will provide a comfortable night's stay.

CAMPING

Trinidad State Park, 32610 Highway 12, 719/846-6951, has more than 60 spots for RVs, trailers, and tents. Reserve sites by calling 800/678-CAMP (2267). The **La Junta KOA** on Highway 50, one and a half miles west of the junction with Highway 109, 719/384-9580, features a playground, pool, and two rec rooms. For information on camping in the **Comanche National Grasslands**, contact Forest Service headquarters, 719/384-2181.

Scenic Route: Highway of Legends

An intriguing legend is told about the Purgatoire River, which parallels the southern part of the Highway of Legends. The full name, El Rio de Las Animas Perdidas en Purgatorio, means the River of the Souls Lost in Purgatory.

In 1594 a Spanish exploration party from Mexico came through this area seeking the fabled seven cities of Cibola. Frustrated with their futile search, expedition members quarreled, and the leader was killed in a heated argument. The party then split; the first faction returned to Mexico, and the second continued to search for the golden cities.

The latter faction then disappeared, said to have perished on the banks of this river. But without the benefit of last rites, their souls roamed endlessly in Purgatory. French trappers later shortened the river's name to La Purgatoire, and later Anglo settlers garbled it to Picketwire. Today the river is called variously the Purgatoire, Purgatory, or Picketwire.

This legend is only one of many surrounding the Highway of

HIGHWAY OF LEGENDS

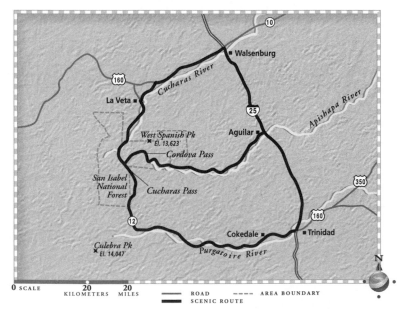

Legends, which can be driven from Trinidad in a day. Along the way are several interesting sights. If you choose to stop at one or several of these spots, it will take a full day to complete the 100-mile loop.

Hispanic plazas are intermingled with historic coal towns throughout the Purgatoire River Valley. In the early 1860s, several New Mexican families migrated permanently to this valley and took up farming and sheepherding. When coal mines opened here in the 1900s, many Hispanic residents started to work in the mines.

Seven miles west of Trinidad is the former company town of **Cokedale**, on the National Register of Historic Places. Established in 1907 by the Carbon Coal and Coke Company, this town housed workers and families until 1947, when the mine closed. Many of the workers purchased homes from the company and incorporated their town in 1948. You can still see ruins of the old coke ovens on the south side of the highway. The ovens removed all moisture, sulphur, and phosphorus from the coal, burning it down to carbon and ash that was used in the process of smelting iron. The former Cokedale Company Store is now a museum, and a guided walking tour of town is available.

As you drive north on Highway 12, you will have first-rate views of the majestic **Spanish Peaks**, which dominate the Cuchara River Valley. These peaks can be seen from several high points throughout southeastern Colorado, and for centuries have been landmarks for those traveling to the southern mountains. The Spanish Peaks are actually two massive volcanoes, with more than 400 volcanic dikes radiating from their bases. Many volcanic dike remains can still be seen in this area, as at **Devil's Stairsteps** and **Profile Rock**, both south of La Veta at mileposts 59 and 61 respectively.

In La Veta, the large adobe structure on the main thoroughfare is the **Fort Francisco Museum**. John Francisco, the area's first settler, built this plaza here in 1862. It became an important trading center for Anglo and Hispanic families living in the Cuchara Valley. The museum is open from Memorial Day to Labor Day. From La Veta, continue following the Cucharas River on Highway 160 to Walsenburg. It's a quick 37 miles south to Trinidad or 80 miles to Colorado Springs on the interstate. ◼

14

COLORADO SPRINGS

General William Jackson Palmer, the ambitious president of the Denver & Rio Grande Railroad, founded Colorado Springs in the 1870s as a genteel and refined community at the foot of the majestic Pikes Peak. But his wasn't the first community in the area. Colorado City had been founded during the Pikes Peak Gold Rush of 1859 and served briefly as the first territorial capital of Colorado. Its bawdy and dusty streets didn't meet Palmer's sophisticated tastes, however, and he chose to develop his exclusive community a few miles south.

Despite his precautions, the two settlements eventually merged into one sprawling city. Today Old Colorado City is a pleasant tree-lined street filled with galleries and restaurants, while the original sections of Palmer's Colorado Springs retain an aristocratic flavor with stately homes, wide avenues, and quiet streets.

Throughout their history, Colorado Springs and neighboring Manitou Springs have attracted people with vision and wealth. Like other communities on Colorado's Front Range, Colorado Springs has seen unprecedented growth during the 1990s. It is also a hub for five military establishments: Fort Carson Army Base, the United States Air Force Academy, Peterson Air Force Base, Falcon Air Station, and the North American Air Defense facility (NORAD), housed within Cheyenne Mountain. In fact, one out of every five workers here is employed by the military. ∎

COLORADO SPRINGS AREA

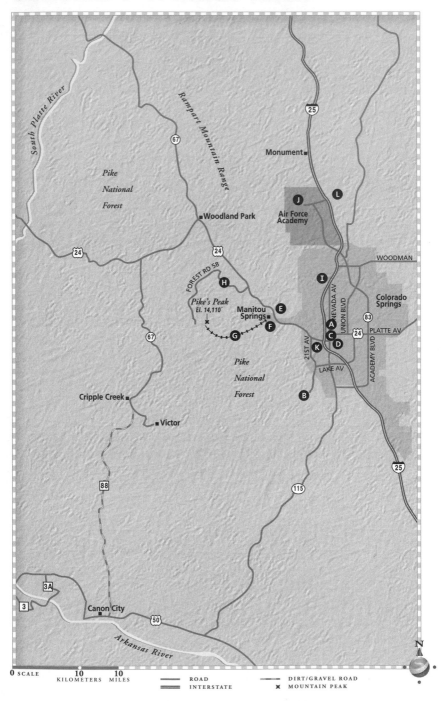

Sights

A American Numismatic Museum

B Cheyenne Mountain Zoo &
Will Rogers' Shrine of the Sun

C Colorado Springs Fine Art
Center

D Colorado Springs Pioneer's
Museum

E Garden of the Gods

F Manitou Springs

F Miramont Castle

G Pikes Peak Cog Railway

H Pikes Peak Highway

I Pro Rodeo Hall of Fame

J United States Air
Force Academy

K Van Briggle Pottery

L Western Museum of Mining
and Industry

Note: Items with the same letter are located in the same town or area.

A PERFECT DAY IN COLORADO SPRINGS

Spend the morning at the Garden of the Gods, named by a Pikes Peak prospector who thought its vermilion-colored sandstone walls and shapes were "fit for the gods." Afterward, drive to Manitou Springs for lunch, then take the Pikes Peak Cog Railway to the summit of the 14,110-foot Pikes Peak.

More adventurous travelers may opt for rising early to hike the 13-mile Barr Trail to the summit of Pikes Peak, then taking the cog railroad back down the mountain. You won't soon forget this exhilarating hike, and afterward you'll really deserve that beer at one of Colorado Springs' microbreweries.

SIGHTSEEING HIGHLIGHTS

★★★ **Garden of the Gods**—The phenomenal sandstone formations protected by this unusual city park tell an amazing geological story of mountain-building and earthquakes. The Lyons Formation, a red sandstone, and the Dakota Hogback, a buff-colored sandstone that caps the ridges of many area formations, were both gradually uplifted beginning 300 million years ago. These formations have since weathered into fantastic shapes, such as Toothsome Rocks, Balanced Rock, and the Kissing Camels.

Most memorable is the park's famous panorama of crimson walls contrasting with the blue-purple and snow-capped mass of Pikes Peak. Adding to the breathtaking scenery are nimble rock climbers spidering across the sandstone walls, as the site is known internationally for its technical rock climbs.

Several hiking trails wind through the formations and a diverse variety of life zones—from plains grasslands to juniper and piñon forests. The Garden of the Gods Visitor Center features informative exhibits on the area's natural and cultural history and a multimedia presentation in its auditorium. A guided tram tour of the park, providing descriptions of the formations and historic sites, starts from the visitor center.

Details: *1805 N. 30th St. Colorado Springs; 719/634-6666. Summer 7–9, winter 8:30–5:30. Free admission. (2–3 hours)*

★★★ **Pikes Peak**—When explorer Zebulon Pike first gazed upon this mountain in the autumn of 1806, he had no idea that one day his name would grace America's most famous peak. In 1859 gold seekers converged on Colorado during what was known as the Pikes Peak Gold Rush. But the mining activity actually occurred in the hills west of present-day Denver, more than 100 miles to the north. Pikes Peak had achieved such notoriety back east that people erroneously assumed the mines clustered around its formidable base.

You can hike, drive, or ride a cog railroad car to the summit of this imposing mountain. The 13-mile (one way) **Barr Trail** departs from Ruxton Avenue near the Pikes Peak Cog Railway station. While Pikes Peak is one of the easiest of the Fourteeners to scale, this is a long trail. Consider making this a two-day trip, staying overnight at Barr Camp. Located about seven miles up the hill, this campsite has two rustic cabins at 10,200 feet. Or take the cog railway one way and hike one way to make the trip in a day.

You can drive the **Pikes Peak Highway** to the summit in the comfort of your own car. However, you should know that this route punishes cars, as it climbs almost 7,000 feet in 19 miles and twists and turns through more than 150 hairpin curves. Stunning views include the lofty peaks of the Continental Divide, the city of Colorado Springs, and even Denver. Even though the road stays open year-round, severe weather might affect your trip. The road begins in the village of Cascade, on Highway 24 west of Manitou Springs. Call 719/684-9383 or 800/DO-VISIT for more information.

The best way to see the summit without having to expend much energy is to take a trip on the **Pikes Peak Cog Railway** (515 Ruxton Ave.; 719/685-5401). The world's highest cog railway train has been carting visitors to the top of Pikes Peak since 1891. The nine-mile trip starts at the Manitou Springs depot, and the round trip takes just over three hours. Train runs late April to October. Advance reservations are necessary. $22 adults, $10.50 ages 5–11.

Details: (3 hours by rail, 2 hours by highway, 1–2 days by the Barr Trail)

★★ **Colorado Springs Fine Arts Center**—An elite group of Colorado Springs residents pooled their talents and resources in the mid-1930s to create this haven of art and culture. The Fine Arts Center continues to thrive as a cherished Colorado Springs institution, with intriguing exhibitions, lectures, and performances. Located at the edge of the Colorado College campus, this world-class collection includes Native American and Hispanic artists' works as well as those of nineteenth- and twentieth-century Western American artists.

Details: 30 W. Dale St. (at Cascade Ave.); 719/634-5581. Tue–Fri 9–5, Sat 10–5, Sun 1–5. $3 adults, $1.50 seniors and students 13–21, $1 ages 6–12, free Sat until noon. (1 hour)

★★ **Colorado Springs Pioneer's Museum**—Situated in the stately El Paso County courthouse, this museum contains several interesting exhibits on the history of the Pikes Peak region, with Indian artifacts, an historical toy exhibit, and—perhaps most entertaining—a quilt once owned by a Colorado Springs woman bearing autographs of famous people of the 1930s, with small illustrations stitched next to their names. Exploring this handsome building, and riding the old-fashioned elevator, is a treat.

Details: 215 S. Tejon St.; 719/578-6650. April–Sept Tue–Sat 10–5, Sun 1–5. Free admission. (30 minutes)

★★ **Manitou Springs**—William Blackmore, an Englishman with a fondness for Native American legends, named the bubbling hot springs at this site after Manitou, the Great Indian spirit in Henry Wadsworth Longfellow's romantic poem *Hiawatha*. While the Utes never referred to their Great Spirit as Manitou, they did frequent these hot springs to heal their aches and pains, as did the Cheyennes and Arapahos.

In the latter part of the nineteenth century, the healthful air of both Manitou and Colorado Springs gained reputations for curing any type of illness, no matter how severe. Tuberculosis patients flocked to the region, seeking bed rest and exercise in the crisp mountain air. Health seekers dipped into the springs at Manitou and drank its soda water to cure everything from cancer to flatulence.

Today Manitou Springs is an eclectic combination of restaurants, antique stores, parks, gift shops, and historic architecture, a great place to wander around for an afternoon. Its historical society has prepared an historic walking tour, and dining establishments often serve mineral water bottled from local springs.

A French priest who came to Manitou Springs before the turn of the century to cure his consumption built the four-story **Miramont Castle** (9 Capitol Hill Ave.; 719/685-1011) to remind him of his European home. The castle's exterior features nine different types of architectural styles, abounding in peaks, balconies, turrets, and dormers, while the interior includes elegant staircases, a gold ceiling in the drawing room, and a 200-ton native sandstone fireplace. Before the Manitou Springs Historical Society restored it into a Victorian museum, the structure served as a sanitarium and apartment house.

Details: *Manitou Springs Chamber of Commerce, 354 Manitou Ave., 719/685-5089 or 800/642-2567. (half–full day)*

★★ **United States Air Force Academy**—Established in the late 1950s on rolling foothills at the base of the Rampart Range, the Air Force Academy includes the striking Cadet Chapel, a B-52 bomber display, and the Academy Visitor Center, with displays on cadet life. If you're there at noon, you will see the ceremonious cadets marching to lunch. A self-guided driving tour of the grounds points out key sights.

Details: *North of Colorado Springs on I-25 at exit 156A; 719/472-2025. Daily 9–5. Free. (1½ hours)*

★★ **Western Museum of Mining and Industry**—Chronicling the importance of mining to Colorado and other western states, this non-profit educational museum collects, restores, and displays mining artifacts. The historic mining equipment has been reconditioned into working order, so you can actually see and hear it run (loudly). Also on the museum grounds are a restored 10-stamp ore mill, blacksmith shop, and working hoist house, all extremely important mining industry innovations.

Details: *From I-25 exit 156A (the north entrance to the Air Force Academy), take the Northgate/Gleneagle Dr. exit and follow the signs;*

719/488-0880. Mon–Sat 9–4, Sun noon–5, Dec–Feb by special appointment. $5 adults, $4 students and seniors, $2 ages 5–12. (1 hour)

✯ **American Numismatic Museum**—Numismatics, the collection and study of coins and paper money, is a fascinating way to learn about world history. This innovative museum interprets how art, economic development, and social change have influenced the currencies of different cultures throughout the ages. Founded under a federal charter in 1912, this sizable collection includes permanent exhibits on Colorado's money, with items from the Gold Rush era and the Denver Mint.

Details: 818 N. Cascade Ave., Colorado Springs; 719/632-2646. Mon–Fri 8:30–4. Free. (1 hour)

✯ **Cheyenne Mountain Zoo and Will Rogers' Shrine of the Sun**— Spencer Penrose arrived in Colorado Springs in 1892 to seek his fortune, which he soon did in the nearby Cripple Creek Mining District. Penrose became one of Colorado Springs' most enthusiastic boosters, masterminding promotional successes and leaving behind a legacy known as the El Pomar Foundation.

Because he had a fondness for European zoos, Penrose built his own zoo on the slopes of Cheyenne Mountain. The Cheyenne Mountain Zoo is still in operation. It continually modernizes its animal habitats, including the Jane Goodall Primate World and a natural Mexican wolf environment, and is known internationally for its success in breeding giraffes.

Later in life, Spencer Penrose began to design his family burial plot high above the zoo on the slopes of Cheyenne Mountain. With his usual promotional flair, Penrose wanted to publicize the beautiful vistas from his cemetery by building an expensive tourist attraction. The result was a monumental stone tower more than 300 feet high, boasting "the Most Complete Amplification System in the World," which played chimes heard 20 miles away. The tower's construction coincided with the death of Will Rogers, a close friend of Penrose. In tribute, he named his monument Will Rogers' Shrine of the Sun.

Details: Take I-25 exit 138 west until you reach the Broadmoor Hotel. Turn right and follow the signs; 719/633-9925. You can visit the shrine with zoo admission, $7.50 adults, $6.50 seniors, $4.50 ages 3–11. (3 hours)

✯ **Pro Rodeo Hall of Fame and Museum of the American Cowboy**—Everything having to do with cowboys, from nineteenth-century ranch work to the evolution of rodeo into a challenging modern sport, is presented here, in two different multimedia presentations and exhibits with cowboy gear and equipment. The Hall of Champions honors contestants from each rodeo, including announcers, clowns, animals, and others.

Details: 101 Pro Rodeo Dr., Colorado Springs; 719/593-8840. Daily 9–5. $6 adults, $3 ages 6–12. (1–2 hours)

✯ **Van Briggle Pottery**—When Artus Van Briggle came to Colorado Springs in 1899 to cure his tuberculosis, he knew he wanted to spend the rest of his life here. He and his wife, Anne, both exceptional artists, created a popular Art Nouveau–style of pottery, utilizing nature motifs and muted matte glazes. Their pottery factory is still run by family members, who produce original Van Briggle designs and modern styles. You can take a free tour of the pottery factory, in the historic round house of the Colorado Midland Railroad year-round, except on Sunday.

Details: 600 S. 21st St., Colorado Springs; 719/633-7729. (1 hour)

FITNESS AND RECREATION

For a relaxing walk on a quiet path, go to **Bear Creek Canyon Regional Park**. Numerous trails here vary in length, but total approximately five miles. The park is open from dawn to dusk and is located at 245 Bear Creek Road; 719/520-6387. From I-25, take the Cimarron Street exit (141) and head west. Turn left at 26th Street, which eventually turns into Bear Creek Road.

The **Monument Creek Trail**, an urban bike path, starts at Monument Valley Park behind Colorado College and travels along the creek a few miles just below downtown Colorado Springs. Or try the **North Cheyenne Canyon Trail**, a nice hike close to town. To get to the trailhead, which is behind the Broadmoor, take exit 140 (Nevada Avenue) southbound from I-25. Turn west (right) on Cheyenne Boulevard until you get to the canyon entrance, where the trail begins on the left side of the road.

There are several excellent bicycle rides in and around Colorado Springs, such as those through the **Garden of the Gods**, **United States Air Force Academy**, or **Palmer Park**. All vary in length and difficulty. Stop in at the Mountain Chalet, 226 North Tejon, 719/633-0732, and ask their helpful staff about trails or any type of outdoor activity in the area.

FOOD

From fine dining in handsome manors to grabbing some beans and rice at a college hangout, there are many options for food in Colorado Springs and Manitou Springs. The best breakfast is found at **Adam's Mountain Cafe**, 110 Canyon Avenue, 719/685-1430, a longtime Manitou Springs institution where you can expect healthy dishes and freshly baked breads and muffins. This vegetarian café also serves lunch and dinner, focusing on international cuisine.

For a wonderful dinner, featuring much of the "new" Colorado cuisine that people are raving about, visit the **Craftwood Inn**, 40 El Paso Boulevard, Manitou Springs, 719/685-9000, specializing in wild game, steak, seafood, and vegetarian options. The creative preparations might include roast duck with cranberry orange sauce, grilled piñon trout with cilantro butter and pine nuts, or braised herbal chicken with green chili and blue cornbread stuffing ($12.50–$30).

Luigi's Restaurant, 947 South Tejon Street, 719/632-0700, is a family-style Italian restaurant that has been serving Colorado Springs residents lunch and dinner for 40 years. With specialties such as pasta, lasagna, meatballs, and sausage, this is the place to go for a hearty meal approved by many Italian mothers throughout the world. **Poor Richard's Restaurant**, 324½ North Tejon, 719/632-7721, is one of those rare treasures you find in college towns, with a coffee shop and bookstore all under the same roof. The food is on the healthy side, with plenty of vegetarian options and excellent pizza. Prices range from $2 for a slice of pizza to $6 and $7 for many the entrees to around $15 for a large pizza.

A great place for a sandwich, soup, or salad in Old Colorado City is **La Baguette**, 2417 West Colorado Avenue, 719/577-4818, a French bakery that entices you with heavenly aromas as soon as you walk in the door. The sandwiches are reasonably priced, around $5. Its croissants, pastries, and other desserts are well worth the extra calories.

Several brewpubs and microbreweries, all specializing in handcrafted quality beers and hearty pub food, have added a new dimension to the nightlife in Colorado Springs. The **Phantom Canyon Brewery** sits on a prominent corner across from the Antler's Hotel at 2 East Pikes Peak Avenue, 719/635-2800. The wonderful restaurant includes fare such as artichoke and asiago cheese dip, roasted chicken breast pizza, and grilled eggplant, portobello mushroom, zucchini, and squash salad. Inside of

COLORADO SPRINGS

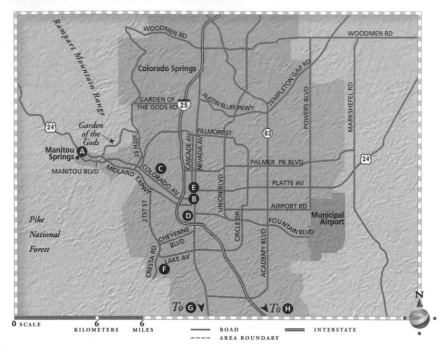

Food

- **A** Adam's Mountain Cafe
- **A** Craftwood Inn
- **B** Josh & John's Naturally Homemade Ice Creams
- **B** Judge Baldwin's
- **C** La Baguette
- **D** Luigi's Restaurant
- **B** Phantom Canyon Brewery
- **E** Poor Richard's Restaurant

Lodging

- **B** Antler's Doubletree Hotel
- **F** Broadmoor Hotel
- **A** El Colorado Lodge
- **E** Hearthstone Inn
- **A** Two Sisters Inn

Camping

- **G** Golden Eagle Ranch RV Park
- **H** KOA Colorado Springs South

Note: Items with the same letter are located in the same town or area.

Antler's is **Judge Baldwin's**, serving a good selection of microbrews and enormous portions of nachos, burgers, and other bar food.

After dinner, stop in at **Josh & John's Naturally Homemade Ice Creams**, 101 North Tejon, 719/632-0299, for a well-deserved treat. The wonderfully rich ice cream can be prepared with mix-ins such as crushed Oreos, M&Ms, or nuts. Go on, you deserve it.

LODGING

Quirky motor court hotels line Colorado Avenue and Manitou Avenue on the way to Manitou Springs. These preserved motels evolved with the American fascination for automobile touring, and luckily, many have been preserved in this area. One of the finest is the **El Colorado Lodge**, 23 Manitou Avenue, 719/685-5485 or 800/782-2246. Built in the 1920s, this classic motor court has individual adobe units with comfortable southwestern furnishings starting at $41.50 in summer. Each room has a Spanish-style fireplace, and the motel will give you wood to make a cozy fire in your room.

If you want to splurge, don't miss the opulence and comfort of the legendary **Broadmoor Hotel**, 1 Lake Circle, 719/634-7711 or 800/634-7711. Built by the wealthy Spencer Penrose in the style of a fine European hotel, the Broadmoor is still a grand establishment, recently updated with new rooms. The main seven-story structure, built in 1918, is embellished with a rich Italian marble and pink exterior. Several fine restaurants, a golf club, ice arena, spa, fitness center, tennis courts, and extensive gardens round out this exclusive resort. Off-season rates are $170 to $235, high-season is $280 to $425. Even if you aren't staying there, drive up to the Broadmoor to experience the fabulous architecture and setting.

The **Hearthstone Inn**, 506 North Cascade Avenue, 719/473-4413 or 800/521-1885, a restored Victorian mansion, sits on a quiet street near Colorado College. The towering old trees that line the street provide a canopy of shade. The private rooms here are perfect for a romantic weekend. Rates, including a full breakfast, start at $70 for a shared bath, and $90 for a private bath.

In Manitou Springs is the charming **Two Sisters Inn**, 10 Otoe Place, 719/685-9684 or 800/2-SIS-INN (274-7466), where the friendly and helpful hosts make your stay wonderful. The Victorian bungalow has five bedrooms and a romantic honeymoon cottage in the back garden. With an entire wall of cookbooks in the sitting room, you will be treated to a creative breakfast. Rates range from $69 to $105 with a two-night minimum on weekends.

Conveniently located in downtown Colorado Springs is the **Antler's Doubletree Hotel**, 4 South Cascade Avenue, 719/473-5600 or 800/528-0444. This new hotel is a renovated version of the historic Antler's, one of the earliest hotels in town. Recent additions include a health club, pool, and microbrewery. The views of Pikes Peak to the west are the best in town. Rates average $145.

CAMPING

Golden Eagle Ranch RV Park, 719/576-0450 or 800/666-3841, has more than 400 RV sites and is located on the grounds of the May Natural History Museum, which exhibits a collection of the world's strangest and largest invertebrates. The park is southwest of Colorado Springs on Highway 115. From I-25, take exit 135 and head west to Highway 115, which is South Nevada Avenue. Drive south five miles until you see the giant beetle.

KOA Colorado Springs South, I-25 exit 132, 719/382-7575, is south of Colorado Springs on Fountain Creek (Widefield/ Security exit). Facilities include an indoor swimming pool, hot tub, and video game room with numerous campground activities. Open year-round.

NIGHTLIFE

Colorado Springs has an excellent symphony, often presenting a varied season with noted performers. Call the **Colorado Springs Symphony Orchestra**, 719/520-SHOW, for more information.

The **Golden Bee**, 719/634-7711 or 800/634-7711, in the Broadmoor Hotel is a must for a rousing night out on the town. With yards of beer, a printed singalong guide, and a rowdy atmosphere, even the most timid patrons find themselves heartily singing along with the piano player in this nineteenth-century pub—actually imported lock, stock, and barrel from England.

APPENDIX

METRIC CONVERSION CHART

1 U.S. gallon = approximately 4 liters
1 liter = about 1 quart
1 Canadian gallon = approximately 4.5 liters

1 pound = approximately $\frac{1}{2}$ kilogram
1 kilogram = about 2 pounds

1 foot = approximately $\frac{1}{3}$ meter
1 meter = about 1 yard
1 yard = a little less than a meter
1 mile = approximately 1.6 kilometers
1 kilometer = about $\frac{2}{3}$ mile

90°F = about 30°C
20°C = approximately 70°F

Planning Map: Colorado

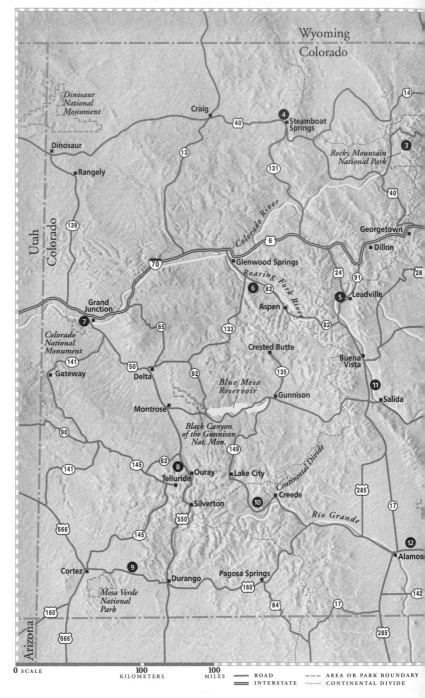

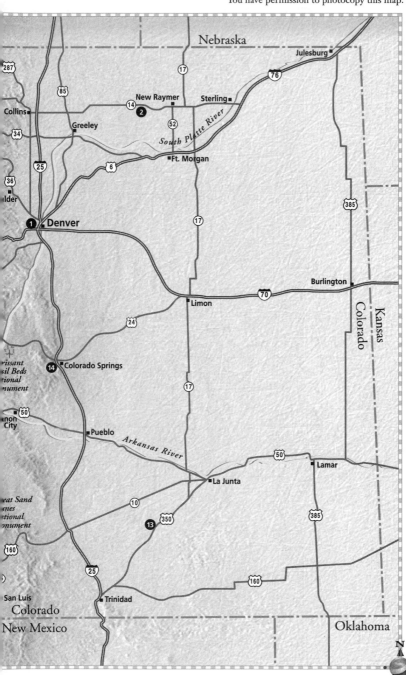

INDEX

Map Index

© Oakley Photography

ABOUT THE AUTHOR

Dianna Litvak grew up in Denver and attended Colorado College in Colorado Springs. In 1991, she worked as the principal researcher and assistant producer for the highly acclaimed documentary *How the West Was Lost*. The series, which aired on KUSA in Denver and the Discovery Channel, focused on the history of five Native American tribes. In 1992 Litvak headed a rejuvenated historical marker program for the Colorado Historical Society. As deputy historian, she traveled thousands of miles across the state planning more than 50 new road-side history exhibits. Litvak currently lives in Denver, Colorado, where she specializes in history writing and is active in a number of historic preservation projects.